The Bone Cave

The BONE CAVE

A JOURNEY THROUGH MYTH AND MEMORY

DOUGIE STRANG

BIRLINN

First published in 2023 by
Birlinn Limited
West Newington House
10 Newington Road
Edinburgh
EH9 1QS

www.birlinn.co.uk

ISBN: 978 1 78027 835 3

British Library Cataloguing-in-Publication Data
A catalogue record for this book is available from the British Library

Designed and typeset by Hewer Text UK Ltd, Edinburgh

Papers used by Birlinn are from well-managed forests and other responsible sources

Printed and bound by Clays Ltd, Elcograf S.p.A.

To Em, Fern, Mara

Tachraidh d' fhiadh fhèin riut fhathast
You'll meet your own deer yet

Contents

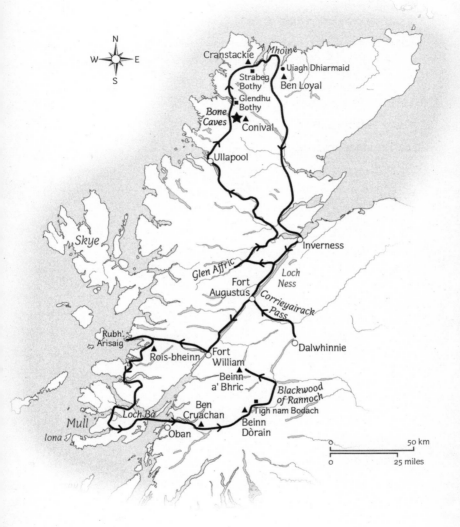

Author's Note on Place-names

The spelling of place-names can be inconsistent, no more so than in Gaelic, where there are sometimes a handful of spellings for a particular place, depending on the map used, reference cited or local usage. This is in part because Scottish Gaelic orthography only began to be standardised in the mid-eighteenth century but also because many of the mapmakers didn't speak the language. Throughout this book, I have used current Ordnance Survey spellings, unless quoting from historical texts.

Introduction: The Other Landscape

This is a book about stories – old stories of people and place, and of the more-than-human world. Hamish Henderson, folklorist and poet, famously observed that traditional culture is like a 'carrying stream', one where the surface ripples and changes, always renewing itself, but where a deep current endures. Hamish's metaphor conjures a landscape of myth and lore that lies within, or adjacent to, the physical landscape, akin to what the mythologist Clarissa Pinkola Estés calls *rio abajo rio*, 'the river beneath the river'. This book's concern is with that other, adjacent landscape, with the stories that shape it, and with the ways that our own lives can be caught in its flow.

What follows is an account of two walks in the Scottish Highlands: one short, in spring; the other longer, in autumn. The walks were not based on established routes like the Great Glen Way or the Cape Wrath Trail. Instead, I used stories as waymarks – folktales and myths, primarily from Gaelic tradition – and I made my way between the places that held those stories according to chance and circumstance. It seemed like a suitably quixotic strategy for a middle-aged man on walkabout, and my hope was that the tales I was tracking – their ambiguity and their otherness – would help to loosen me, make me more pliant to the land I was walking through, deepen my relationship with it.

We tend to think of folktales as belonging anywhere and nowhere, like the fairy tales of the 'Cinderella' and 'Jack and the Beanstalk' variety; tales where a hero or heroine sets out on an adventure, surmounts various challenges, and gains at the end great riches and the hand in marriage of a prince or princess. Many such tales have been gathered from Gaelic oral tradition – in the 1860s, John Francis Campbell of Islay published *Popular Tales of the West Highlands*, which contains numerous examples of the type, and which is still considered to be one of Europe's finest folktale collections.

The tales I'm interested in are of a different order: they're less abstract and more specific, more rooted in place. A monstrous boar scars the side of a mountain, a scar still known today as Sgrìob an Tuirc, the 'Furrow of the Boar'. A hunter raises his gun to a deer, but before he can shoot, the deer takes the form of a woman. Another hunter receives an uncanny gift from the Cailleach – an elusive figure who is remembered in place-names throughout the Highlands, and whose presence haunts this book.

While tracking these stories – mapping that other landscape – I discovered a depth of meaning to them that provides an unfamiliar perspective on contemporary issues such as land ownership and ecological stewardship. And at a time when so many questions are being asked about our relationship to place and to the other species that we share place with, I'm convinced that these stories deserve to be shared more widely, that they remain vital in the sense of being both alive *and* necessary.

Chapter 1

Cleaning the Cailleach's Well

The wind was fierce on the ridge. At the summit I sheltered in the lee of the cairn, crouching among stones and moss, the tiny green hands of alpine lady's mantle. I stayed too late on top, thrilled by the views as the sun set behind the peaks and ridges of Lochaber. Below me, the moor began to heave and shift in the dark as though it was *un*moored, as though the lochs dotted across it were the only fixed points, glinting the last of the light. Dropping down from the summit, I searched along the western slope of the ridge, among banks of turf and exposed peat hags. Water seeped to the surface in dips and creases, but you wouldn't call them pools.

It was late and time to stop even before I stepped into the bog. When I pulled out my leg it was cast to the knee in wet, black peat, and it was heavy, like a false leg, or someone else's, so that I had to shake it until it felt like my own. I pitched my tent in the dark on a patch of firm ground, pulled off wet clothes and put on all my dry spares, and then crept into my sleeping bag. My head torch threw shadows that billowed with the tent in the wind.

Dòmhnall Donn-shùileach, 'Brown-eyed Donald', is camped one evening on the ridge of Beinn a' Bhric and is striking a flint to light a fire to cook his supper, when the Cailleach appears at his side out of the darkness. 'Greetings, mistress,' he says, with as much calm as he can muster, 'and from where did you come?'

'Oh well, I was on top of Beinn a' Chrùlaiste when you struck the first spark of your flint, Donald of the brown eyes,' she replies, casually.

'You will have been running then,' says Donald, just as casual, knowing full well that Beinn a' Chrùlaiste is a full day's walk to the west.

'Oh, no,' says the Cailleach, 'just strolling along, I was.'

They continue with their banter as Donald builds the fire and sets a pot on it; and even though he is ravenous hungry, having spent all day hunting on the hill, even though his teeth are swimming in his mouth at the thought of the venison bubbling in the pot, Donald is sure to offer the Cailleach the best portion of the meal. They share their supper in companionable silence, and then the Cailleach thanks Donald and disappears into the dark, leaving him to spend a fitful night, wrapped in his plaid, wondering if she might return and insist that she snuggle her bony, crony body next to his.

This is the first part of a tale I heard many years previously, told in a pub in Edinburgh by traditional storyteller Jamie MacDonald Reid. It stayed with me, in part, because the mountain is so intrinsic to the narrative – the tale's rootedness in a specific place, Beinn a' Bhric, where I was now camped, gave it substance and lodged it more vividly in my memory. The significance of the encounter between the Cailleach, the 'Old Woman', and Brown-eyed Donald the hunter, and their relationship to a wider body of Gaelic folklore, was not yet clear to me; but I was excited to be tracing the tale's provenance on the mountain, like following a stream to its source.

Beinn a' Bhric means 'Speckled Mountain', speckled like a brown trout or like the back of a red deer calf. It's one of the mountains that form a rim around the wide, elevated bowl of Rannoch Moor – a bowl that held the last ice of the last Ice Age. Twelve thousand years later, Rannoch Moor is still rising by a few millimetres each year: a long, slow decompression after the burden of a mile's depth of ice. No roads cross the moor, but there is a railway line, and the Glasgow-to-Fort William train trundles along it twice a day and back again. Once, as a passenger on the train, I experienced a kind of agoraphobia – at least I think that's what it was.

I was in my mid-twenties, travelling north to Fort William in February, one of only a handful of passengers spread between the two carriages. We crossed the moor late in the afternoon, and it looked dismal in the half-light of winter. Thin, wet snow smeared every surface, the lack of definition confusing the space between things. Peering out of the window, the mountains seemed both far away and looming, and I became disorientated, holding onto my seat while at the same time floundering out on the moor. The sensation was brief but overwhelming. I've never been so lost. I pulled myself together – that's how it felt, as though I had to haul some dislocated part of me back onto the train – and spent the rest of the journey unnerved, buried in a book for distraction, grateful as night fell that the windows reflected back the lights of the carriage, keeping out the dark.

Twenty-five years later, and I was out on Rannoch Moor again, or rather, above it, sleeping fitfully. The wind jolted me awake, and for a moment I thought that the tent had untethered and was slipping from the ridge. I lay in the dark, pressed to the ground while the wind beat at the flysheet, and thought about my family, my two daughters when they were young – those times when they would wake in the night in a storm, afraid, and I would pretend that the house was a ship, heaving on the sea's swell, so that I staggered as I walked from the bedroom door to their bunks, asking, 'Avast me hearties, what ails thee?' Teenagers now, they still remember the stories I'd tell to soothe them, and the funny house that we lived in, with its straw-bale walls and timber mezzanine – a house that you would imagine might sail and list in the wind. The memory of being there for them was a solid truth, like a stone, weighting me to the side of the mountain.

Beinn a' Bhric is twin-peaked – the summit to the west, which gives it its name, is smaller in height and less shapely than its neighbour, Leum Uilleim, 'William's Leap'. The pair stand shoulder to shoulder, conjoined by a curving ridge, with Coir' a' Bhric Beag, the 'Little Speckled Corrie', clasped between them. The mountain rises above Corrour Railway Station at the north-western edge of Rannoch Moor and provides the backdrop to a well-known scene in the film *Trainspotting*. Fans still catch the train to Corrour, the highest railway station in the British Isles, to take pictures and pose at the spot where Renton delivers his soliloquy on national identity: *It's shite being Scottish . . .*

*

By morning the wind had eased and cloud huddled around the ridge of Beinn a' Bhric. I was inside the cloud, the air wet and cold, and there was no summit or sight of other mountains. I cut out a small circle of turf on a level bank and unpacked the bag of kindling and the half-dozen lengths of firewood that I'd carried in my rucksack. My fire was a compact sun, unnaturally bright against the grey of the mist. I set a pot of water to boil and willed the flames to lift the cloud and conjure the actual sun. I made tea, ate oatcakes and a cold, sweet apple, and carefully tended my fire on the mountain in the clouds. It was the morning of 1 May, Beltane according to the old Celtic calendar – the word's meaning most likely a compound of 'bright' and 'fire'.

After the fire died, I poured water over the ashes and replaced the circle of turf, tramping it firm, then took down my tent and packed my rucksack. The wind had shifted, thinning the cloud so that gaps were opening and I could look down into

Gleann Iolairean, and across to the grey lochans on the plateau of Meall a' Bhainne. I took out my map and gauged my position relative to what I could see around me, checking that I was in the right place.

When I'd sat down to look at Beinn a' Bhric on a large-scale map, before setting out to climb it, I'd noticed below the summit the name Fuaran Cailleach Beinn a' Bhric, the 'Well of the Old Woman of Beinn a' Bhric', and felt the thrill of discovery. Jamie MacDonald Reid's tale didn't mention a well, but here was confirmation of an association between the Cailleach and the mountain, as well as a hint of other stories still to be found. As for the location of the well: in Gaelic, *fuaran* usually means a well in its natural state, an undug pool or spring, so it was possible that the peat bog I'd stumbled into the night before, with its few inches of surface water, might be all there was to find.

The side of the mountain steepened below me. I clambered down to where a stream had formed a gully between two crags, and then followed its course back up amongst the folds of the slope, hoping it might lead to what I was looking for. Rags of cloud drifted across the mountainside. I startled a hare that was crouched in a dip to the left of the stream, encroaching on the tolerated space between us as though I had nudged a trip-wire. It sprang away into the mist and left my body charged with adrenalin.

I found the Cailleach's well tucked in a hollow, hidden from above and below. Even at a short distance, you could walk by without noticing it. It was an oval pool, gravel-lined and clear, like a portal, with the stream I had followed pouring from the lip of it. The water tasted like stone. I filled my water bottle and cupped my hands and washed my face.

Local tradition tells that the Cailleach cleans her well on the first morning of May. In her absence, I rolled up my sleeves and cleared some of the silt that had built up around the outflow. After a few minutes of scooping and splashing, my arms were numb with cold. When I stopped, the pool returned to stillness.

Dropping beneath the cloud, I followed the stream back to the gully, intending to scramble down into Gleann Iolairean, and to walk out from there via the head of Loch Treig to the railway station at Corrour. A bird flew past, contouring the crags: a swallow, unexpected in this place and at this height. It tilted its body away from me in alarm, flashing its orange breast and looking back with a tiny, black eye. Small, quick life, heart the size of a tic tac, following an old ellipse from Scotland to Africa and back, carrying the sun from the south on its breast. Now I was blessed. Now it was the first day of summer.

Chapter 2

The Stag and the Blade

Stories attach themselves to places, building up layers of meaning over time. On my first visit to Beinn a' Bhric, I uncovered one of those layers, tracing the presence of the Cailleach in the mountain's topography. That visit was a reconnaissance, an initial foray into tracking stories in the landscape. As I waited for the train at Corrour Station, I'd looked back up at the mountain and understood that this was the beginning of an abiding relationship with it.

Through the summer, I delved into the traditions and lore associated with Beinn a' Bhric, uncovering more folktales in books and recordings, as well as fragments of song and pibroch tune. They were all place-specific, a density of meaning concentrated on a single mountain. Such a concentration is not, of course, unique to Beinn a' Bhric; wherever you dig, you find that the land brims with culture, and I soon discovered a whole body of corresponding tales that related to the Cailleach and to the hunting of deer.

My trip to Beinn a' Bhric kindled the desire to go for a longer walk, one that would offer more glimpses of that other, storied landscape, and so, one autumn morning, I found myself travelling by train through Perthshire, past ploughed fields and stubble fields, and wind turbines on low hills, blades gleaming in the sun; past a field with grazing cows that were clustered in groups like guests on a lawn at a wedding.

It was five months to the day since I'd camped on Beinn a' Bhric, and now I was setting out with the whole of October ahead of me; my first solo, long-distance walk since marriage and parenthood. There had been other trips – day walks and the odd weekend – but this was different, a chance to walk without timetables or the need for a swift return. It felt timely: I'd turned fifty; my children, as teenagers, were beginning to shape their own lives; and I'm lucky, my wife and I both understand the gift of occasional solitude.

North of Blair Atholl, the fields become moors and the hills become mountains, and the train's engine strained as it pulled us up and over the Pass of Drumochter, before easing as we approached Dalwhinnie at the head of Loch Ericht. The loch fills a cleft between Ben Alder and the mountains west of Drumochter – a spear of water nearly fifteen miles long, pointed at Rannoch Moor. A way in, or rather, a way out: the loch is one of a number that formed when glacial ice melted and spilled from the great bowl of the moor.

Dalwhinnie was quiet and dull beneath a cloudy sky, and I was the only person to step off the train onto the platform. Surrounded by mountains and sitting at a height of over a thousand feet, the village is one of the least sunny and most consistently cold in the UK. I noticed the chill as I walked past a straggle of houses to the village edge, where I stuck out my thumb and gained a quick hitch along the A889 to Laggan. The driver was a cheerful estate agent whose black Labrador leaned forward from the back of the car and licked my face – 'kisses' said the estate agent, chuckling, as I wiped dog slaver from my cheek. And then I was walking west into the wind, following the course of the River Spey, with the mountains ahead, and beneath my feet, under the tarmac, General Wade's Military Road.

Rain scoured my face, driven by gusts of wind. I wrapped myself in waterproofs, pulled my hood low, and followed Wade's Road as it skirted a nameless grey loch that had been formed by the damming of the River Spey. Two wooden boats were moored close to the shore, one painted green, one painted blue, both straining at their moorings in the wind. The rain came in squalls, with sunshine bursting through the clouds in between, turning the grey loch luminous.

After the 1715 Jacobite Rising, General George Wade was commissioned to construct a network of military roads in the Scottish Highlands, to help enforce the rule of the British State. The most challenging of those linked the barracks at Ruthven in Strathspey, fifteen miles to the north of Dalwhinnie, with Fort Augustus at the head of Loch Ness. It did so by crossing the Monadhliath Mountains via the Corrieyairack Pass. Wade and his road builders breached the pass in 1731, completing the commission. Fourteen years later, it was the Jacobites, under Charles Edward Stuart, who gained most advantage from the use of the network. On 27 August 1745, British troops under the command of General John Cope retreated from their intended march over the Corrieyairack. Fearing an ambush near the top of the pass, they went north instead to Inverness, leaving uncontested the main route into Perthshire for the Jacobite clans of the North-west Highlands.

I'm not much interested in the doings of Charles Edward Stuart, an aristocrat whose failed quest to claim the British throne brought terrible consequences to the people of the Highlands; but I'd always wanted to climb the Corrieyairack Pass. During those intense, joyous, exhausting first years of parenthood, I would occasionally dig out my Ordnance Survey map of Northern Scotland and trace a line along the shore of a loch or over a bealach, or pass, between two mountains. It was a vicarious pleasure, imagining myself there by reading the topography of the map; but it was also a form of commitment to walks I might take in the future. The Corrieyairack Pass was one I often traced, and now, though the rest of my route was to be guided by chance and by folktales – that most unreliable of narrative forms – the pass seemed an appropriate place to begin a journey into the north and west.

*

Late in the afternoon, I crossed a bridge over the River Spey and passed an estate yard bustling with 4x4s, trailers and Argocats. Through the open door of a shed, I saw the body of a red deer stag hanging by its tied hind legs from a hook on the ceiling. A ghillie was in the shed, standing with his back to me, his attention focused on the carcass. It was an odd first encounter with one of the creatures that would be, more than any other, my companions on the journey. I was glad the ghillie didn't notice me, and I walked on quickly, as though I'd witnessed something illicit or profane: the stag upside down, the bucket catching its blood; the ghillie with an apron over his tweeds, busy with knives.

An hour later, at dusk, another stag, very much alive, paused as it crossed the road ahead of me and turned to look. It was young, only a couple of tines on each antler. I stopped too, and for a moment we regarded each other in silence.

When I think about red deer, I think about how there are too many of them – the population stands at around 400,000, which is more than there's ever been in Scotland – and how they overgraze the land, stripping young trees of their foliage and decimating seedlings, so that there is no chance for woodland to regenerate naturally. I think about how some estate owners maintain high numbers of deer, even feeding them in winter, to ensure there's plenty to be killed in the shooting season. And I think about the fact that, in many parts of the Highlands and Islands, there are more deer than people.

Abstract thoughts disappear when you meet a young stag at dusk on General Wade's Road, with forestry pressing either side, and with the silhouette of its head and antlers unmistakable, like an imprinted memory or a pattern recognition handed down from hunter ancestors.

I had no wish to harm the stag and felt instead a wary empathy – two strangers meeting on a night-time road, each surprised and curious to find the other there. The stag jumped the road-side fence and disappeared. I followed it into the forest, clambering over the fence with none of its elegance, hoping to find a place to camp for the night.

The ground was poorly drained, and the trees, mostly spruce, were spindly. Storms had uprooted many of them, and I had to manoeuvre around and over those that lay criss-crossed on the forest floor. In places, fallen trunks were useful as bridges for crossing patches of bog. A stand of tall larch trees signalled drier ground not far from a bend in the Spey where it looped around the forest plantation, and I could hear the murmur of the river through the trees. Fallen needles formed a thick carpet beneath the larch and were heaped in wind-drifts against their trunks. I pitched my tent, gathered dead branches, and cleared space to light a fire to cook my evening meal.

Throughout the month, I planned to cook on open fires where it was practical and sensible to do so. It's a contentious issue in the Highlands. Every year, campers cause damage with badly looked-after fires, especially in the dry months of early summer; but in October the ground is usually damp with autumn rain, and I was a careful and conscientious fire-tender. I also carried a stove in my rucksack, a mini Trangia, but was keen to preserve fuel when possible. More than that, to set my campfire and tend it after dark served a deeper need than the means to cook a meal: it was the day's walk rewarded, the hearth around which a forest or a glen became home for the night.

The moon rose above A' Bhuidheanach, 'The Yellow Ridge', and glowed amongst the crowns of the trees. I was grateful to be warm, dry and fed. My only concern was the pain that throbbed in both my feet.

I'd made a mistake. My old walking boots were cracked and no longer waterproof. I was on a tight budget but didn't want to buy cheap, so I had replaced them with a second-hand pair, bought on eBay for £40; the same brand as my old ones, listed as my size and barely worn. When they arrived, they were too tight. I took them to the cobblers to be stretched, tried them out on a couple of day walks in the weeks leading up to October, and convinced myself they would be fine, especially if I wore thin socks. They weren't.

In the last of the firelight, I applied plasters to the blisters on my heels and my toes, then went to bed and slept beneath trees that surged and keened in the wind. October is rut month for red deer, and in the night, I heard stags roaring on the other side of the Spey.

The Gaelic for 'deer' is *fiadh*, the same word for 'wild'; they are also traditionally known as *crodh-sìthe*, 'fairy cattle'. In the folklore of the Highlands, there is no creature more other-worldly, more fey, than the *fiadh*. In many tales a hunter will raise his bow or gun to shoot a deer, only for it to take the form of a woman – always a woman – turning to a deer again when the weapon is lowered. Murdoch Macpherson, seventeenth-century hunter of Strathspey, known as Muireach Mac Iain, is said to have met one of these shape-shifting deer on An Dùn, a hill near Dalwhinnie, to the east of where I was camped.

It is late in the afternoon and Muireach Mac Iain, with skill and guile, has stalked a deer so close that he can look it in the eye. He raises his gun, and the deer takes the form of a woman, fairer than any he has seen; but when he lowers his gun, it's a deer again. After much to-ing and fro-ing between forms, from deer to woman and back, eventually the deer stays deer, and Muireach succeeds in shooting it.

Immediately after the kill, overcome with weariness, he rolls himself in his plaid and falls asleep next to the body of the deer. At dusk, he's woken by a voice thundering in his ear: 'Muireach, Muireach, you have this day slain the only maid on An Dùn!'

Muireach Mac Iain jumps to his feet. 'If I have killed her, you may eat her,' he says, and he leaves An Dùn as fast as he might, taking home no venison for the larder that evening.

Like the Cailleach's encounter with Brown-eyed Donald on Beinn a' Bhric, this is clearly not a typical folk or fairy tale: Muireach Mac Iain is no hero, and he's certainly not returning with great riches; nor is it a fable, for there's no moral imperative. Instead, Muireach's encounter with the deer-woman explains nothing and speaks only of a relationship to a world that is mysterious, beautiful, savage – a hunter's world.

*

In the morning, I discovered that my map – the one I had traced with imagined routes during those early years of parenthood – was out of date. It didn't show the construction track for the upgrade of the Beauly–Denny power line, or the new 165-foot-high pylons, marching up and over the Corrieyairack Pass. It didn't show the industrial compound between Garvamore and Melgarve, with its corrugated sheds and wire fence festooned with blue 'KEEP OUT' signs, its coils of arm-thick cable and stacked ceramic insulators as big as my children, and its giant diggers with their orange lights flashing; the glare and growl of it all.

The Scottish Government has set an ambitious target for renewable energy production. Much of our electricity already comes from wind turbines and from hydropower, and the capacity of the existing transmission network is inadequate to cope with further expansion. Hence the Beauly–Denny upgrade, so that more power generated in the Highlands can be sent to the Central Belt.

The Garvamore compound is situated close to where a friend of mine is adamant that he once had an encounter, not with shape-shifting deer, but with little silver buddha-men, fat-bellied and glowing by the river.

He'd been camped by one of the Spey's many pools and had got up to relieve himself in the night. Because he was only half-awake, it seemed unremarkable that the silver men should be there; bewilderment came with full waking in the morning. My friend is level-headed, not one for such encounters. Whatever it was he saw – or dreamt he saw, despite his insistence – it is unlikely to be repeated now that the pylons dominate the glen, and the compound with its bright lights looms above the pools.

The tarmac road ends at Melgarve, and the old military road continues, climbing up into Corrie Yairack. The meaning of the name is disputed, but it seems to be an anglicisation of Coire a' Gheàrraig, suggesting 'Corrie of the Short Burn or Spring'. Either way, to climb the corrie is to appreciate the toil of building the road: each stone you step on has been excavated from the hillside, carried and carefully planted; mile upon mile of back-breaking work, in all weather and for poor pay, no doubt.

After a particularly steep section, where the road is forced to zigzag up the side of the corrie, I stopped to rest and eat lunch by a cairn. It was a sheltered spot, surrounded by crags and gullies – a good place for an ambush – and I understood why General Johnnie Cope might have had second thoughts about leading his redcoat soldiers up into it. Looking back, despite the wide strath of the Spey and the Cairngorms rising in the distance, what I saw was the line of giant, antlered pylons. Somewhere on the hill a stag was bellowing, as though he too was affronted by the sight of them.

*

An ugly concrete shed stands at the top of the Corrieyairack Pass, at a height of 2,500 feet. On its locked, rusted door a sign reads: *The safety of men's lives depends on the equipment stored in this shed.* The shed is a remnant from the first power lines that ran over the pass. Taking shelter from the wind in its lee, I caught my breath before turning my back on Speyside. The land continued to rise either side of me, north to the top of Corrieyairack Hill, south to Carn Leac; but this was where I wanted to be, at the pass, with Glen Mor, the 'Great Glen', opening below.

The Great Glen Fault splits Scotland diagonally, stretching south and west from the Moray Firth and the North Sea to Loch Linnhe and the Atlantic. It is part of a major fault in the Earth's crust and can be traced northwards all the way to Svalbard in the Arctic. In Scotland, physically and culturally, it's not as significant a divide as the Highland Boundary Fault which runs roughly parallel, some fifty miles to the south, and which marks the transition from the Lowlands to the Highlands. Instead, Glen Mor is like a great sword stroke slicing across the shoulders of the Highlands, severing one mountainous region from another. Not as significant, but a severance nonetheless: beyond Glen Mor, the landscape of the North-west becomes one of the most remote, rugged and sparsely populated in Europe.

My feet were sore, my rucksack heavy on my back after the climb out of Corrie Yairack, and around me the mountains were saturated and grey; but I was elated to be here, to be crossing over like so many had done before: the drovers, packmen, merchants and reivers, the people who had used this pass long before General Wade and his road builders pitched up; an old route for cattle and commerce, for the exchange of news and the passing back and forth of stories.

It is a fine day and Donald Cameron, known as Dòmhnall Mòr Òg, 'Big Young Donald', is out on the moor with his dog and his

gun. He's as renowned a hunter as Muireach Mac Iain of Speyside,
but he is from Lochaber, to the west of the Monadhliath. His step
is light on the moor, and the sun is warm on his face. Early in the
afternoon he encounters some people cutting peats at a bank. They
are strangers to him, but they invite him to join them and to share
their food. He's not hungry, but they insist, calling him by his
name. Donald's dog wants nothing to do with the strangers; it
keeps its distance, hackles raised.

   The tairsgeirean, *the peat spades, are set aside, and a blue*
woven cloth is spread. There's butter, cheese, oatcakes, finer than
any Donald has tasted. After the meal, he thanks them, and they
bid him farewell, calling, 'Long may it be, Dòmhnall Mòr Òg,
before you bring down a deer.'

   'I'll hope not,' he replies, taking his leave; and sure enough, it
isn't long before he reaches the heights of the moor and sees a fine
strong stag. He raises his gun to shoot, but taking aim, it's a woman
that is in his sights, with pale complexion and curling red hair. He
lowers the gun, and it's a stag, raises it, and it's a woman, and he
sees that she is combing through her hair, and that with each stroke
of the comb, lice are falling from her curls like winnowed chaff.
Three times he raises his gun, and on the last he loads it with a
bent silver sixpence instead of a lead ball. This time the stag stays
stag, and he shoots it dead, the silver sixpence piercing its heart.

   When he goes to gralloch the stag – to take its guts out – he finds
in its belly the same butter, cheese and oatcakes that he had eaten
with the strangers at the peat-bank. He stands and folds his gun
under his oxter, and he and his dog go home without venison for
the larder that evening.

It was raining hard as I followed Wade's Road across the boggy
watershed of the Monadhliath. Cloud shrouded the mountains on the other side of Glen Mor, occasionally lifting enough
to reveal wind turbines arranged in neat patterns on the slopes.
An eight-wheeled Argocat passed me on the track, driven by a

young ghillie, who waved. It was followed minutes later by a smart, black 4x4 pick-up. I nodded to the driver and saw the shapes of two figures in the rear seats of the cab, the clients, obscured by tinted windows. The stag that they'd shot was sprawled in the open back, sodden with rain, its slack head bumping against a wheel arch.

The popular image of modern hunting in Scotland is of honourable ghillies practising their craft with skill, regard for tradition and patient tolerance of the behaviour of their clients, as though it's they, the ghillies, who ennoble the act and govern the relationship. There is some truth in this, and I have a good deal of respect for many of the ghillies and stalkers I've met, although the persistence of illegal poisoning and trapping on some private estates suggests that not all live up to the ideal; and when it comes to the relationship between ghillie and client, everyone knows who really wields the power.

A friend once told me a family tale about his grandfather, who as a young man worked as a ghillie on a Highland estate between the wars. He was tasked with rowing a party of women across a loch to their picnic spot. Because they were fashionable young ladies, they were smoking cigarettes. 'You must think it scandalous to see us smoking,' one of the women said to the ghillie, who replied, perhaps without thinking, perhaps mischievously: 'Och no, we see the tinker-wives doing it all the time.' He was dismissed from service later that day. His children's children remember his perceived insolence with pride.

Roads and power cables cross the mountains. The land is not wild land. The deer which roam the hills are a commodity, stocked and then stalked in the shooting season. There are shiny black cars outside the big house on the estate. The upper reach of the Spey, one of Scotland's finest rivers, has been dammed to divert extra water to the aluminium smelter at Fort William. The Spey dammed and diverted is not the same Spey. The hills bristle with the blades of wind turbines.

It's complicated. During my month of walking, many of the locals I met were in favour of sporting estates, wind farms and fish farms, hydro-electric power stations, mono-crop forestry. They want jobs for themselves and their children that don't rely solely on the tourist dollar; and for sure, given accelerating climate change, wind and hydro are attractive alternatives to oil and gas.

I actually like the look of wind turbines, despite their intrusion: the elegance of their slow, enormous turning, especially when there is a group of them, like choreographed dancers or those whirling Sufi mystics. But the bigger question is not about aesthetics or jobs or ownership; it's about whether this is tenable, whether a system that relies on ever more industrialisation of the land, and extraction from it, can or should be sustained.

I camped for the night by the bridge at Lagan-a-bhainne, the 'Hollow of the Milk'. My feet were cramped and sore, my left heel badly blistered, and I was painfully aware of how stupid I'd been to set out wearing tight, second-hand boots. That evening, the rain was too persistent for a fire, so I crouched in my tent and cooked dinner on the stove by the light of my head torch.

*

In the morning, I followed the old stone road as it curved round and down the southern side of Glen Tarff. Mist clung to the hills, and where the sun filtered through, thickets of birch glowed. The wind turbines and the pylons were out of sight, and wildflowers grew in the road's verges, with self-heal still in flower. Below me, by the river, a sparrowhawk glided from one thicket of birch to the next. On the slope above, a stag and half a dozen hinds studied and then dismissed me. Around a bend in the road, the pylons veered back into view, and the white-washed cottages of Fort Augustus gleamed in the distance, clustered at the head of Loch Ness.

A rusted sign on the gate at the bottom of the glen proclaimed: *Wade's Road is a scheduled ancient monument. Any person causing damage is liable to prosecution by the Secretary of State.* I closed the gate behind me and thought about the construction tracks of the Beauly–Denny power line, gouged into the hill; the industrial compound between Garvamore and Melgarve; the metal march of the pylons.

Chapter 3

The Loch beneath the Loch

The Caledonian Canal passes through the middle of Fort Augustus before opening out into Loch Ness. Designed by Thomas Telford and William Jessop, its construction early in the nineteenth century, linking Fort William to Inverness via Lochs Oich, Lochy and Ness, means that there is a continuous body of water running the length of the Great Glen Fault. Strictly speaking, this makes an island of the North-west Highlands.

A crush of tourists was taking selfies on the canal bridge when I crossed over. I was limping with the pain in my feet and thought about booking a pitch at the campsite in the village, but its name, Cumberland's Campsite, strengthened my resolve to carry on. Naming your business after a duke whose epithet is 'the Butcher', and who, in the aftermath of Culloden, encouraged his troops to commit what nowadays would be considered war crimes against the defeated Jacobite soldiers, as well as against the local civilian population, doesn't seem sensitive to the history of the area. The village itself is also named for the duke, William Augustus, who was youngest son of King George II. Before being re-named, it was known in Gaelic as Cille Chuimein, after Saint Cummein of Iona, who reputedly built a church there in the seventh century.

It was a busy place, for October. I found a public telephone and phoned my wife, asking her to post my old walking boots to Ullapool, care of the Ceilidh Place, and to book me a bed in their bunkhouse for a couple of nights.

During my month's walk, I wanted to step away from the world of phone calls and texts, emails and 24-hour newsfeeds, so I hadn't brought a smart phone or a radio. It meant no GPS or weather forecasts, but I had a map and compass, and suitable kit to engage with whatever weather autumn in the Highlands might present; and I'd packed a non-smart mobile phone, wrapped in a waterproof bag in my rucksack, in case of emergency.

I gave myself five days to reach Ullapool, time enough for the Royal Mail to deliver my old boots while I stopped to rest my feet and then hitched my way there. At the local shop in Fort Augustus, I stocked up on food supplies and blister pads, and bought myself treats. I'd planned to eat simple camping food on my journey – porridge, oatcakes, stew – but I'm no ascetic: after three days on General Wade's Road, I was glad of the chance to buy chocolate and whisky.

The woman serving at the counter lamented that there was never now a quiet season, that this year was the busiest ever and that the cheap pound just kept the tourists coming. Everyone I spoke to in the village offered an opinion on the busy-ness. Because I was a walker with a rucksack, it seemed that I was spared their reproach. When I stopped to check times at a bus stop, an old woman – small, thin-lipped, wrapped in a beige raincoat – told me, unprompted, that it was '*Outlander* that was bringing them'. She went on to explain that normally it would have quietened down by now, but instead, 'The bloody campervans are still clogging up the roads.' It was a complaint I was to hear again and again: the campervan craze, and the lack of infrastructure to accommodate them.

There was no bus due, so I walked to the edge of the village to hitch north on the A82, following the shore of Loch Ness. I knew of a quiet place to camp and hoped to reach it later that day.

*

'Where are you from?' The question was friendly but probing, and very Scottish – that insistence that the place where you were born is more important, when assessing character, than your profession or social standing. The driver, a middle-aged man, was quick to tell me that he himself had lived in the area for over twenty years, though he added, quietly, as though regretful of the fact, it wasn't where he was from.

I grew up on the outskirts of Glasgow, on one of the new estates that bulges at the edge of the city; brick and pebbledash terraced and semi-detached houses for the aspirational work-ing class. My parents moved there from Springburn when they married, part of the exodus from inner-city tenements, and my mother still lives in the house that they bought. But when I left home, I moved around and made choices that dislocated me ever further from 'where I'm from'. As we drove into Invermoriston, I answered the driver nonetheless: 'Glasgow originally, now living in the south-west near Lochmaben, if you know it.' He nodded, satisfied, placing me.

My next lift was from a Yorkshireman who had moved to the area and who was self-building a house. He was a practical man who told me how much he enjoyed working his way through the different stages of the build. He had just finished the roof and was now cladding the walls, and he hoped that his house would be wind and watertight before winter set in. He also told me that he had seen the Loch Ness Monster. I laughed, thinking that he was joking, but he said it matter of fact: how one morning on the loch-side he'd seen it, its head and arched back rising above the water. He had no reason to lie, though he acknowledged it was unlikely I would believe him. I told him it was the last thing I expected to hear from a down-to-earth Yorkshireman. He wasn't embarrassed.

'I saw what I saw,' he said.
'I'm sure you did,' I replied.

In the sixth century, Colmcille, Irish prince and founding abbot of a monastery on the Isle of Iona, encounters a monster while crossing the River Ness, which flows from the foot of Loch Ness into the Beauly Firth. Colmcille, nowadays known as Saint Columba, is on his way to Inverness to convert a Pictish king. As befits such a high-power holy man, he makes the sign of the cross with a flourish of his hand and scares off the monster, saving the lives of the monks who are travelling with him. A century later, Adomnán, 9th Abbot of Iona, writes in his hagiography of Colmcille that 'the beast, as if pulled back with ropes, fled terrified in swift retreat'.

Between St Columba's encounter and the twentieth century, there is scant mention of a monster in Loch Ness. But in the 1930s, a flurry of sightings began, producing amongst others the famous 'surgeon's photograph' of a small-headed, long-necked creature emerging from the water. Long suspected of being a fake, it wasn't until the 1990s that the truth of the photograph surfaced, when one of its creators, by then a very old man, admitted that the monster's head and neck was a model mounted on a toy submarine. You'd think that would have done for Nessie, but her story continues to fascinate and to feed a need for the inexplicable, projecting that need out onto the landscape. The scholar Ronald Black, writing in *The Gaelic Otherworld*, believes that the mistake most Nessie-hunters make is to search Loch Ness for a creature of flesh and blood, one which inhabits the physical world. If she's to be found at all, he suggests, it will be in the 'otherworld' – that landscape contiguous to ours, *the loch beneath the loch*, to paraphrase Clarissa Pinkola Estés or, as the poet Kathleen Raine has it, 'the bright mountain behind the mountain'.

A tale of the Loch Ness Monster was not what I expected to hear on my travels, but it was a useful reminder that we all accommodate different experiences of reality. It would be easy enough for me to disbelieve a Yorkshire builder who says, with absolute conviction, that he has seen the Loch Ness Monster, just as I might dismiss my friend's half-awake encounter with little silver buddha-men on the banks of the Spey; but by doing so, I would be narrowing my vision, lessening my chance of a glimpse of the 'bright mountain'. Instead, I took it as a positive sign that, as soon as I'd crossed the Great Glen Fault, I was being confronted with a lived experience of that other landscape I was looking for.

My favourite account of Nessie comes from the storyteller Douglas Mackay, who grew up in Inverness and who tells a story about his father Hugh, when he was out fishing with a friend just at the point where the loch pours into the River Ness.

It's dusk and the two men are casting out onto the river, with the chill of the evening held at bay by frequent sips from whisky flasks. A disturbance in the water catches the attention of one of the men, and he sees, snaking its way across the mouth of the river towards them, the tall head and curved humps of a serpent-like creature. Incredulous, fearful, the men gesture to each other and point to the approaching beast.

To their surprise and relief, they watch as a red deer stag steps out of the water, followed in line by three hinds and their calves. The deer shake the water off their coats like dogs, then slip between the trees that crowd the bank.

It seems apt that the fishermen were confused by the deer, *na fèidh*, our wild, fey companions, swimming across the Ness and blurring the boundary between myth and reality.

The Yorkshire builder dropped me at Drumnadrochit, stopping his van outside Nessieland, a tourist attraction and café with a large fibreglass sculpture of the monster towering above the outdoor picnic tables. As I opened the van's door and climbed out of the passenger seat, we both looked up at the sculpture. The driver raised his hand in salute, though I was unsure whether to me or to the monster, and then he drove off towards Inverness. It began to rain as I walked out of the village, heading west towards Cannich on the A831, each step sore.

*

My last hitch of the day was from Ron Bury of Tomich. Ron was retired, but he was an active volunteer, conducting surveys for wildlife charities and setting up motion-sensor cameras in woodland to record the presence of red squirrel, pine marten and other mammals – even occasionally a Scottish wildcat, though he told me he'd only recorded two in six years.

Ron detoured out of his way to drop me at my destination, and when we parked the car by Eas a' Choin, the 'Dog Falls', he walked with me into the woods, 'for the sake of the conversation'. Charlie, his dog, ran ahead, tail wagging, but Ron himself was slow from a gammy leg – the result of a crash during his 'irresponsible motorbike days'. I was grateful for the pace, given the state of my feet. After a mile of walking and chatting, I left Ron under a Scots pine, rolling a cigarette and looking for chewed pine cones – red-squirrel evidence; a gap-toothed, grizzly-man, untroubled beneath the trees.

Glen Affric – from Gleann Afraig, 'Dappled Glen' – holds a remnant of the pine forest that once covered large parts of the Highlands. Its oldest trees, the 'granny' pines, were around when wolves were in the glen. Their growth is frugal in the northern climate, producing coarse needles and skeletal branches, bark that is plated and cracked like a veteran's armour; but in the evening their trunks glow orange-pink with the setting sun, as though warmth is radiating from inside of them. The glen was just the place to camp and to rest my blistered feet.

Glen Affric is not a wild place. Most of it has been owned by the Forestry Commission, now Forestry and Land Scotland, since the 1950s, and careful management is required for its protection and regeneration. But walking through it, you sense that a measure of its old, wild self is being restored, as though it's returning to somewhere older than Scotland – that nation state of industry and commerce that felled its trees, drained and ploughed its moors, built its roads and cities. There's nothing like the fauna that there was, the lynx and bear and boar, the wolves; but it's the kind of place where you would expect such creatures to be, and, being there yourself, it's possible to imagine their return.

It was late in the afternoon when I took the track west through the glen and stopped on the ridge below Carn Fiaclach, 'Toothed Cairn', looking down through pine and birch to Loch Beinn a' Mheadhoin, 'Loch of the Middle Mountain'. The sun silvered the water, small islands were crowned with trees, and the leaves of the birch were golden yellow. The view held me till the light faded and I went looking for a place to camp, eventually finding a clearing on a promontory that curved out into the loch from its southern shore. The clearing was surrounded by pine, birch, willow, a rowan stripped of its berries. Lichen hanging from the branches of the trees thrived in the clean air, and the ground was thick with blaeberry and heather, and with thin grass where the canopy cast most shade. At the centre of the clearing lay a well-used hearth: a circle of stones, brimful with ash.

By the time I pitched my tent and gathered dead branches for a fire, the night sky was black. When I took off my boots, I shouted aloud with the pain. Tending to my blisters, I was impressed by their weeping; my left heel in particular was a puckered, red mess.

I cooked stew in my pot on the fire and cut a hunk of bread and buttered it – I'd bought a whole pat from the shop in Fort Augustus. A barn owl shrieked not far from the clearing, and I imagined mice scurrying for cover on the forest floor, their tiny hearts quickened like mine. I had heard that shriek before – so unlike the affable hoot of a tawny owl – but even still, its witchy-ness had me peering into the dark between the trees, aware that my fire was a beacon, letting anyone, or anything, know I was here. In Gaelic, a common name for an owl is *cailleach-oidhche*, 'Old Woman of the Night'.

Dòmhnall Donn-shùileach is on the ridge of Beinn a' Bhric. His plaid is dun-coloured like the mountain, like the deer he's stalking; they're congruent with each other. He's moving on the mountain with the deer as though it's a dance, or as though his mind is cast on the deer; but it slips. The deer veers off the ridge, leaping down the slope of Coir' a' Bhric Beag like a stream in its course. Donald crawls to the edge and looks down. In the corrie's bowl he sees that the deer has found its herd and that a familiar figure stands in their midst. Donald lowers his bow.

This is another part of the tale I heard Jamie MacDonald Reid tell, in that pub in Edinburgh. There are many versions and fragments. In some, the hunter is identified as Dòmhnall mac Fhionnlaigh nan Dàn, 'Donald, son of Finlay of the Lays', who lived in Lochaber in the sixteenth century, and who was born near Fersit, some thirty miles south of Glen Affric. A compatriot of Dòmhnall Mòr Òg, who encountered the strange peat-cutters, this Donald was both hunter and bard. His poem, *Òran na Comhachaig*, the 'Song of the Owl', is considered by folklorist Calum Maclean to be one of the greatest ever to have been composed in Gaelic. Four hundred years later, in the 1940s, it was still being recited as part of the living oral tradition of Lochaber.

The moon was up, and the barn owl shrieked again, charging the air with its otherness. When I planned my walk, I was not so worried about the weather or the toil of rough terrain: it was the shortening days that concerned me, the acceleration towards darkness, and being spooked at night on my own in a forest, far from house or village. I huddled by the fire and drank whisky from my tin cup, thinking of Brown-eyed Donald and his first encounter with the Cailleach, when he'd so calmly invited her to share his meal. I was impressed again by his composure and wished for a measure of it myself.

*

The tent's flysheet was patterned with birch and rowan leaves in the morning. It was so quiet I could hear the wing beats of small birds as they flew between the trees. The air breathed, loosening more leaves and catching the tallest frond of a clump of bracken, twisting it, like a key turning.

I lit the fire, boiled water, made tea and then followed the path to the shore, grateful to be walking bootless on a carpet of leaves and moss. The day unlocked. When the sun cleared the ridge, the loch was intense with light, a bright mirror for the mountains that held it, a wild loch, older than Scotland. I took three quick breaths and walked in, my pale Scottish legs turning bronze in the peaty water. *There was a man, there wasn't a man.* There was a loch. I plunged under it, the cold shocking and the water a dark, deepening landscape. My arms thrust forwards and down, a few quick strokes, and then I was up and gasping and whooping and swimming back towards the shore, my head raw.

It was joyful to stand waist-deep in a loch of whisky-coloured water, to splash and wash away the sweat of previous days on the Corrieyairack Pass, to walk back under the trees to the fire, the loch an unbroken mirror behind me, as though I'd never been in, or never came back out. If anyone had been walking on the forest track above my camp, looking down through the trees, they would have seen a naked man dancing an awkward jig around the fire, scuffing fallen leaves and flailing a thin travel towel, warming himself at the flames.

Like the rest of the glen, Loch Beinn a' Mheadhoin isn't really wild. The head of the loch was dammed in the 1950s to feed the hydro station at Fasnakyle, and the shore of the promontory is strewn with the stumps of dead pine, remnants of trees that once grew down to the old shore, before the dam was built. The trees were felled, the water raised, and eventually the drowned stumps released their grip, floating to the surface and washing ashore where they dried and weathered like bones.

After breakfast, I returned to the shore, unclasped my folding saw, and cut a load of arm-thick roots from the stumps, carrying them up to the clearing for firewood. They burned clean on the fire, and what little smoke they gave was pine-scented, astringent; decades under water and then bleaching on the shore in the sun, and still they held the sharp smell of their growth.

Something in me shifted. The man who might have stayed ashore, whose head was busy with the surface of things, gave way to the man who'd swam in the deepening landscape of the loch.

The high pasture of the corrie of Beinn a' Bhric is where the Cailleach leads her deer in summer, to graze the sweet grasses and mountain herbs. In the evenings she milks the hinds, singing to soothe them, and when the hunters of Lochaber hear her song, they know fine to keep away from Coir' a' Bhric Beag. But the Cailleach is having trouble this evening. The hind she's milking is restless, despite her attempts at soothing. It kicks the cogan, the milking bowl, out of her hands, spilling the evening's milk, and then runs off up the slope. Knowing that Donald's there, watching from the ridge, the Cailleach shouts after the hind, 'I wish Dòmhnall Donn-shùileach's arrow was in you!'

Donald makes no show of the strength required to bend the great Highland bow, and his arrow, released, finds the heart of the hind. The Cailleach of Beinn a' Bhric is mighty pleased to be rid of such a troublesome beast, and she offers Donald a gift in return, asking whether he would prefer the sense of sight or the sense of smell to be taken from any deer that he hunts.

'You take the nose, and I will take the eye,' Donald replies, meaning that he can conceal himself from the deer by moving skilfully through and around the features and contours of the land, but that he cannot deceive their keen sense of smell.

'Henceforth,' says the Cailleach, 'you can stalk upwind of any deer. But mark this,' she says, raising her hand as though to bless him, 'one day you will shoot a great stag, and when it is gralloched, you will find a ball of blue worsted yarn in its belly. That will be your last kill, Donald of the brown eyes.'

I don't know any hunters. I've met people who like to shoot guns at birds and other creatures, but that's not the same thing. In my early thirties, when I was working as a self-employed gardener, one wealthy, rural client gave me a tour of his gun room. He also showed me his family sword, which was wielded during his wedding ceremony. He wasn't much older than me, but he held his entitlement like the sword, between us. On autumn days while I pruned roses and dead-headed the dahlias, the woods beyond the garden were loud with the blasts of his shotgun and with the squawk of dying pheasants.

My head was spacious in the evening in the forest of Glen Affric. Thinking about my old client and his imperiousness didn't rattle me. I took my cup of whisky to the shore, to see the last of the light. Trout rose for autumn gnats, casting circles on the water, and the sky was heavy with cloud. When I walked back under the trees and followed the path through the heather and blaeberries to the glow of the fire, I tried to imagine how it would be to be a hunter here. Or maybe it was the other me who imagined it, the one who stepped into the loch in the morning and didn't step out – my bronze, peaty double. Maybe he was walking back down through the silt of the loch to a camp on the old shoreline, one that we left such a long time ago.

When glacial ice retreated from the Highlands of Scotland, all kinds of flora and fauna established themselves, some species returning to land they had inhabited during earlier inter-glacial periods, some altogether new. Eventually, humans arrived, and for thousands of years our ancestors made home here as hunter-gatherers, living so lightly that the only evidence they were here at all is a few fragments of tools shaped from bone and antler, some flint microliths, and a couple of shell middens in the Hebrides. It's hard to guess the human population density during that Mesolithic period but safe to assume it was sparse: a scattering of extended family groups, clans if you like, each with a large territory. In evolutionary terms, they were just like us, physically and cognitively, although the environment in which they lived, and their attitude towards it, was very different.

There are, of course, no eye-witness accounts from Scotland's remote past, but the geological record allows a glimpse of its landscapes and of the wildlife that those hunter-gatherers lived alongside, and we can study accounts of similar landscapes untouched by industrial civilisation. In 1769, when Captain Cook anchored his ship, HMS *Endeavour*, off the coast of New Zealand, the botanist onboard, Joseph Banks, recorded in his journal that although they lay a quarter of a mile off the shore, the clamour of birdsong during the dawn chorus was 'deafening'. Sailing up the coast of Mesolithic Scotland, the forest that crowded its shores would have been just as loud with life.

*

I spent four days and nights in the forest of Glen Affric. On the morning of my last full day, blue tits and coal tits were busy in the trees around me, a treecreeper worked the pine next to the hearth, and a pair of chaffinches beat the bounds of the clearing. I had seen no humans since parting with Ron Bury, the camera-trap man. The only human-caused noise I'd heard was on the previous day, when a boat's engine buzzed like an aggravated wasp somewhere on the loch.

A blustery wind shook down wet leaves, and the sky and the loch were grey. Despite the company of birds, I was cold and damp and dull, like the weather. I made tea, wrapped myself in warm clothes and waterproofs, and scrambled up through heather to sit beneath a pine tree, the roots of which gripped the exposed rock at the highest point of the promontory. As I sat looking at the loch and at the way the wind ruffled it, and at the trees swaying on the islands, and at the solid ridges of mountains rising into cloud, my mood brightened, and I felt buoyant, as though I was perched on the prow of a boat, as though looking, yielding my senses to the landscape and the elements, was a gift back to myself.

Although I have no experience of hunter culture, I have met people who are not so estranged from that way of life as we are in the modern West. A couple of years after I left my gardening job with the sword-wielding pheasant shooter, my family and I lived for a year in New Zealand. We didn't sail like Captain Cook but flew the 10,000 miles in a couple of days, stopping over in Singapore. I found work in a large garden that was open to the public, in a town close to Auckland. My youngest daughter was born there, and we lived in a bach – a simple wooden cabin – on the coast, with a short walk down through native bush to a beach. Our neighbours, who lived in the bach across the lane, were a large Maori family.

One of the few conversations I had with the man of the house took place on the beach. He was in his thirties, a big man, overweight, wearing a t-shirt, shorts, flip flops. He had been fishing and was walking back along the shore with his catch in a cool-box. He stopped when I approached, and we both turned to look out to sea. I asked about the fishing.

'Good enough,' he said. 'I'm down here most days, feeding the family.' He laughed slowly, softly: 'Government pays the bills, and the fishing's pretty easy.'

We always said hello after that, and although I've no idea if his attitude was typical of wider Maori society, it was clear that his priorities were different to those associated with modernity – the imperative to 'get on', to be upwardly socially mobile, to accumulate wealth, status, property.

I won't romanticise my neighbour's life; the impacts of colonisation on indigenous people are well known: the loss of land and culture; the inter-generational trauma so often manifested in alcoholism and drug use; the struggle to maintain identity. But I was glad that he'd found a way to play the system we Europeans, we *Pākehā*, had imposed: carrying on with feeding his family and living 'pretty easy', just as his people would have done in Aotearoa, 'Land of the Long White Cloud', in the days before Dutch explorers pitched up and called it Nova Zeelandia.

The weather shifted over Glen Affric through the day. By evening, when I went to the shore to wash dishes, the surface of the loch was completely still and reflected a clear sky, turning from deep blue to red as the sun set. It took a long time to wash my pot and spoon. When I returned to camp it was dark, and I had to blow hard on the embers to coax the fire back into flame. The night settled around the clearing, and, four days in, the thought that I might have been anxious to be here alone, after dark, seemed absurd. I added the logs I'd been drying, let the fire flare for a last time, then sat with it till it faded to a core of embers and a curl of smoke.

Dòmhnall Donn-shùileach hunted the mountains of Lochaber for many years and was renowned for his uncanny skill as a stalker. In old age he lived in a small cottage at the head of Loch Treig, below Beinn a' Bhric, and was looked after by his granddaughter, who lived nearby.

One autumn evening, he spies from his bench outside the cottage a great antlered stag that has come down to the shore to drink from the loch. The stag is as beautiful as any he's seen. He asks his granddaughter to step inside and take down his bow from where it hangs, unused, on the wall, and to see that the bow string is supple. He asks her to choose the best fletched arrow, and to rub it smooth on the hearth stone if it sits rough in the cleft of the bow. And although he is too weak to draw the bow – the great Highland bow that requires the strength of youth – his granddaughter is there to help. They bend the bow together, and their arrow finds the heart of the stag. When his granddaughter goes to the shore with her knife to gralloch the stag, she finds a ball of blue worsted yarn in its belly.

'The Cailleach's prophecy,' says Donald. 'My last kill.'

He bids his granddaughter goodnight, and she takes the path home to her family. In the morning she finds him slumped on the bench outside his cottage, with his head fallen forward and his white beard like a ruff on his chest. Dòmhnall Donn-shùileach's granddaughter wraps his body in the skin of the stag they killed, and with the help of her people he is borne up and buried on the eastern slope of his beloved mountain, Beinn a' Bhric, the Cailleach's mountain. His granddaughter sheds her tears into the stream he's buried by, a stream that is still known today as Allt Nighean Mhic Dhomhnuill, the 'Stream of Donald's Granddaughter'.

There's a lot going on beneath the surface of this story, and the ball of blue worsted yarn discovered in the stag's belly intrigues me. It appears in other tales of the Cailleach and is perhaps a symbol of the end of a way of life: the hunting culture that held sway up until the eighteenth century, when the introduction of sheep farming, wool production and the making of yarn had such an impact on the people and the landscape of the Highlands. Equally, I'm fascinated by the bond between the hunter and the Cailleach, and curious about his deference to her and his offering of food, as well as her ability to manipulate the deer and to give her blessing and approval for the hunt. It seems to me that the tale speaks of a very old relationship in the human story, one that is crucial to an understanding of Highland deer-lore.

*

I rose early after a calm night, unpitched my tent, packed my rucksack and prepared to leave the clearing beneath the trees – its hearth, the loch, the spaciousness. I'd hardly worn my boots in four days and dreaded putting them on again. A jay flew overhead, bright bundle of colour and noise. Its *scraich* at the sight of me prompted a long-drawn *pee-ouw* from a buzzard on the other side of the loch. Walking on the track back to Eas a' Choin, I passed trees that were covered in lichen and looked like raggedy old men.

After the Corrieyairack Pass, I'd thought I might walk through Glen Affric to Kintail and Loch Duich, and then perhaps cross to Skye to climb Beinn na Caillich – another story-rich mountain – or else stay on the mainland and travel north to Torridon; but that was before my second-hand boots began to bite. Now they were already pinching as I walked the mile and a half to Eas a' Choin.

At the car park, I met an elderly couple with their dog, a lurcher, who looked at me in that worried way that lurchers do. The couple stopped when I approached and were clearly curious to know where I had come from, so early in the morning. They were the first humans that I'd seen in four days, and I wanted to tell them about witches shrieking in the woods, about Donald the brown-eyed hunter, about the other landscape beneath the loch; but I wasn't sure that my reality and theirs would cohere, so I simply bid them a fine morning instead.

There were ripe brambles in the verge on the road to Cannich, and devil's-bit scabious in flower, and the red hips of dog rose. I stuck my thumb out. Three hitches took me the seventy miles north and west to Ullapool.

Chapter 4

West Coast Male

'Where are you from?' That question again, this time asked by a Cannich man who gave me a lift to Muir of Ord.

'A small clearing on a wooded promontory, mirrored on the surface of Loch Beinn a' Mheadhoin,' was what I wanted to say, was the answer that might serve the deeper current of the question: who are you, and how might I place you?

Growing up on the edge of a city, you're neither in nor out, and it was only after I left school that Glasgow properly claimed me. Aged seventeen and with few qualifications, I found myself standing alongside hundreds of other teenage boys in the main hall of the Scottish Motor Trade training centre, adjacent to Hampden Park in the city's south side. We were there to be enrolled in a youth training scheme and were told to join one of three queues, with the choice of becoming a mechanic, panel-beater, or parts-man. I was clueless and hesitant. A tall boy standing next to me said that being in a parts department would be better, 'less manky', than being in a workshop. It was the only career advice I received, other than from my mother, who told me that I should join the army, that that would 'sort me out'. I paid heed to the tall boy – he was wearing a Joy Division t-shirt – and for four years I worked as an apprentice in a parts department in the basement of a garage in Partick, living in a rented room in a flat off the Great Western Road. The garage, at times, was a brutal place, and I didn't thrive there.

From Muir of Ord my second hitch was in a bashed, muddy hatchback. Inside the car, the rear seats had been removed, and a strimmer was strewn in the expanded boot, along with waterproofs, wellies, fuel cans. Everything was covered in a layer of flailed vegetation that had dried to a pale green fur. I settled in the passenger seat, clutching my rucksack in front of me. There was a web of cracks in the windscreen, spinning out from the point where a passenger's head would hit in a crash. My instinct was to get out, but we were already moving, so I buckled my seat belt and tested it. The man in the driver's seat didn't notice, and nor did he ask where I was from. He looked as broken as his car; a big man, in his twenties I guessed, but with a worn face and red, swollen eyes. I could smell the drink on him, and it was no assurance to be told, as we accelerated round a bend, that he knew the roads like the back of his hand.

I was grateful that he couldn't take me far: in my short time in the car, I felt anxious for my life and for his. He told me that he used the hatchback for work and that he had an Audi in his garage at home. Unsure if he needed me to believe him, I said nothing. He told me about fighting and splitting with his girlfriend, and about the death of his brother, and him the only one left. When we stopped at the junction, his body shook as though he was flinching from a series of blows. I thought he might be having a fit, but his eyes were wet with tears.

'I'm a fucking mess,' he said. 'I need help.'

I began to say something, the smallest gesture towards his suffering, but he flinched again, and the space in the car contracted, became volatile. When I opened the door and climbed out, it was as though my lungs had seized and were only now starting to work again. His parting words were implacable: 'Don't worry, the booze will finish me off,' and he laughed in a way that wasn't laughing, 'as you would expect, me being from the West Coast.' The car sped away, and I stood dazed by the side of the road, breathing hard, with all the balance and spaciousness I'd found in the forest of Glen Affric jolted out of me.

The A835 was busy and loud, and I was buffeted by the slipstream of lorries as I walked along the verge of the road through Strathconon, the main route from Inverness to Ullapool. It was pointless to hitch: there was nowhere for cars to stop even if they wanted to, and after a mile or so I reached a lay-by and hopped the fence into a field that sloped below it, walking down to a line of trees that marked the course of the Black Water, a tributary of the River Conon. I took off my rucksack and sat beneath the trees on the bank, grateful to be resting my sore feet, happy to let the river drown the noise of the road.

There was no dun-coloured plaid for the hatchback driver, no congruence with the deer on the hill. His was a wounded and disparate life, and I wondered about his parents, whether they were still alive, the anguish they would be suffering; or whether they had been the cause of anguish – the passing down of alcoholism and violence is a well-enough-known tale in the west of Scotland.

How would it be to live a balanced life, filled with meaning and ceremony, in a place where you were from and where your culture's stories told you that you had always been from – and then to be severed from that? In the Highlands, the archaeology of severance is everywhere: the ruins of townships tumbled amongst heather and bracken. In the Lowlands, the Acts of Improvement levelled the old *fermtouns*, burying them under ploughed fields and modern steadings, whereas here, the landscape wasn't 'improved' in that way – sheep farming requires no plough and few buildings. The houses belonging to people cleared from their land remain in plain view – homes built by ancestors that can still be named and remembered. Meanwhile, sheep find shelter in the lee of ruined walls, and it's no wonder there are wounds that struggle to mend.

It was mid-afternoon, and I was due at the Ceilidh Place. I stood at the lay-by with my thumb out, facing down the traffic, and waited half an hour for a lift; the car that stopped took me all the way to Ullapool. As we drove through Strath Garve, its loch opened out into beauty beneath the foothills of Ben Wyvis.

Native of Strathcarron, craftsman, actor, musician, Calum had moved the few miles north to Ullapool for work and raising children, but he had a patch of land back home and would one day build a house on it. Another big man, he had an ease about himself, a geniality, and a quiet assurance that was the opposite of my previous lift, as though, on the road to Ullapool, I was being introduced to the flip sides of the West Coast male psyche.

It was no hardship to spend an hour in Calum's car, and the conversation flowed as we drove up towards the watershed between Strath Garve and Loch Broom. The land was rugged, treeless, and we passed few houses apart from the Aultguish Inn, sitting forlorn below the concrete brutalism of the Loch Glascarnoch dam. As we crossed the pass at Dirrie More, the sky cleared to the west, and An Teallach, 'The Forge', rose like a mountain in a fable, thrilling to see, its ridge a jagged shadow as the sun dropped behind it.

Streetlamps were lit along the shore road in Ullapool. Calum and I shook hands when he dropped me off by the pier, which jutted out into Loch Broom, the sea loch that opens to the Atlantic: the West Coast, where my compass is always pointed.

*

It took a while for me to find the courage to leave my job in the garage in Partick. I was serving an apprenticeship, gaining a trade, a solid, working-class aspiration, but I had no enthusiasm for it. A fellow apprentice used to take engine diagrams and parts lists home at night, so that he could memorise the part numbers, while an older colleague told me that in thirty years, he had never taken a day off sick. Rather than respect their diligence and dedication, I thought they were mad. Looking back now, I see a fearful young man, dully conscious that he was being crushed in the basement of the garage, but with no tools to lever himself out. It was only the greater fear of thirty years there and a head crammed with part numbers that forced me to act.

When I told my mother that I had handed in my notice, she was furious, warning me that I was throwing my life away. I found a job in a bar on the Great Western Road, working alongside people my age, many of them students. It was a brief, bright spell of inhabiting an entirely different Glasgow to the one I had known, although the intense friendships and the whirlwind nights were shadowed by too much drinking and too many drugs: it was the late eighties, peak Thatcher, and I and everyone I knew was taking more acid than was good for us.

One weekend, a friend invited me to visit his parents' home in Argyll, the place where he was from. Alastair's dad was a lock-keeper on the Crinan Canal, and the job came with a whitewashed keeper's cottage, built on three floors into the side of an embankment between the canal and Loch Crinan, which opens out into the Sound of Jura. It was autumn and already dark when we arrived in Lochgilphead off the bus from Glasgow. His mum picked us up by car, and there was mention of a party and a bonfire.

The party was at Crinan Ferry on the other side of the loch, which we crossed in a borrowed boat at slack tide, the loch a black mirror pricked with stars. We were rowing a dinghy across the sky, the rhythm of Alastair's oars like wing beats. Halfway across, I noticed that the blades of his oars, cutting through the water, trailed stars – not the fractured reflection of stars, but something actually sparkling beneath the surface of the loch.

'Phosphorescence,' said Alastair, grinning at my bewilderment. 'You know, in the water.'

I didn't know, at least not then, that at certain times of the year, when tide and atmospheric pressure are right, *Noctiluca scintillans* rises towards the sea's surface and, when agitated, glows with a greenish-blue light. Billions of single-cell algae, waiting for their moment to shine.

Being out in the dinghy on the loch, the Milky Way above and below us, Alastair at the oars and me trailing my hand in the water and watching it flame, makes me think now of the tale of the monks at Clonmacnoise in Leinster in Ireland, who witnessed a boat floating in the air.

The story is from the eighth century, and there is no context, no linear narrative about where the boat came from or where it was going; it's just a snapshot of the everyday miraculous, the otherworld and this world co-existent, like the images seamlessly woven into the text of an illuminated Celtic manuscript.

The monks of Clonmacnoise are about their business when they see a currach and its crew sailing across the sky. The boat is trailing its anchor on a length of rope, and the monks grab hold of it, but one of the sailors swims down to them, as though the air is water, seeking to free the anchor. The monks grab him too, but he shouts to be released, making it clear that he will drown. They let him go, and he pulls himself back up the rope with the anchor behind him, and the currach sails on through the heavens.

It's not so far to cross Loch Crinan. As we rounded a promontory, Alastair and I saw the glow of the bonfire on the shore and the shadows of people gathered there, and heard the sound of fiddle and guitar and laughter across the water. When we pulled the boat ashore, the welcome to Alastair was generously extended to me.

On the bus back to Glasgow, I mourned the growing-up I might have had: bonfires at the weekend and learning boat-sense on a sea loch; bearded dads rolling joints and long-haired girls who played fiddle and spoke with soft accents. The West Coast was imprinted on my mind as a place for the everyday miraculous.

My life in Glasgow was floundering. Returning one evening to the flat that I shared, I found that it was on fire. My flat-mate's boyfriend was a dealer, and in revenge for her infidelity, he had turned up at the flat, high on cocaine, clutching a can of petrol, which he'd poured onto the carpet and set alight. We were lucky no one died. Around the same time, another friend had taken to buzzing glue and aerosol. I found him one night, standing outside his flat, froth spilling from his mouth, a can of lighter fluid in his hand. He was in a dark place, unable to recognise me or himself.

Casting around for a rope to pull myself up, I spotted an advert in the jobs section of the *Glasgow Herald*: 'Help wanted on a small Hebridean island.'

*

At the reception desk in the Ceilidh Place, I discovered that its bunkhouse was fully booked for an event and that my wife had paid for me to stay in one of the guest rooms above the inn instead. The parcel she'd sent had also arrived, and I was grateful to find my old boots waxed and wrapped in paper inside. The room was spacious and lovely, with a dormer window that looked down the street to Loch Broom, an en-suite bathroom with a cast-iron bath and white cotton sheets on the king-size bed – a room beyond my budget. I smiled at the thought that two nights here probably cost more than I would have spent on a pair of new, properly fitting boots. My eBay frugality had saved nothing in the end and caused my feet a deal of pain; but then, I had gained the wealth of four days in Glen Affric and now this simple luxury.

Being inside, it was more noticeable that my clothes were damp and dirty, and that I smelled of earth and sweat and wood smoke. I made camp in the bedroom, emptying my rucksack, spreading my tent to dry, and airing my sleeping bag. I scrubbed my pot, mug and spoon in the sink, washed socks and underwear, hanging them to dry on the radiator, and then I sank into a deep, hot bath. By the time I dined downstairs that evening, I was reasonably groomed, though disheveled on the inside – adjusting, still, to having swapped my clearing in the woods for an inn full of people.

*

Ullapool bustles, even in October. I liked its big-village, small-town size, and with broad streets and expansive views, it's less compressed than other West Coast ports like Oban or Fort William. In 1788, the British Fisheries Society invited Thomas Telford to design and build a centre for the West Coast herring fleet. The 'herring boom' was short-lived, overfishing decimated stocks, and by the end of the nineteenth century Ullapool was a pretty town with few prospects. It survived the twentieth century by offering sheltered anchorage to deep-water trawlers, and then, in the 1970s, at the height of the Cold War, Loch Broom became the unlikely base for a fleet of Russian and East European 'klondykers'. These factory ships were anchored in the loch for months at a time, processing mackerel caught by smaller boats and shipping the catch east to the Baltic in refrigerated vessels. For many years the town's pubs and shops were kept busy by sailors from behind the Iron Curtain.

Ullapool remains a working port. The previous day, when Calum dropped me off at the waterfront, half a dozen fishing boats were huddled at the pier, there were yachts moored in the bay, and the Stornoway ferry, the MV *Loch Seaforth*, had arrived and was disgorging its cars and passengers.

My toes could move again, my old boots moulded comfortably to the shape of my feet. I spent the morning buying food supplies, proper trekking socks and more blister pads, then went for a stroll along the shore, glad to be by the sea for the first time on my journey. A cormorant welcomed me, surfacing a few yards offshore and then spearing back under the water.

I ate lunch on the pebble beach next to the pier, mobbed by a handful of herring gulls who hoped to share my oatcakes. A young one stood in front of me, insisting on my attention. It hadn't developed the plumage of adulthood, the yellow-ringed irises or the yellow beak with blood-red tip. It was black-eyed, black-beaked, and even the toes of its webbed feet were black. Little goth, its cry was both pathetic and indignant – *tzwee tzwee tzwee* – like a rusty foot pump. The other gulls flew off when they saw I wasn't for sharing, but the young one stood there, truculent, pestering me until I left the beach. The day was cold, wet, blustery, the weather no worse than it had been at times in Glen Affric, but knowing that my warm room was only five minutes away, I lacked enthusiasm to be out in it.

That evening, after dinner, I chatted to a retired fisherman in the inn. He was bald and broad-shouldered and had a sharp nose and large thick-lensed glasses. Once we had established where we were from and he heard I was now living near Lochmaben, he was delighted: the man who'd trained him so that he could sit his boat-masters' licence was originally from Lochmaben.

'He was one of those blokes who could take words that were this big,' the fisherman said, opening out his arms as though he was measuring a prize salmon, 'and coup them down to a size that I could understand.' He sipped his pint thoughtfully. 'That's why me, who was no good at school – English, maths, any of that – was able to pass the exams I had to sit, and become the boat-master I am.'

I liked his idea of couping words down – from the Scots *coup* 'to fall or push over', pronounced as 'cow' with a 'p' on the end. The fisherman blinked his eyes like the burly owl he resembled, and we raised our pints to his old instructor.

Later, I went out for a walk along the waterfront. The night sea was black and swollen against the pier. I turned back towards my bed in my room in the Ceilidh Place, grateful for the civilising comforts of the inn and yet, at the same time, eager to be on my way in the morning. Unseen in the dark, on the far side of Loch Broom, Allt na Caillich, the 'Stream of the Old Woman', continued on its course, tumbling down the side of a ridge, pouring itself into the sea loch.

The Cailleach is everywhere in the Highlands. Writing in the 1930s, the folklorist J.G. McKay describes her as 'the most tremendous figure in Gaelic myth today'. Her name is attached to countless streams, lochs, mountains and other landscape features, and often there's a tale associating her with these places. Sometimes it's more than association. Cailleach na Mointeach, the 'Old Woman of the Moors', is a ridge of low hills on the Isle of Lewis. Viewed from the north, the ridge takes the form of a reclining figure: it *is* the Cailleach, asleep in the land, demonstrating that in Gaelic tradition, as with other indigenous cultures, the distinction between the literal and the symbolic is supple, easily blurred, able to be one thing *and* another, like the shape-shifting deer-women encountered by Muireach Mac Iain and Dòmhnall Mòr Òg.

The Cailleach herself is supple, ambiguous, a composite figure gathered from various strands of myth and lore, and I was keen to unravel some of those strands, coup them down, as the owl-eyed fisherman would say, into a useful understanding.

She's perhaps best known in Scotland as the land-shaping giant who creates the Hebrides by accident, dropping from her apron the boulders she is carrying; and who uses the Gulf of

Corryvreckan and its whirlpools as her washtub, spreading her plaid to dry on the Paps of Jura – so clean and white you would be forgiven for thinking it was snow on the hills. My favourite story of her giant self tells of an encounter on a trip from Scotland to Ireland.

She's wading across the sea, the water only up to her knees, and she is carrying, as usual, an apron full of boulders. A French ship sailing into the Firth of Clyde passes between her legs, the tip of its topmost sail brushing her inner thigh. Such a delicate touch discomposes the Cailleach, and in a fluster, she drops the boulders from her apron. Thus, today, Ailsa Craig, a rocky bump of an island, sits ten miles off the Ayrshire coast.

Naturally, it had to be a French sailing ship for such a risqué encounter, and the details playfully blur the boundaries between legend and myth. More seriously, the Cailleach is also 'the old woman of storms', crone of winter, a blue-faced, one-eyed hag, who smites the world with frost and snow, and who creates thunder and lightning by striking her great hawthorn staff on the tops of mountains.

In all these traditions there's a correlation: she is elemental, a force of nature, like the Irish Cailleach Beira and like other 'earth-goddess' figures of Old Europe – that pre-Bronze Age, pre-Indo-European culture that can be traced in the archaeological record and in surviving fragments of myth and folklore.

But there is another Cailleach, a different tradition, one that seems to be aboriginal to the Highlands, though there are parallels elsewhere. This is the Cailleach whose well it is that I found on Beinn a' Bhric, who sings to the deer in Coir' a' Bhric Beag, and who mediates between the deer and the hunters. She's more human-sized than giant, though she is more-than-human – after all, she makes the leap from Beinn a' Chrùlaiste to Beinn a' Bhric in the time it takes to strike a flint and light a fire.

It is stories of her, and of her deer-women, that I was most keen to track on my walk. Many of those stories are centred around Lochaber and Rannoch Moor; but for now, I wanted to push my journey outwards, define its limits and look for traces of the Cailleach and other deer-lore in the far north.

*

Hitching out of Ullapool in the morning, a signpost informed me that John o' Groats was 170 miles away. I was on the A835, which is now part of the North Coast 500, a promoted touring route that has increased the volume of traffic on once quiet roads, many of which are single-track and not suited to such a volume.

That morning, the traffic was sparse, but after a few cars passed, a local woman in a Land Rover stopped to give me a lift. I was always conscious, on my journey, that it's easier to be a man when walking and camping and hitching solo, and that my own daughters will grow up assessing the potential risks of such a journey differently. It made me especially grateful whenever a woman offered me a lift, as I knew that her generosity was also, to a different degree than that of a man's, an act of trust.

As we drove north into Assynt, we entered a landscape unlike any other in the British Isles, and soon the distinct shapes of the mountains began to rise around us, mountains whose names form a well-known litany: Stac Pollaidh, Cùl Beag, Cùl Mòr, Suilven, Canisp.

Like many, I first became acquainted with Assynt through reading the poetry of Norman MacCaig. MacCaig was born and raised in Edinburgh, and as an adult he worked as a primary-school teacher in the city; but every summer, along with his family, he spent the long school holidays in Assynt.

Many of his poems celebrate its landscape, its wildlife and its people, so that reading MacCaig's poetry in my twenties, I felt more intimate with Assynt than I had any right to. Now I was looking forward to testing that intimacy against the hard rock of the place itself – the old, hard rock.

Assynt's mountains are mostly sculpted out of Torridonian sandstone, which was formed around 1,000 million years ago. Some of them are capped with Cambrian quartzite, whilst at their base is a layer of Lewisian gneiss. Exposed in places, this rock is around 3,000 million years old – the oldest in Europe. As well as sandstone, quartzite and gneiss, there are seams of limestone, marble and granite. The complex geological and meteorological forces that have acted on them over such spans of time drew the attention of professional and amateur geologists alike to Assynt in the nineteenth century, during the early years of the scientific study of geology. That attention is ongoing, and the area now lies at the heart of the North-West Highlands UNESCO Global Geopark, one of a worldwide network of sites of exceptional geological significance.

Assynt's geology makes it the most rugged district of a rugged region, one that covers most of the far north of Scotland. Named Suðrland, 'Southland', by Norse settlers – which it was to them – Sutherland, as it is now spelled, initially referred to lands south of Caithness but today stretches from Dornoch on the east coast to Lochinver on the west, and north to Cape Wrath and Durness. As a region, it has the lowest human population density in Europe, with under three people per square kilometre. In comparison, Scotland as a whole averages seventy people per square kilometre, while England averages 432. These figures support the popular notion of Sutherland as a vast, empty, wilderness, one that is divided into a few large sporting estates, mostly owned by multi-millionaires, with some crofting and fishing around the edges.

Figures are no use when trying to conjure a sense of place. I prefer stories for that, or songs, or the kind of elegant poetry that Norman MacCaig wrote: poetry that, through a wealth of noticing, counters the idea of Sutherland's emptiness and responds to the issues of land ownership with a challenge: 'Has owning anything to do with love?'

Chapter 5

The Bell in the Bone Cave

The stag knew I was there. He could smell me, but it didn't discourage him: he stood at the mouth of the cave and roared. I was inside the bell of his voice, the cave ringing with it. It was dark, but there was moon enough to mark the shadow of his antlers on the floor, and I could see the shapes of the hinds passing, hear their hooves drumming the path. The stag muttered, begrudging me, then strode off, following the hinds up towards the slopes of Breabag.

Earlier that day, the woman in the Land Rover had dropped me off at the foot of the glen, and I'd followed the path up to Creag nan Uamh, the 'Crag of the Caves'. All afternoon, I had sat in front of the caves and watched the deer in the glen: small groups of hinds, their heads bowed, young ones at their sides, grazing the autumn grass; and to each group a stag, lording it over them.

The rutting season is called *am bùireadh* in Gaelic, 'the roaring'. The stags bulk up from summer, and a coarse ruff of hair bristles on their necks; they roll in soiling pools, coating themselves in thick, black peat that is soaked with their own urine, and they chew on mosses and lichen until they smell rank. One stag I was watching, with his hinds on the slope opposite the caves, began to bellow as another stag approached, crossing a boundary. They hurled themselves at each other, the bone-clack of their antlers sounding clean and dry like a gunshot in the glen. With brute strength, driving the intruder backwards, the dominant stag defended his estate.

I didn't come here for the rut. I only knew that, in my month of walking, I wanted to loosen boundaries rather than define them. That afternoon, sitting at the mouth of the cave, watching the deer in the glen as the day began to thin, Ullapool's bustle slipped from my mind, and my body began to relax, as though I had removed a coat that was too tight.

The cave system at Creag nan Uamh has been forming for hundreds of thousands of years, water patiently dissolving the limestone seams. Excavations, early in the twentieth century, unearthed brown bear and reindeer bones. Later digs revealed the remains of arctic fox, lynx, wolf, and wild horse. A found fragment of polar bear skull is 20,000 years old. People were here too – unearthed human remains have been carbon dated to as far back as the Neolithic era – and the old shielings by the stream below the caves are a reminder that, until recently, we were integral to the ecology of the glen, our removal just another small, harsh deed in the history of land ownership in the Highlands. The nearest village now is the crofting township of Elphin, ten miles away.

Light slipped from the glen as the sun dropped behind Canisp. I set up my stove on flat ground at the cave entrance and cooked my evening meal. Two ravens returned to roost on the crags above, complaining at my presence. A group of hinds, followed by a stag, crossed the stream and began to crop the grass below the cave, the stag herding and strutting as though it was him who had made the decision to cross.

Three of the caves at Creag nan Uamh can be explored on foot. Those who excavated them gave them names: Badger, Reindeer and Bone Cave. Beneath them, and the slopes around, lie systems of passage and chamber accessible only with climbing gear, including a cavern that could house Edinburgh's Usher Hall. Bone Cave slants down and in for thirty feet. At the back there is an alcove with a clear pool.

Ripples, reflected by my torch, danced on the ceiling as though the water was glad of the light. A low passage, opposite the pool, narrows to a porthole, a child's squeeze, through to Reindeer Cave. The passage was sheltered and quiet, away from the wind at the entrance and from the noise of water dripping from the crags. I made camp there, unrolling my mat and sleeping bag and lighting two small candles.

Reindeer antlers form the bulk of the animal remains found during excavations of the caves, having been washed into them from the slopes above. Carbon dating of antler fragments reveals that reindeer were here as early as 50 000 BCE, and that, as glacial ice advanced and receded across the glens, they retained an intermittent presence up until the early Holocene. In a study of several hundred of the antler finds, the over-whelming majority were from female reindeer. The few others were from immature males.

Reindeer are unique amongst cervids in that both males and females carry antlers. Adult males shed theirs in winter, adult females in early summer at calving time. The females seek high, remote terrain for calving. They return again and again, in large herds, to the same grounds. Yearling males will occasion-ally accompany their mothers, but no adult males will be present. For thousands of years, it seems, the reindeer of Assynt used the slopes above Creag nan Uamh as their calving grounds. I was camped in a cave that had become an ossuary for their remains.

*

When I was a boy, growing up on the edge of Glasgow, we found a shark down the burn at the end of my street. When I say 'we', I mean the gang of kids who played in the gully through which the burn flowed – the Manse Burn, though I only learned its proper name as an adult. It was always just 'the burn' to us, and the name meant more than running water: it was the gully itself, thick with hawthorn and sycamore, and the clearings where we played Dead Man's Fall and Kick the Can; it was where we built dens and dams, climbed trees, lit fires, caught sticklebacks in jars; it was the place where child-hood happened; it was where I was from.

The burn marked the boundary between our estate, Bonnaughton, and the neighbouring estate, Baljaffray. Both were built in the sixties and seventies, an expansion of Bearsden, one of Glasgow's leafiest suburbs, and named after the farms whose fields they were built on. Kids from the two estates claimed the burn; sometimes we played together, sometimes we fought.

The shark, *Akmonistion zangerli*, is three feet long and 330 million years old. Back when it was young, a large chunk of Scotland sat near the equator, and Bonnaughton and Baljaffray were part of the bed of a shallow marine lagoon bordered by swamp forest.

Everyone knew you could find fossils amongst the outcrops of slate and shale on the banks of the burn, and we all dug for them, prising apart thin sheets of slate like opening pages in a book; but it required knowledge beyond ours to decipher the pressed shapes that we occasionally found. One of the Baljaffray boys took his findings to a neighbour, Mr Wood, who happened to be a palaeontologist and fossil expert. Intrigued by what he was shown, and with support from Glasgow's Hunterian Museum and the Nature Conservancy Council, Stan Wood organised a dig.

It was, of course, he and his team who found the shark, but we consoled ourselves with the knowledge that if it hadn't been for *our* excavations, no one would have thought to look for it.

You can visit *Akmonistion zangerli* in the main gallery at the Hunterian Museum in Glasgow. Thanks to the mud that preserved it at the bottom of the lagoon, it's the most complete fossil of a shark from the Carboniferous Period that has ever been found; so complete, that its last, partially digested meal, a fish, can be seen lodged inside its stomach.

The shark unspooled time for me, my young head dizzy with the notion that you could prise open, with your fingers, 330 million years, and that the burn where I spent my boyhood, a place that was so familiar to me, held a story older and stranger than any I might have imagined. The experience stayed with me, fuelling a fascination for how the past is layered in a landscape, and for the ways that those layers can be revealed. With encouragement, I might have pursued the study of palaeontology or archaeology – I think I've the temperament for it: the slow, fastidious work, the careful uncovering of hidden things. But around the time the shark was found, my father left home and never came back.

It turns out that beneath my parents' marriage lurked the secret of his affair with another woman. After he left, we muddled through, my sisters and I, and my mother, who didn't cope so well. There's a black-and-white photograph of her in a box of family photos, taken when she was young and single, working as a secretary in the late 1950s. She's on a day trip to Aberdeen and is standing at the pier with two friends, arm in arm, their hair thrown back by the wind. My mother is wearing a white blouse and a dark, flared skirt. She looks happy, carefree. I've never known that person.

I'm told that as a child I was self-contained, content to play on my own, 'always away somewhere' in my head. After my father left, self-containment became a strategy, a retreat from what was happening around me, although some moments were vivid enough to draw me back: my parents in the kitchen – he must have come back to gather his things – and her pulling a chopping knife from the drawer, brandishing it at him, shouting 'You won't take my children away from me!'

Perhaps death is less complicated than divorce; perhaps to lose a partner or a parent that way, the grief is like a bone broken clean. In the years after my parents split, I never saw or spoke to my father. He tried to arrange for us to meet, but I refused out of loyalty to my mother, who told me only, 'He left you too, you know.'

Many unkind words were spoken in those years, all of us carrying our wounds, though I was rarely able to articulate my own feelings. My mother didn't want to hear that I missed my father, and I didn't know how to speak of it to my sisters or my friends. I would stand at the work bench in the shed at the back of our garden, handling tools that he'd left behind: artefacts from someone who was no longer in the world – in my world. I was in my mid-twenties before we met again.

*

The stag's bellow in the night, at the mouth of Bone Cave, startled me out of a thin sleep. After he and the hinds had gone, I lay with my eyes open. I could still hear a faint roaring, but not from the stag: this was continuous, perhaps an underground river flowing somewhere in the caverns below. The passage I was lying in, which led to Reindeer Cave, was like the ventricle of a shell, and it was as though I was hearing the echo of the water that had once rushed through – like pressing a sea-shell to your ear as a child and hearing the sea.

Wide awake at the back of the cave, reeling from the stag, my senses tripping in the dark, I slipped furthest from the form of me that is husband, father, taxpayer. I lit a candle and looked up at the ceiling of the passage, which was pitted and ribbed like the roof of a mouth. In the flicker of candlelight, cracks and bumps and stains formed themselves into leaping deer, with antlers that curved upwards and became plumes of smoke.

It's easy enough to dismiss pareidolia, the perceptual quirk that persuades us to construct images out of random patterns, but that night in Bone Cave, with only a candle to keep back the dark, I imagined an otherworld pressing through from the other side of the ceiling. The distance between me and the people and the houses of Elphin felt more than ten miles.

*

Grey light seeped along the floor of the cave. The morning was cold and wet, and I brewed tea on the stove while wrapped in my sleeping bag. Outside, I could hear stags somewhere further up the glen, still roaring. I packed my rucksack and left Bone Cave, climbing up onto the stone fields of Breabag. The path I followed wasn't just a hillwalker's path towards the summit; it was another path, drummed by hooves, an old path, leading to the birthing place of reindeer. Below me, the two ravens were in the air above Creag nan Uamh, reclaiming it after my intrusion, descendants of descendants of the ravens who once watched over these calving grounds, attending each birth, eager for the bright, wet afterbirth.

The *Orkneyinga Saga* mentions the hunting of reindeer in Caithness to the east of Sutherland, in the twelfth century. The historical accuracy of the Viking sagas has often been confirmed by archaeology, but in this case the presence of reindeer so recently in Scotland's past is dismissed as unreliable, not least because the saga was written at a distance, in Iceland, by an author who would have based their knowledge of game on memories of a Norwegian homeland, where both red deer and reindeer were present. All other evidence, including carbon dating of the remains found at Creag nan Uamh, suggests that reindeer became extinct in Scotland some eight thousand years ago, their demise as likely the result of the warming climate as from predation by man.

It's a pity, because the fossil record disproves one of the explanations given for the origin of tales about the Cailleach of Beinn a' Bhric and other deer-women. It's an explanation that the story collector, John Francis Campbell, was particularly keen on. Born in 1821, Iain Òg Ìle, 'Young John of Islay', was something of a Renaissance Gael: he became a barrister in London and later a courtier to Queen Victoria, and had expertise as a scientist and inventor in the fields of geology, optics and photography. He was also a linguist who spoke several languages and travelled widely. Contemporary accounts describe Campbell as a self-effacing man who never married and who never sought fame or fortune. To his peers, he was 'the man who followed the fairies'; to those with an interest in Gaelic language and culture, he was a pioneer, one who performed a great service at a time when Gaelic was dismissed as an inferior language – a few decades before he was born, it was described as 'the rude speech of a barbarous people' by Samuel Johnson, the distinguished writer and author of *A Dictionary of the English Language*. Campbell's response, and legacy, is his four-volume *Popular Tales of the West Highlands*, a treasure trove of what he called the 'literary excellence' of Gaelic oral culture.

In the introduction to Volume 1 of the *Popular Tales*, Campbell describes an encounter he had in 1850, while travelling in Sweden, with a family of Sámi reindeer herders, known in his time as Lapps. Witnessing their appearance, living conditions and culture, he was convinced that the Picts of Scotland were a kindred race to the Sámi, and that tales of the Cailleach milking her deer, as well as other tales of fairy women and their 'fairy cattle', are a folk memory of when the Picts, like the Sámi, were reindeer herders.

Our old friend Muireach Mac Iain, the Speyside hunter, is involved in a tale that would seem to bear this out.

He is hunting in the forest of Gaick in Badenoch, when he spies a herd of hinds. To his astonishment, each hind is accompanied by a woman, small in stature, clad in green. These fairy women are milking the hinds. One of them has a hank of yarn, hoisted over her shoulder, and the hind she is milking grabs at the hank and swallows it. The angry woman strikes the hind and curses it: 'May an arrow from Muireach's quiver pierce your hide.'

In the course of the day, Muireach Mac Iain stalks and kills a hind, and when gralloching it, he finds the yarn in its belly.

This story has obvious parallels to the encounter between Brown-eyed Donald and the Cailleach, but to suggest that it is part of an oral tradition that remembers a time when Pictish women herded and milked reindeer is far from the mark. Unfortunately for Campbell's thesis, Pictish culture flourished between the late Iron Age and early medieval period, several thousand years after reindeer had become extinct in Scotland; and as for the notion of kindred races, the Sámi are Finno-Ugric, whereas the Picts were a Celtic people.

There is much to respect and admire in the scholarship of John Francis Campbell of Islay, but it's clear that a different explanation is required for the origins of the tales I was tracking.

I picked my way along the ridge of Breabag, across quartzite slabs and patches of loose scree, heading north towards Conival. Up on the ridge, after so long an estrangement, all traces of the reindeer have been scoured away – there are no layers of sediment to act as an archive. But place holds memory in myriad ways. Kneeling in the rain amongst the scree, I looked for and found a form of lichen, delicate and curled amongst moss in crevices of the rock, known in Gaelic as *crotal rèin-fhiadh*, 'reindeer lichen'.

Chapter 6

Conival

Three ridges meet at the summit of Conival. The name reflects this, although it has been anglicised. A stream tumbling down a crag on the northern ridge remembers the Gaelic: Allt a' Choinne' Mhill, the 'Stream of the Meeting Hill'. The crag is formed from off-white quartzite, 100 million years old and showing its age: the glen below is littered with rocks and shards that have eroded and fallen from it, some small, like arrow-heads, others, sheared-off blocks as big as horses. The crag guards the low point of the ridge, which continues north, rising again and widening to become a slope of Beinn an Fhuarain, the 'Mountain of Springs'. The low point, the col, would have had a name once, but even the oldest maps have forgotten it.

I was climbing a path to the right of the Allt a' Choinne' Mhill, having gambled that the weather would improve and that I might gain the view from the top of Conival. After my time in the depths of Bone Cave, the mountain's summit seemed like a useful corrective, and if nothing else, I hoped the altitude would clear my head of the fug of a disturbed night's sleep.

The path zigzagged up the crag and was steep enough that I had to use hands as well as feet. The quartzite was coarse against my fingers. Above me, Conival disappeared into cloud, the same cloud that rolled like smoke over Breabag to the south, smothering the ridge where I'd walked in the morning. The rain at least had stopped, and when I reached the col, I paused to rest by a small tarn. I munched oatcakes and was grateful that my feet had mostly mended. Both heels were still tender, but they were padded with bandages and new socks, and my old boots fitted snugly. Cushions of thrift hugged the ground around me, a few of their seed heads still hanging from thin stalks, and a moth's wing floated on the surface of the tarn: just the one, chalk-white, and the water so clear it was as though the wing was suspended in mid-air.

To the north, two stags were on the slope of Beinn an Fhuarain, keeping a distance from one another. They were too far away for me to gauge their size, but they weren't bellowing, and there was no sign of any hinds. I guessed that they were immature, not yet strong enough to challenge at the rut. Beyond them, out of sight on the far side of the slope, lay the graves of six Royal Air Force crew members, buried at the site where their aeroplane crashed.

On the morning of 13 April 1941, in the midst of World War II, Anson N9857 XF-F took off from RAF Kinross on a cross-country training mission. The plane successfully crossed to the West Coast, but the crew sent a radio message stating that weather conditions were bad. They flew up the coast and, as the weather continued to deteriorate, requested an emergency landing at RAF Stornoway. The runway there was blocked with snow, and they were unable to land. A short while later, the wireless operator at RAF Stornoway received a message from the plane: 'Icing up . . . lost power in port engine . . . losing height . . . descending through 3,000 feet . . .'

The snowstorm is remembered in Assynt as one of the worst of the century. On the day of the crash, three local shepherds died whilst trying to gather their sheep into shelter. The Avro Anson was presumed lost at sea, and after a few days, the air search was suspended. Six weeks later, a shepherd found wreckage on Beinn an Fhuarain and alerted the authorities.

Two of the crew survived the crash and tried to stay warm during the storm. Their bodies were found inside the broken fuselage of the plane, swaddled in the silk of opened parachutes. A third crew member had also survived: Sergeant Charles McPherson Mitchell from Ballater in Aberdeenshire, the oldest of the men at thirty-one. He was, presumably, the only one able to walk and had set off into the blizzard to try to reach help. He climbed down the wrong side of the mountain, east instead of west, away from the nearest settlement at Inchnadamph, though he wouldn't have known that. His body was found on the lower slopes, slumped in the lee of a boulder.

The graves of the six crewmen are covered with a cairn of stones. At over 2,000 feet, it's the highest grave site in the Britain Isles. In 2013, the Commonwealth War Graves Commission replaced the rusted metal cross that marked the cairn with a granite memorial stone, delivered by Chinook helicopter and set in place by a team of RAF servicemen and volunteers.

The sky was clearing to the west, cloud barely snagging the summit of Canisp, but above me the ridge of Conival was lost in mist. I thought of the young men in their Avro Anson, caught in a storm with only one engine working, flying blind through cloud, losing height and praying for a field to crash-land in. They probably didn't see the mountain before it hit them.

Mortality rates for trainee aircrew were high in the years leading up to and during the war, with thousands of crew members killed in training missions before they had the chance to fly in active service. In Sutherland alone, several mountains bear the wreckage of military aircraft, and in recent years there has been increasing interest in such sites. People visit to photograph the wreckage and sometimes to salvage engine parts or instrument dials or battered panels of fuselage – a ghoulish treasure hunt.

I left the remains of the Avro Anson and its crew in peace, following the path south instead, up towards the summit of Conival. The ridge rose steeply, dropping away on both sides, and soon the mist was around me, skewing my senses so that I was glad the path was well defined.

Conival is only slightly lower than its neighbour, Ben More Assynt, the highest mountain in Sutherland. With the summit swaddled in mist, I had no sense of being at any height at all; height was like depth, the air dense and saturated, as though I was back beneath the surface of Loch Beinn a' Mheadhoin in Glen Affric, peering into a dark, deepening landscape.

The summit cairn is C-shaped: a curved dyke of piled stone, three feet high. I wrapped myself in spare clothes and crouched in the curve; cold, tired, still hoping the cloud would lift. The cloud thickened; Conival was making no concessions. Norman MacCaig writes that these mountains are unmanageable: 'intractable in any terms / that are human'. The thought made me wary and euphoric all at once, and I wanted to stay high, to walk the east ridge that links Conival to Ben More, to experience both mountains in all their intractability. But it was late afternoon, and it would be slow-going, scrambling along a mile of shattered quartzite in the mist. The prospect of being on the ridge after dark tempered my euphoria, and I turned back, making my way slowly and carefully down to the col.

Stepping out of the mist, nothing had changed: cloud still snagged the summit of Canisp, and Breabag continued to smoulder. From the col, I could see the course of the Allt a' Choinne' Mhill as it flowed west into Gleann Dubh, and then down towards the settlement at Inchnadamph, the 'Meadow of the Stag'. I knew that there was a hostel down there and that if I was quick enough, I could check in, grab a shower, and still have time to go for a meal and a pint in the nearby hotel.

Two bowls indented the hillside at the head of Gleann Dubh. Looking down on them from the col, there was a symmetry to how they sat in the land – one filled with water: Loch Mhaolach-Coire, 'Loch of the Brow of the Corrie'; the other a bog: Cùil Dhubh, the 'Black Hollow'. Two bowls, one full, one empty, the loch shimmering with what light was left in the day while the hollow darkened. I made my choice, walked east instead of west, across the col to the edge of Coire a' Mhadaidh, 'Corrie of the Wolf'. There was no path, so I scrambled down a scree chute and then followed a stream as it dropped in a series of falls to a lochan cupped in the corrie. In places, it was too steep for deer to graze, allowing wildflowers and other vegetation to flourish: sedum and asphodel, hawk-bit, butterwort, different kinds of fern and grass. In early summer, the walls of the corrie would be bright with mountain flowers.

Ungainly, the weight of my pack aslant on my back, I lowered myself between ledges, hands clutching at turf, feet blind. When I reached the lochan and glanced back up behind me, I saw a deer watching from the col, as though it had been looking out for me while I scrambled down – maybe one of the stags I had seen on the slope of Beinn an Fhuarain. I offered up my thanks, grateful, in the gloom of the corrie, with cloud pressing down on the ridges, that another living mammal was up there, negotiating its own relationship with these remote, intractable mountains.

By the time I unpacked and pitched my tent, it was too dark to see if the deer was still there. Later, curled in my sleeping bag, glad that I had chosen the corrie and not the hostel, I imagined myself up on the col with the deer as it settled for the night. And even though I'm not a traditional hunter, by think-ing about the deer, by visualising myself alongside it, I gained some small insight into how it might be to live a life so entan-gled with such creatures; and it struck me again that so many of the stories traced on this landscape acknowledge the depth and ambiguity of that entanglement.

Dòmhnall Mòr Òg has been up since dawn, and after a fruitless morning's stalk, he is resting on a ridge through the heat of the afternoon. His yew-tree bow and sheath of arrows lie at his side. A soft voice asks if he is asleep. 'Not now,' he says, jumping to his feet.

Before him is a red deer hind with chestnut flanks. He stoops to gather and draw his bow, fixing an arrow in one fluid move. When he raises the bow, the deer takes the form of a woman, her chestnut hair flowing down her back, her cheeks pale as bog cotton. 'It grieves me, young Donald,' she says, 'that you are bent on shooting hinds.'

'I have never fired at a hind when I could find a stag,' replies Dòmhnall Mòr Òg.

'That has served you well,' she says, 'but your sharp arrow is in my haunch since last Wednesday.' And he sees the truth of her words in the blood from the wound in her thigh.

'Little did I expect it of you, young Donald,' she says, 'after the days we have spent together, sporting and playing, sucking honey in the breast of the wood.'

A mist comes down on the ridge, so that he can't see the shaft of his bow in front of him. When it lifts, she is gone, and he never sees her again.

This is the same Dòmhnall Mòr Òg of Lochaber who encounters the peat-cutters on the moor, and who kills the deer-woman by loading his gun with a bent silver sixpence. The fact that he is now hunting with a bow is a reminder that the years slip in these tales; that even when the protagonists are identified as known historical figures, the stories themselves exist outwith the chronological certainty of calendar time.

As to their origin, seventy years after John Francis Campbell of Islay claimed that tales of deer-women are a folk memory of reindeer-herding Picts, J.G. McKay, offered a different explanation. His 1932 essay, 'The Deer Cult and the

Deer-Goddess Cult of the Ancient Caledonians', proposes that the Mesolithic hunter-gatherers who first pushed north into the Highlands brought with them, along with bone tools and flint knives, a belief system based on the worship of a deer-goddess. McKay goes further, suggesting that an order of priestesses dominated society at that time, and that it was they who led the rituals associated with the goddess and with the hunting of the deer. McKay supports his theory by citing tales that include women-to-deer transformations, such as the encounters of Dòmhnall Mòr Òg. The stories, he claims, are simply the fossilised memory of priestesses donning and doffing their deer-skin robes and antlered headpieces as part of a ritual performance.

J.G. McKay was clearly influenced by the work of his contemporary and fellow Scot James George Frazer, author of the *The Golden Bough*. He follows Frazer in promoting the idea that all societies progress in a linear fashion from archaic 'primitive' to modern 'civilised', with an attendant intellectual evolution from superstition to scientific rationalism. So far, so Social Darwinist; and like Frazer, McKay makes a number of speculative leaps, moulding the evidence to suit his theories rather than the other way around.

McKay's essay usefully gathers a range of traditional material relating to the Cailleach and to deer-women, but his interpretation of the material is too simplistic, too literal. He insists, for example, that descriptions of deer-women shifting form three times in succession is concrete evidence that the tales originate as ritual performance. It's an odd insistence, given that the 'rule of three' is universally applied in folk narratives, where things happen thrice not because of ritual but because such repetitions build rhythm and tension, as well as being a useful memory aid.

If J.G. McKay is wrong, if stories of shape-shifting deer-women don't derive from dancing priestesses, and if they are not John Francis Campbell's reindeer-herding Picts either, then the question remains: where do they come from?

*

The flysheet was wet with dew when I clambered out of my tent in the morning. Camped at nearly two thousand feet, the temperature dropped below freezing in the night, and I had to keep my clothes on in my sleeping bag to stay warm. The tent was pitched on raised ground at the north-eastern edge of the corrie, just above where the Garbh Allt, the 'Rough Stream', spills out of the lochan into a small pool, before tumbling over a waterfall and on down the hill. The pool was just the right size and depth for a plunge, but the sun hadn't cleared the ridge, and the thought of the shock of the water convinced me to set up my stove instead, and to boil water for tea.

The sky was patched with high, light cloud, and the peaks of the mountains were clear. It would be a fine day. Holding the hot tin of my mug with both hands, I sat on the corrie's lip and absorbed the view. My breath, tea-warmed, condensed in the air as though I was blowing smoke.

From Coire a' Mhadaidh, Ben More's ridge looks more like the sharp outline of a dune than a mountain, with the scree on its flanks like grey-pink sand. To the north, Na Tuadhan, an outlying spur of Beinn an Fhuarain, towers above the corrie. The quartzite exposed on its flanks is twisted in kinks and folds, a dramatic example of the geological upheaval which, in part, makes the area such a mecca for geologists. The name, Na Tuadhan, is from the Gaelic for 'hand-axes' and is likely to be descriptive, perhaps named after the two spikes of rock on the peak of the spur, jutting up like the blades of axes.

The slopes below the corrie, all the way down to Gorm Loch Mòr and Fionn Loch Mòr, 'Big Blue Loch' and 'Big White Loch', are strewn with rocks and boulders that have tumbled from the mountains, or been carried down as glacial erratics.

It's a wet, barren landscape, and the archaeological record suggests that no one ever settled here. The meadowlands of Inchnadamph and Elphin have long been occupied – a chambered cairn at the foot of Gleann Dhubh is evidence of Neolithic human settlement – but on this side of the Ben More range, the nearest shielings are six miles to the north in Glen Coul; whilst east, it's even further to the farmed land on the shores of Loch Shin.

All of which makes Coire a' Mhadaidh a fine, remote home for the animals that give it its name, a home that hasn't changed much in the 250 or so years since they last lived here: the lochan continues to be transformed when sunlight clears the shadow of the ridge in the morning; den sites are still to be found amongst the crags and the rockfall above the lochan's shores; and the rise on the lip of the corrie, where I was camped, remains an obvious vantage point from which to survey the land that opens out below – the great interior of Sutherland.

I tried to look at the land the way I thought a wolf might. Its looking would be sharper, more alert, than anything I could manage, but I took my time, doing my best to assimilate the shape and line of lochs, ridges and rocks. For a while, the only movement I saw was the shadows of clouds on the slopes of the hills, but then I noticed first one and then a handful of deer in the distance, picking their way amongst boulders beneath a crag that hid Loch Bealach a' Mhadaidh, 'Loch of the Pass of the Wolf'.

If I was a looking wolf, my ears would prick and my focus intensify, and I would study each individual deer, gauging sex and age by size and movement, taking note of their position in the hierarchy of the herd, looking out for signs of weakness or injury; I would watch the herd as a unit, judging how bonded it was and how confidently it moved in the terrain. As my muscles tensed in anticipation, I would calculate the herd's direction of travel, the distance between us, the orientation of sun and wind, and I would decide, even before I began to move, the optimum pace, and place, for interception.

A grey rock, prominent on the crag above the deer, was roughly the right shape and size. I willed it to shift, to lope to the crest of the crag and raise its muzzle, to gather its pack and strike. Nothing stirred – the rock was just a rock – and the deer, without concern, wound their way around the side of the crag.

Polson of Wester Helmsdale, along with his son and another lad, track a wolf to Glen Sletdale in the east of Sutherland. They're sure it's a she-wolf, and that she has cubs hidden in a den on the rocky slope of Càrn Garbh. They watch and wait until late in the day, when she emerges from a cleft on the slope, sniffs the air, then lopes off towards the head of the glen.

Polson and the two lads clamber up to the den. The entrance is a narrow fissure, too narrow for Polson, so he sends the lads to squeeze in and kill the cubs while the mother is absent. As they go about their grizzly business, the wolf returns, alerted by a scent in the air or by a mother's sixth sense. She lunges past Polson and scrambles into the fissure, but before she can reach her cubs, Polson grabs her by her bushy tail. His son in the den shouts, 'Father, what is keeping the light from us?' And Polson replies, 'If the root of the tail breaks, you'll know soon enough.'

The wolf is stuck in the fissure, unable to turn to defend herself. Polson, with his free hand, unsheathes his dirk and stabs again and again at the wolf's haunches, until she's so weak that he can pull her out and finish the job. Thus he kills the last wolf in Scotland.

A stone plaque, just off the A9, a few miles south of Helmsdale, commemorates Polson's deed, which took place in the year 1700, though the 'honour' is disputed. Apparently, it was actually Sir Ewen Cameron of Lochiel who shot the last wolf at Killiecrankie twenty years earlier, while a popular tale insists

that it was MacQueen of Ballachrochin, a handsome and peer-
less hunter who stood six foot seven inches tall, and who killed
the last wolf near the River Findhorn in 1743. My favourite
account is that of a woman in Strathglass who'd gone to borrow
a cast-iron griddle from a friend in Struy, and who was attacked
by a wolf whilst walking home. Undaunted, she dispatched it
with a fierce blow to its head with the griddle, thus ensuring
the extinction of the species on Scottish soil.

Most poignantly, in his book *The Last Wolf*, the nature writer
Jim Crumley imagines a lone female, not stalked and beheaded
by a heroic hunter, but old and withered, seeking refuge on
Rannoch Moor, curling up beneath a Scots pine and wrapping
her tail over her nose as her breathing begins to slow.

Over on mainland Europe, wolves are doing well, reclaiming old territories, present now in every country on the continent, even the densely populated, intensively farmed
Netherlands, whose lack of 'wild' land makes it an unlikely
home for wolves. Scotland would be an easier fit, and nowadays two of the biggest landowners in the Highlands are keen
on wolves. They're also significant local employers. Does that
sway opinion? Should it? Who gets to choose, and how can we
have the debate when positions seem so entrenched?

Once, during a conversation with the tea-trolley man on the
Glasgow-to-Fort William train, I was told that wolves were
fine elsewhere, in places like Canada or Norway, but not here.
He wasn't interested in my question about what might happen
if the people of Canada and Norway adopted his stance.
Alternatively, the Caithness-based academic, Magnus
Davidson, has suggested, only half-jokingly, that 'Kelvingrove
Park would be a great place to reintroduce wolves. It would
attract more tourists and have very little impact on farmers.'
His point being that many of those who loudly advocate for
wolves know full well that they won't have to live with the
consequences.

I don't expect wolves to be re-introduced in my lifetime, though I would wish for it. It's a wish that has nothing to do with arguments about the economic benefits of eco-tourism over agriculture, or public versus private ownership of the land, or even how that land might best be stewarded. It's to do instead with the same understanding that the intractability of this landscape is good for us, that to be in the presence of something outwith our control, something that might be more than a match for us, teaches perspective, humility even. Wolves at home again in Coire a' Mhadaidh would do that for sure.

I've only once encountered a large predator in the wild, and that was fleeting. My wife and I spent six months in Portugal before we were married, working on a small farm in the north, near the village of Pedrógão Grande. We had been out for a day in an open canoe, paddling on the Rio Zêzere that flows through the foothills of the Serra da Estrela. The section of the river was remote, far from any settlements, the banks wooded and pathless. We both saw it at the same time. It was more a register of movement and colour than a fixed sense of a shape: swift, sleek movement – not a goat or boar – and a mottled coat and tail. That was all: something moving fast, with sleek purpose, crossing a clearing above a river. But it thrilled me, and continues to thrill me, to have been in the presence of a creature that was going its own way; that would, by choice, have nothing to do with us, but nonetheless imposed itself on our senses like a charge of electricity. Our best guess was that it was an Iberian wolf, though it's possible that it was the even rarer Iberian lynx.

*

After breakfast, I unpitched my tent, packed, and made ready to leave the corrie. Before donning my rucksack, I went to gather water from the Garbh Allt. Crouching next to where it pours out of the plunge pool below the loch, I filled my water bottle and then leaned forward until my face was just above the surface of the stream. It was flowing too fast to hold my reflection, a blurred shadow that could have been anything. I scooped water with my hands and gulped it down in a place where thirsty wolves would once have bowed their heads to drink.

Walking north from the corrie under a bright sky, I picked my way amongst streams and bogs, and small lochans spiked with reeds that were like ink brushstrokes, waving in the breeze. Boulders were everywhere, some split – great eggs cracked open – some balanced like abstract sculptures. I passed one boulder that was the size of a small house but shaped like a squat, fat hen, its head turned quizzically; a twice metamorphic rock. When I walked beneath it, I hunched my shoulders and ducked my head, wary of the peck of its blunt stone beak.

A large yellow frog with black markings and gold-rimmed eyes was crouched on a knoll by Loch Bealach a' Mhadaidh, though I pretended not to notice it as I approached. It shuffled away anyway. To my east, in the distance, Ben Klibreck was shapely and blue-black against the light. People never settled here, but the land was known and named: each lochan, each stream, each knoll well kenned by those who hunted here, in days when maps were carried in the head. It struck me how rarely those names are now used, that watching it reflect the blue of the sky, I might have been the first person in days to say aloud 'Gorm Loch Mòr', and that weeks might have passed since someone sat enjoying the light at Grianan a' Choire, 'Sunny Spot of the Corrie', or quenched their thirst on Cnoc an Fhuarain Bhàin, 'Hill of the White Springs'.

I passed a black peat hag with the bones of trees protruding from the peat, and stopped to dig out an arm-thick length. The surface was bleached where it was exposed to the sun, but when I split it open the inside was dull orange, like ochre: it was an alder root, tannin-rich, but not resinous like pine. This boggy landscape may never have hosted the Scots pines that were once extensive in the Central Highlands, but there would have been trees nonetheless: alder and willow in the wetlands, stands of birch and rowan on drier ground, oak and hazel in sheltered places, montane scrub on the high slopes.

Like much of Scotland, a combination of factors deforested Sutherland: for centuries, timber was felled for fuel and to clear land for grazing; from the eighteenth century, sheep farming was introduced; and then in the nineteenth century, the popularity of sport shooting on Highland estates resulted in the exponential growth of the red deer population. That growth continues through the twentieth century and into the twenty-first, with numbers more than doubling in Scotland since the 1960s.

That morning, the only trees I passed were a few rowans growing on the tops of boulders, their roots wedged in cracks, their branches too high to be stripped. As I approached one boulder-perched tree, gold-leaved and basking in the sun, a bird tumbled out of it and flew off erratically, banking and twisting as though it was dodging bullets. Not much bigger than a thrush, the same dun-brown colour, but with pale bands on its tail feathers: a female merlin, the smallest of Scotland's birds of prey. There is life and beauty still amongst the bog and the boulders, but there could be so much more.

It's well known that wolves are a keystone species, their presence felt in every link of the food chain, so that when they are removed the ecosystem is impoverished, thrown out of kilter. If wolves were back in Coire a' Mhadaidh, they would help reduce deer numbers to a sustainable level and keep those that remained on the move, so that they no longer grazed one place long enough to strip it of all that dared to sprout. Even here, in the wet, slow-growing north, old habitats would re-emerge in a handful of years, and with them a flourishing of flowers, insects and birds.

I'd met no one since I was dropped off on the verge of the A837 and walked up to Creag nan Uamh, two days previously. When I left Bone Cave and climbed onto the flanks of Breabag, I'd spotted two walkers in bright waterproofs at the foot of the glen, making their way up to the caves. I was glad to have been packed and gone before they arrived. My head was still ringing from the encounter with the stag at the cave mouth in the night, and from the feeling that some part of me had slipped in the depths of the cave. I would have been in no fit state to give a useful account of myself. Walking now amidst silence and spaciousness, I became absorbed in the landscape and was consciously grateful that I lived in a country where undisturbed engagement with the natural world is possible. It's something I have never taken for granted.

Once, in my late twenties, I hitched to Torridon and reached the head of Loch Maree in the evening. It was late June, the forecast was fine, and I was keen to climb and camp on top of a mountain, not least to escape the midges that seethed in dense clouds above the shore of the loch. I set off up Slioch – from An Sleagach, 'The Spear' – but when I reached a grassy shoulder below the summit where I'd thought to camp, I found a German couple who'd thought so too. Their tent was pitched, and they were sitting quietly outside. We exchanged polite hellos, but I could tell they were as disappointed as I was to find themselves in company. I left them in peace, though it wasn't easy, on top of a spear-pointed mountain, to find another spot that was level and out of sight. That night the sunset was tremendous, the mountains on fire around me, and after dark, the moonless sky brimmed with stars. Knowing that others were camped close by didn't spoil the experience, but it did alter it.

The couple had gone by the time I rose in the morning, or else had shifted form into the pair of wild goats that eyed me impishly from the path above. The goats were part of a small herd that, in contrast to my own cautious scramble to the top, casually negotiated the crags and gullies below the summit. Twenty years later, the memory of being there is clear in my head: a windless, silent morning; Beinn Eighe and the mountains of Torridon rising sharp into blue sky above a cloud inversion that smothered Loch Maree. There was so little vegetation on the summit, I can only assume that the goats were up there too to appreciate the space and the silence, and to breathe air that was like gulping the view of mountains into your lungs.

*

A mile north-east of where the Avro Anson crashed on Beinn an Fhuarain, I skirted a ridge called Cailleach an t-Sniomha, 'Spinning Old Woman'. The name is associated with a boulder, Clach na Caillich, that sits somewhere on the ridge, though my map didn't detail where, and with countless boulders to choose from, I didn't go looking.

There's no lore that I can find associated with the name, but it is likely there was once a tale of the Cailleach being turned to stone here, just as she has been at Creag na Cailleach in Argyll, at Cailleach Point on the Isle of Mull, and at so many other places where her figure is said to have been petrified in the landscape. The ridge seemed an appropriate place for the Cailleach as winter's hag: stony and desolate, a fierce place, no doubt, when the wind is blowing from the north and snow is drifting on the ground. I thought about Sergeant Charles McPherson Mitchell, who had walked away from the wreckage of his aeroplane and stumbled down off the wrong side of Beinn an Fhuarain wading through snow, desperately looking for the glimmer of a lamp in the window of a cottage.

Somewhere close to here, he stopped, exhausted, and sat down with his back to a boulder. I wondered if he survived the night and woke to a view that would have brought despair: a waste of snow and ice, and no sign of cottage or track. How does the land seem then: intractable, indifferent or like an enemy? I wonder if he felt stalked, crouched in the lee of his boulder, hiding from the death that was coming for him like a pack of wolves unleashed from Coire a' Mhadaidh, or like a blue-faced, one-eyed hag, spinning before him on the ridge. I hope hypothermia lulled him. I hope he tucked himself beneath a blanket of snow and that the last thing he saw was Gorm Loch Mòr, dazzling blue under a bright sky, like a vision of some other landscape, away from wartime Scotland.

Six weeks is a long time for a body to lie, waiting to be found; I took care skirting the ridge and crossing the stream that fed Gorm Loch Mòr. Walking north towards the bealach between Beinn Leòid and Meallan a' Chuail, I stopped to look back and saw that the Ben More range was crouched in the land like a beast: the ridge of Conival was its spine, curving around the corrie; Ben More's flanks were its fine strong haunches; while Na Tuadhan was its angular head. The two spikes on the summit were not the blades of axes after all, but ears, pricked, like those of a wolf.

Chapter 7

Bealach Horn

A couple of months before setting out on my walk, my wife passed on to me a book that had been passed to her, on the chance that it might be of interest. Reading it jolted my understanding of stories about the Cailleach and about deer-women.

Rane Willerslev, a Danish anthropologist, lived for a year with a group of indigenous Siberian hunters, the Yukaghir, who are based around the Upper Kolyma River in the Russian Republic of Sakha. Willerslev first visited the Yukaghir in 1993, before returning to begin an extended stay in 1999. Whilst there, he spent most of his time accompanying hunters as they stalked elk and trapped sable in the larch forest, the sub-arctic taiga, that was their home. His book *Soul Hunters* is an account of the relationship that exists between those indigenous hunters and their prey. The parallels with the Scottish stories that I was tracking are uncanny.

On one occasion, Willerslev describes watching as Spiridon, the elder of the hunting group, dressed in elk skin, captures the attention of a female elk and her calf in a clearing in the forest. As the elk walks cautiously towards him, with the calf trotting behind her, he raises his gun and shoots them both. Later, Spiridon explains: 'I saw two persons dancing toward me. The mother was a beautiful young woman and while singing, she said: Honoured friend. Come and I'll take you by the arm and lead you to our home.' The old hunter goes on to say that, had he gone with her, he himself would have died.

Despite time and distance, despite one being a verbatim account told as simple truth and the other being one of many versions of an old folktale, the experiences of Spiridon and of hunters such as Dòmhnall Mòr Òg or Muireach Mac Iain mirror each other. Reading Willerslev's book was like swimming in Loch Beinn a' Mheadhoin in Glen Affric and seeing for the first time the landscape that dropped away beneath the water, and understanding that the loch's surface and everything reflected above it was only half of what was going on.

*

Late in the afternoon, walking down to Loch Glendhu, 'Loch of the Dark Glen', the tidelines and bladderwrack on the shore were unexpected, even though I knew that at its far end the loch flowed through a narrow strait or kyle – from the Gaelic *caol* – out towards the open sea, with the Kylesku Bridge elegantly spanning the strait. I'd been walking all day in an inland landscape of moor and ridge, so it was strange to meet the sea and smell the tang of it.

When I reached the shore, the sun had dropped below the ridge south of the loch, though its light still touched the crags above me. The loch's surface was static and black. In the distance, a small fishing boat with a red hull sat lopsided in the water, the fisherman leaning over the gunwale, hauling lobster creels from the depths of the loch. Nearer, a pair of eider ducks puttered around close to the shore, the male with his brilliant white feathers grabbing all the attention.

Glendhu Bothy was in shade, its windows blank. Inside, it was well kept but gloomy and cold. According to the visitors' book, it had been days since anyone had stayed.

Bothies are often former shepherds' or stalkers' cottages, set in remote glens and far from public roads. They're there to be used by hillwalkers and climbers, and the shelter they provide has, many times, saved lives. Over a hundred bothies, mainly in the Highlands, are maintained by the Mountain Bothies Association, a volunteer-led charity. On my month's walk they offered an occasional, and welcome, alternative to the cramped cocoon of my one-man tent.

When I lit a fire in Glendhu Bothy's hearth, and fed it with the dead branches I had gathered from a straggle of trees in the glen, the room glowed as though the bothy shared my gratitude, as though a fire in the hearth restored it to being a home.

We've made fire for at least 100,000 years and possibly much longer, the hearth resting at the heart of human culture, and it's only been fifty or so years since we replaced it with the television. Throughout my journey, whether in bothies, clearings in woods, or on the shores of lochs, the fires I lit never felt intrusive. Instead, at night, in the dark of a depopulated glen, creating a glow of light and warmth, and cooking food over it, was like a small act of restitution: each fire a reminder that we belong here.

When I finished my meal, I went outside to wash my pot and spoon in the nearby stream, then I closed the door to the night and rolled out my mat and sleeping bag in front of the hearth. The bothy was now snug, and luxurious after my cold camp at altitude the night before. I fell asleep watching the flicker of embers in the grate.

*

It was early and dark when I woke in the morning. After tea and porridge, I climbed away from the shore of Loch Glendhu before the sun had cleared the ridge, following a deer path through rusted bracken up onto the slopes of Beinn a' Ghrianain – named after the ruined settlement of Grianan, the 'Sunny Place', that lies below it to the west. Or perhaps it was the other way around, with the settlement named after the mountain. Either way, Grianan is a pre-Clearance township now no longer marked on Ordnance Survey maps.

A red deer stag postured above me on the hill, antlers raised, grumbling at my interruption to his morning. I placated him, acknowledging how handsome he was, and promising to keep my distance if he kept his. After my encounter with the stag in Bone Cave, my attitude towards the deer I met shifted, as though the bell of the stag's voice announced a new, heightened awareness of how we might connect. The shift was there in the rush of emotion and gratitude I felt when I noticed the deer watching me from the col as I scrambled down into Coire a' Mhadaidh; and here it was again in a more playful form, on the slope of Beinn a' Ghrianain, as I engaged in mock-earnest conversation with a grumpy, early-morning stag.

The Yukaghir of the Upper Kolyma River ascribe 'personhood' to the elk that they hunt, as well as to other creatures of the taiga – most notably fellow-hunters like bear and wolf and lynx. It's a form of respectful anthropomorphism that seems to me to be at least as sophisticated, and certainly less reductive, than modern science's insistence on a separation between humans, with our inner life of emotions and intentions, and animals, mere biological automatons. This view remains orthodox, and anthropomorphism – endowing animals with what we consider to be human qualities like the ability to feel empathy, jealousy, love – continues to be dismissed.

The Yukaghir see no such separation. For them, each time they hunt an elk, it involves an encounter with a distinct individual, and they talk about the spirit or soul of the elk – they use the word *ayibii* – as a person with whom they must engage. That engagement involves mimicking the elk to a degree that becomes a kind of shape-shifting. The hunter wears a coat of elk hide with the fur turned outwards and headgear with protruding elk-like ears, and his skis are covered with elk skins so as to sound like the animal when moving on snow. He doesn't fully become elk, but nor is he still himself. Rather, by donning his elk skins and mimicking the behaviour of the elk, he inhabits a dimension, a landscape, where he and the elk are congruent with each other, where they 'see' each other. It's the same betwixt-and-between place where the San Bushmen of the Kalahari Desert hunt kudu, a form of antelope, describing their experience of the hunt as entering 'kudu mind'. It's the same place where Dòmhnall Mòr Òg sees the hind as a wounded woman on the hill, or where Dòmhnall Donn-shùileach moves with the deer like a dance on the ridge of Beinn a' Bhric.

It's a fraught business. Hunters are boundary-crossers, moving between the human world and the wild, and there is no guarantee of a safe return. For the Yukaghir, the *ayibii* of the elk they hunt is always a woman, never a man, irrespective of whether their prey is male or female. Thus, hunting becomes a form of courtship where the elk is enticed to 'give itself' willingly to the hunter. The idea of hunting as courtship is not, of course, unique to the Yukaghir: it forms part of the world-view of hunter-gatherer cultures from the circumpolar north to the prairies and forests of the Americas and the bush deserts of South Africa and central Australia. What I hadn't appreciated, before reading Rane Willerslev's book, is the degree to which tales of hunters and deer-women from Lochaber and other parts of the Highlands are synonymous with that world-view.

*

Loch an Leathaid Bhuain lay before me, 'Loch of the Lasting Slope', and adjacent to it, Loch na Creige Duibhe, 'Loch of the Black Crag'. These are straightforward place-names, descriptive and instructive, waymarks for when we forget and need guiding back into relationship with the land – like the cairns of stones you find by mountain paths, there for when the mist comes down. Ben Stack, from the Gaelic *stac*, meaning 'steep', peeped over the hill ahead, and Quinag, from *cuinneag*, a 'milking pail', rose behind me: an impossible-looking mountain, its two northern peaks dominating the view to the south of the kyle.

As I picked my way down towards the gap between the two lochs, a large bird cast itself off from one of the crags on Beinn a' Ghrianain: a golden eagle, the first I had seen on my walk. It wheeled high above me and then drifted south, becoming a dark speck against the bulk of Quinag.

*

When I cast myself out of Glasgow in my early twenties, I landed on the Isle of Iona. My reply to the 'help wanted' advert in the Jobs section of the *Glasgow Herald* led to three years' work at one of the island's hotels, first as general assistant and then as gardener, growing vegetables and salads for the hotel's kitchen – a leap of faith on the part of the owners, as I'd never grown anything before.

An eagle-high view would pick out Iona as a significant waymark in my life, but before moving there, I only knew that it was a small island off an island, off the West Coast of Scotland. It was the 1980s, there was no internet to scroll for information, and at that time I had no grasp of my country's history. Friends from the city couldn't understand why I chose to move somewhere so remote, so peripheral. After three years there, I understood that it was unlikely I would live anywhere again that felt quite so centred.

Spend time on any Hebridean island and you can't help but engage with its natural and cultural ecologies: the wildflowers on the machair, the oystercatchers and arctic terns, the place-names and what they mean, the sea and all its dispositions, the lives embedded in a landscape. Iona rekindled the wonder I felt as a boy when *Akmonistion zangerli* was discovered down the burn at the end of my street, and whilst living on the island I began to think about gaining an education. I found myself drawn less to the study of material artefacts, to archaeology or palaeontology, and more to the study of what UNESCO calls 'intangible cultural heritage' – folklore and tradition, Hamish Henderson's 'carrying stream'.

When I left Iona, I enrolled on an Access Course for mature students at the University of Edinburgh and went on to study Ethnology – folklore – at the university's School of Scottish Studies, co-founded of course by Hamish Henderson in the 1950s. A world opened to me.

*

A seam of hard rock puts a step in the land between Loch an Leathaid Bhuain and Loch na Creige Duibhe, with a single, narrow waterfall dropping between them, like a bowl of water being carefully tipped into another. Both lochs reflected the deep blue of the sky. I crossed above the waterfall, hopping from stone to stone, while a dipper bobbed on a rock on the shore below me, its white bib gleaming.

In my thirties, during those early years of parenthood, this was the journey I dreamed: passing between two lochs on a bright morning; steering a path around crags and peat hags, their edges scabbed with moss; climbing a ridge in the company of deer, a string of hinds keeping ahead of me as though I was herding them; watching an eagle drift until it became a dark speck on the horizon.

From the top of the ridge, mountains rose all around. I was walking north and reckoned it would take three or four days to cross the mountains, reach the North Coast, and walk east to a place and a story that I had long been keen to visit. Ahead, I could trace my route to the Bealach Horn, the high pass between Arkle and Meall Horn. To reach the path to the bealach, I had to climb down off the ridge I was on and pass through the village of Achfary. Walking the road into the village was the first time in days that I had felt the jolt of tarmac.

Achfary is incongruous. With its trimmed hedges and mown lawns, planted specimen trees and picket-fencing, it looks like a southern hamlet that has been spirited to Sutherland. The village is part of the Reay Forest Estate and owned by Hugh Grosvenor, the 7th Duke of Westminster. When still in his twenties, the young duke inherited the 39,000-hectare estate from his father, as well as a £10 billion fortune and several other estates and properties, including a large chunk of Mayfair and Belgravia in London.

I don't know Hugh Grosvenor, he's maybe a lovely man; it's his position as laird that unsettles me, and the power gifted to him through our land-ownership system. Walking through Achfary, I thought about the settlement over the hill at Grianan and the remains of the buildings that are there: homes tumbled back into the land, 'the stones that made walls / become cairns', as Aonghas MacNeacail writes of a similar settlement in his poem '*gleann fadamach*'. I wondered whether there would still be people living at Grianan, that 'sunny place', if their ancestors had owned the land themselves back in the eighteenth century, with the power to make decisions about their own lives and futures.

I saw no one alive in Achfary, despite it being late in the morning. For me, its neatness was soulless, and there was none of the clutter and clatter of messy, noisy village life; but maybe the people who live there would tell a different story. On the outside of the estate office there's a marble plaque in memory of the 1st Duke of Westminster, who died in 1899. It was erected by his foresters and servants to 'express their deep respect and regard' – as though they would have been able to express anything other. In the redundant telephone box nearby, a defibrillator has been installed.

A wren cut across my path, carrying a chink of light on its beak, disappearing into the gorse on the other side of the track. A blustery wind put white caps on the waves being blown across Loch Stack. From a distance, scree on the slopes of Arkle looked like sand or filings that were heaped in skirts around the mountain's base, the work of frost and ice – winter's beak sharpening itself on the mountain, slowly grinding it down.

The bothy at Lone was locked. It stands below Arkle by a bridge that crosses the river which shares its name: Abhainn an Lòin, 'River of the Marshy Meadow'.

*

When I hitched to Torridon in my late twenties, and climbed and camped on top of Slioch, I walked north the next day to Carnmore Bothy. Carnmore is basic, just the one long room of a stone byre, owned and maintained by the Letterewe Estate, with a tin roof, earth floor and no fireplace. It was evening when I arrived, and outside the bothy, the midges were fierce. Inside, an old man was cooking bacon and beans on a meths stove. After we'd said hello and eaten our respective meals, the old man and I sat across from each other and swapped whisky and roll-ups as the light faded. He was entirely at ease with himself and spoke quietly with an Aberdeenshire accent, his sentences laced with Doric. That evening he shared a wealth of bothy lore.

This was before the Mountain Bothies Association website, before bothy bibles and location guides, so that the only bothies I knew were the ones I had heard of through word of mouth or else discovered whilst walking. I dug out from my rucksack my OS Travel Map that covered all of Northern Scotland, and we spread it between us, lighting a candle to see by. The old man donned reading glasses and began to mark small crosses on the map with a pencil, reciting names of bothies and remembering his visits to them, recommending one for its proximity to a good trout loch, another for the availability of firewood, or as a base to climb a particular mountain, or simply for the beauty of its location. He marked crosses for MBA bothies and for those that were maintained by estates, like Carnmore; he marked others too, that were special, hidden, their locations shared with discretion. It was an evening of initiation, and I understood it to be so: the exchange of whisky and tobacco, the elder and his knowledge, our faces in the candlelight surrounded by shadows.

The map is now tattered and stained, with Sellotape holding the folds together. It's the same map that I pored over as a young parent, imagining the walks I would one day make. It's a treasure map, and although I have no memory of the old man's name, I've often had cause to be grateful that he entrusted me with his recommendations, so that I might carry them forward in turn; accepting, of course, that some may now be out of date.

So it was with Lone Bothy, one of the X marks on the map. It was only midday, but the wind was strengthening, and I'd considered stopping there for the night. I could spend a restful afternoon pottering by the river and tackle the Bealach Horn in the morning. The Reay Forest Estate's decision to lock the bothy removed that choice. A mean decision, it seems to me, to close a bothy that has been used by walkers for years.

I could have camped, of course, but the wind had the feel of something building, so I pushed on, climbing the path to the Bealach Horn, hoping to cross over and reach the shelter of another bothy, Strabeg, by the evening. It was a hard push, my pack heavy on my back and my heels pinching, despite the comfort of old boots. Halfway to the top, three red deer hinds and their yearling calves watched me from the other side of a gully. The hinds' coats glowed chestnut in the sun as they turned and cantered away, the young ones following behind them.

*

My dad was a keen mountaineer, and I retain a vivid memory of trudging along a mountain path behind him. It must have been not long before the divorce, and we'd gone off to spend a weekend in the hills. It was late in the afternoon and raining; my head was down, my shoulders hunched beneath an orange nylon rucksack that was too big for me, and I was focused on the only colour ahead in the gloom: the red of the gaiters my dad wore above his boots, splattered with mud, guiding me on.

Of my two daughters, the younger has most inherited my own love of hillwalking. The first mountain we climbed together was Beinn a' Bhùird, 'Table Mountain', in the Cairngorms. It was late June and exceptionally hot, nearly thirty degrees, but Ear-choire Sneachdach, the 'Snowy East Corrie' on the flank of Beinn a' Bhùird, still held significant patches of snow. One patch, the size of a five-a-side football pitch, had four stones protruding from the middle of it. When we approached the snow's edge, the stones stood up and loped away: mountain hares that had been sitting stone-still in bowls they'd scraped in the snow, to cool down. We kicked steps up to the bowls, finding in the centre of each a cluster of droppings, small fibrous pellets, like offerings. The glare of the sun on the snow stung our eyes. We carried on, kicking our way off onto a ridge that would take us to the top and stopped to rest by an outcrop of granite, leaning into its shade and gulping water from our bottles. On the final section of ridge, the stones beneath our feet radiated back the heat of the day. Our pace slowed. It was strange to feel the sun so intense in Scotland. Nearing the summit, my daughter acknowledged that she had suffered on the steep bit, her leg muscles sore, but that she never thought of turning back. I was glad we'd waited until she was fifteen: too young, and the day might have been torturous, putting her off mountains for life.

It was a privilege to walk in that high land with my daughter. The south summit of Beinn a' Bhùird sits at just under

4,000 feet and is marked by a simple cairn on a plateau that stretches over a mile to the north summit. We took our time looking around, as though to absorb all the views at once would have been too much. At Bloodhound Buttress we peered over the edge and down into Coire an Dubh-lochain. Even on such a bright day, the lochan lived up to its name: peering back at us, a black eye in the corrie's socket. We met no one on the mountain, apart from four men who were wearing similar blue t-shirts and khaki shorts – 'the blue boys' we called them. Their pace was relentless. They didn't stop to enjoy the summit but pushed on, explaining that they had more Munros to claim. As we looped around the plateau and began to make our way back down, we could see their bright blue t-shirts far ahead of us and their bald, hatless heads gleaming under the sun.

My own pace on the path over the Bealach Horn was far from relentless. I stopped and filled my water bottle from a stream, at a place where it tumbled into a small deep pool. The water sparkled in the sun.

Sometimes it feels like the greatest privilege of parenthood is to be a good conduit, to pass on from your own life the best of what was passed to you; and I wonder, occasionally, if my dad hadn't left, how much more time we would have spent in the hills together.

After my daughter and I climbed Beinn a' Bhùird, we bivvied for the night in Glen Quoich, beneath a cluster of Scots pines. Our cooking fire was set in an old hearth, a well-used circle of river stones. After dinner and a mug of hot chocolate, my daughter fell asleep in her bivvy bag on the other side of the fire. I lay and watched the embers burn down, enjoying the cool of the night after the heat of the day. There were stars and no midges. I knew I would sleep lightly, on guard despite trusting there was nothing in the glen to harm us, but in that moment the responsibility was a blessing.

In the morning, when we forded the river, an adder was submerged in the shallows, cooling itself, only its head breaking the surface. We gave it a wide berth as we crossed, and its head swivelled, watching us pass. After an hour's walking under the sun, we stopped to swim in a pool, the water a cold shock with snowmelt still running off the mountain. It was absolutely translucent. We called it our Paradise Pool, and it struck me then that words like 'ownership' are tricky when it comes to landscape. The usual, phlegmatic rules of capitalism are inadequate. It might be a simple truth that someone can purchase, and thus own, a watch or a toaster – but a mountain? At what depth of legitimacy does that apply? Can someone really own the pool in the river that we swam in; and again, as Norman MacCaig reminds us: 'Has owning anything to do with love?'

My daughter and I walked out of Glen Quoich together, parent and child, but also now fellow mountaineers. In our two days there, we had acquired a relationship to that part of the Cairngorms that had nothing to do with the exchange of capital, and that felt reciprocal. Maybe at some level, ownership becomes an attitude; maybe, to paraphrase an old ballad, if we choose, we can all be lairds of as much land as we'd walk in a long summer's day.

*

There's little soil or turf on the stone fields of Arkle – only a thin, patched pelt. To the north, the long ridge of Foinaven, 'White Mountain', was sharp-edged like a blade. The quartzite of the ridges and summits around me gleamed white, othering them, making them mountains from somewhere else, some higher-altitude, desert place. As I crossed the high point of the Bealach Horn, the wind unsteadied me, and the low sun stretched my shadow thin. Euphoric and exhausted, I sat down and dug out oatcakes from my rucksack, eating them with smoked cheese while my head tried to accommodate the view around me, the measure of its beauty. In the gap between Foinaven and Arkle, I could see a blue triangle of sea, and to the east, in the far distance beyond Ben Hope, another mountain: Ben Loyal, the northern pivot around which my month's walk would turn.

Chapter 8

Cranstackie

I was sitting on a chair by a table at a window, drinking tea from my tin cup. The table was stained and blistered with candle wax, and the sun above the ridge was warm through the window. A grey wagtail fluttered at the glass, as though it was trying to find a way in. Three times it flew to the glass before being cast aside by the wind. Its breast was pale yellow, like primroses. Earlier, I had opened the front door and all the internal doors, to let the bothy breathe; the doors had to be wedged with old roof slates to stop the wind from banging them shut. The space inside the bothy seemed to expand like a lung, stirring ash in the hearth and swirling dust that sparkled with the let-in light.

The evening before, when I crossed the Bealach Horn, it was dark by the time I scrambled down off the last ridge into Srath Coille na Feàrna, 'Strath of the Alder Wood'. I had to use the line of a deer fence as guide, clutching the wire in places to lower myself. There was no moon and few stars, and my legs were aching after all the day's miles; it took a long time to walk the last two to the bothy.

Strabeg Bothy is marked as 'special' on my bothy map, and the old man at Carnmore was right to recommend it. It's a former shepherd's cottage, with upstairs bedrooms and a bathroom with a toilet that flushes into a septic tank. There is no running water, but there are buckets to fill from the river. The cottage sits on a knoll at the bend where Srath Coille na Feàrna opens out into Srath Beag, the 'Little Strath' from which the cottage takes its name.

From my chair at the window, I could see a silver birch tree growing out of a ruined stone byre. The sun was full on my face. It was a dazzling day, a high-energy day, but too windy to go anywhere exposed, despite the attraction of the stony ridge of Cranstackie to my west. Up there today I would be beaten by the wind, cast aside by it, so I went out to wash my socks in the river instead and to gather dead branches for firewood. The wind pummelled the reeds on the slope that led down to the river, so that the slope was alive with their movement. It looked like an attack, as though the reeds were sweeping up against the solidity of the bothy. I hung up my socks to dry in the birch tree.

The wind increased through the day, toppling my stack of drying firewood and flailing the alder trees by the river. At sunset, I watched clouds barrelling across the summit of Cranstackie, while the wind bellowed in my ears and the mountain glinted like gun metal. Inside, the walls muffled the sound of the wind, but at times the force of it shook the ceiling and it felt again like an attack, one that the bothy was only just withstanding. After dinner, I sat by the fire, the storm amplifying the pleasure of small treats: clean, dry socks; two chocolate digestives; a measure of whisky in my cup; and I thought about the people who had lived their lives here, without electricity or telephone, with no road in and their nearest neighbour two miles away. When I went outside before bed, bands of pale green light were rippling across the sky, fading, then strong, then fading again: aurora borealis; *Na Fir-chlis* in Gaelic, 'The Nimble Men'.

The beings who brighten the night sky above Scotland do so not in dance – despite being called 'The Merry Dancers' in Orkney and Shetland – but in battle. 'When the mirrie dancers play, they are like to slay,' the saying has it, and the word 'mirrie', which has been corrupted to 'merry', actually means 'shimmering'.

They're fallen angels, maybe, or offspring of the Cailleach, as some would have it. Whoever they are, the frenzy of their combat flares across the heavens, and on ferocious nights, the blood of the wounded and slain forms a red pool in the sky, with drops spilling to Earth. Which is why, if you're lucky, you might find on a pebbled shore a piece of 'bloodstone' – a form of jasper flecked red with the congealed blood of the Nimble Men.

In the morning, I walked up the strath in the wind and rain, keeping to the tree-line below Creag Shomhairle, 'Sorley's Crag'. The path I was following dodged its way between boulders that had split and fallen from above, and across the river, Cranstackie rose in armoured plates of stone. I found myself involved in the strath, as though I wasn't just passing through, as though the chores of gathering firewood and scooping buckets of water from the river were a form of participation. Earlier, at breakfast, when I rekindled the fire in the hearth to boil water for tea, it was done in association with all those who'd previously kindled fires here.

The woodedness of Srath Coille na Feàrna is a delight. A note in the bothy explains that the deer fence is in place to protect the trees that are there, and to encourage regeneration, with the eventual aim of extending the woodland further. Why would you not want to protect the trees, if you owned such land? Why would you not want to extend the woodland further?

In 2017, the Scottish Government announced as part of its draft Climate Change Plan, that it aimed to increase the nation's woodland cover from 17 to 25 per cent by 2050. To reach that target, 10,000 hectares of forestry needs to be planted every year. Given that trees are pretty efficient at absorbing carbon and releasing oxygen, governments around the world have realised that afforestation is a useful strategy in the struggle to minimise Climate Change.

Some folk are not so keen on the idea. When the Government made their announcement, Mountaineering Scotland and the Scottish Gamekeepers Association – an unlikely alliance, given their different and often opposing agendas – issued a joint statement expressing their concern. You might expect the Gamekeepers Association to oppose afforestation: they want to manage the land in the way they believe works best for their members, and if that means muirburn, raptor and hare control and high numbers of deer on the hill, resulting in no woodland regeneration, then so be it. Less expected was the view expressed by Neil Reid on behalf of Mountaineering Scotland citing the impact that afforestation might have on Scotland's 'dramatic open views and vistas', and arguing that visitors don't want to go for 'miles-long wanders through woods'.

Miles-long wanders through woods – the idea thrills me. To be fair to Mountaineering Scotland, though, their main concern is the introduction of yet more large-scale monocrop plantations of Sitka spruce, and following a backlash from many of their members, they now concede that allowing native woodland to return is no bad thing. But if you encourage the notion of the land as an outdoor gymnasium, then for sure, what you want is quick, easy access, plenty of signposted paths and 'open views and vistas'; and if gun sport is your thing, then trees only get in the way of your shot.

How do we relate to the land? How best do we steward it, and for whom? That's what this is about; that's what it's always about.

There's a useful comparison to be made between the Highlands of Scotland and south-west Norway. Both areas have a similar climate and geology, and from the Bronze Age onwards, as woodland was cleared for agriculture, both suffered large-scale deforestation. Their paths diverged, however, in the eighteenth century when, in the Highlands, people were removed from the land, often without choice, to make way for large-scale sheep farming and then, in the nineteenth century, for sporting estates. We know the consequences: the deer, the grouse, the empty townships, 'the stones that made walls' becoming cairns, the land as green desert.

South-west Norway also witnessed a dramatic population decline, with extensive emigration to the United States in the nineteenth and early twentieth centuries, but the land the emigrants left behind was never consolidated into large estates. Nowadays, rural south-west Norway remains a patchwork of owner-occupied smallholdings, providing income from farming, forestry, hunting and tourism. That diversity, including sustainable levels of animal grazing, has resulted in the regeneration of the Norwegian forest, with woodland cover now standing at 33 per cent.

Go visit Glen Affric, or Glen Feshie in the Cairngorms, or Srath Coille na Feàrna. The 'open views and vistas' are still there, but rather than the monotony of a man-made wasteland, you look out across a rich mix of woodland, moor and mountain, supporting a fine diversity of habitats and species.

The wind had dropped a little in the night, but it was still too strong for the heights, so I kept to the wooded side of the river, with the intention of gathering enough firewood so that there would be a dry stack for whoever next visited the bothy. Towards the head of the strath, there is a bealach that leads over and down into Srath Dionard, below Foinaven. It's called Bealach a' Chonnaidh, 'Pass of the Fuel'. Early maps show that Srath Dionard has long been treeless, so it's likely that the people who lived there, at a settlement called Carrachandubh, would have crossed the bealach to Srath Coille na Feàrna to gather firewood as fuel for their fires. The name evokes the act, and I thought of gathering a bundle of dead branches and carrying it over Bealach a' Chonnaidh as a way of honouring it;

but it would be a wasted journey, for there are no longer people to welcome the wood at Carrachandubh.

The further up the strath I went, the more I was drawn to Cranstackie. Despite the weather, I wanted to walk on the glinting stone of its ridge, and I had packed my waterproofs and some oatcakes just in case. When I crossed the river, I gave up the pretence of looking for firewood. On the far bank, a heron was disturbed by my presence. It flew upriver, landed, then flew again.

The Cailleach who lives in the woods is causing a sickness to spread amongst the cattle and the people. The parish priest, through strength of prayer and splashes of holy water, drives her from the woods but is unable to banish her completely, and the sickness continues to spread.

It's rumoured that she has taken up residence at a cairn by a loch, and at night she is glimpsed in the air, flying to and from the loch, going about her unholy business. An old sergeant, retired from one of the Highland regiments and fearful of no one, is determined to rid the parish of her presence. Late one night, he loads his gun with a crooked sixpence and a handful of silver buttons, and lies in wait below the cairn for her return. At last, in the grey light before dawn, the old sergeant hears a soughing like a gust of wind, and she's there, hovering above him, exposed to the barrel of his gun.

A shepherd finds the sergeant in the morning, slumped below the cairn, semi-conscious, both his gun and his collarbone broken. Lying next to him is a large, dead heron, and from that day forth, there's never been sight of the Cailleach in the parish, though the loch is still known as Loch na Caillich.

I followed the course of a stream up onto the mountain and soon found myself walking across a large patch of unbroken rock: dark grey gneiss, almost black, like the flank of a giant whale that had breached through the crust of the Earth. Veins of white quartz rippled through the gneiss. The rock was so smooth that each step had to be measured, like walking on ice, even with the grip of the Vibram soles of my boots. Nothing had changed here since glaciers scoured the rock. Such scales of time were beyond me.

I had set out to gather firewood but found myself on the ridge of Cranstackie. The wind made the skin of my face ripple against the bone of my skull, and to move forwards I had to lean into it, walking at an angle to my balanced self. There were no detached stances up here: it was too real, too risky, too hypothermic. With my hood pulled low and my chin tucked into my fleece, I crouched on the ridge and peered west, directly across at Foinaven. I've never been so intimidated by a mountain: its northern flanks rose sheer, twisted with seams of gneiss and quartzite, and around its summits, clouds fumed; it was no place for a warm-bodied human to be.

Some tales tell that the Cailleach as 'old woman of storms' retreats to Skye at the beginning of spring, to Beinn na Caillich, or that she skulks through summer in a north-facing corrie of Ben Nevis, waiting for the light to thin again. I think if she goes anywhere, it's to this stony north land, to the twisted peaks of Foinaven or the ridge of Cranstackie, where life is scoured away by wind and rain. Down in the strath, amidst the birch and the alder, I could imagine her as mistress of the deer, but here on the ridge she is winter's hag, death's crone – an ancient figure out of Old European cosmology.

The Cailleach's association with the heron in the tale hints at that strand of her lineage. Cranes, and crane-like birds, are often depicted as companions to the underworld goddesses of Old Europe, and are deployed by them as psychopomps – guides that lead the souls of humans to the realm of the dead. Hence, perhaps, the once common Highland superstition that the sight of a heron in flight is a portent of a death to come.

Cranstackie would be a fitting place to bring the dead. Up here, eagles and ravens would be glad of the feast, the cairns of our bones picked clean and then scattered, though it would be quite the ask of family and friends to carry a body so high.

The ridge was barren, pathless, a jumble of broken quartzite stretching for more than a mile to the summit. Confronted by so much stone, life is more obviously precarious. I thought about the poet Hugh MacDiarmid, and the time he spent in another stony landscape.

For nearly a decade, through the 1930s, MacDiarmid lived with his second wife, Valda, and their young son on the island of Whalsay in the Shetland Isles. They lived in poverty in a cottage with a peat fire and wooden crates for furniture, surviving their first winter there on a diet of fish and potatoes gifted to them by neighbours. It was a difficult time, physically and psychologically. MacDiarmid writes in a letter that he was a man 'brooding in uninhabited islands'. From that brooding he wrote 'On a Raised Beach', a long poem that contemplates the stones of West Linga, a small island off Whalsay. Facing up to the hard stuff of material reality, the 'lithogenesis' of creation, MacDiarmid sought to articulate his faith in a creative force that lay at the essence of things.

The poem's language can be alienating – it reads at the start like a glossary of geological terms – but there are also lines of great beauty and insight. Borrowing from Hebrews 12:27, MacDiarmid writes of the stones:

> Their sole concern is that what can be shaken
> Shall be shaken and disappear
> And only the unshakable be left.

I picked my way along the ridge, jarred by the wind but aware of how present I was, how sharp my attention to what could be shaken. Below me, Srath Beag was green and ginger with moss and deer grass.

Loch Eriboll lies at the foot of the strath. The name is from the Old Norse *eyrr-ból*, 'farm on a gravel bank'. The loch is ten miles long, opening out into the north Atlantic, the only sheltered, deep-water anchorage between Cape Wrath and the Pentland Firth. During World War II, it was an important base for Allied ships, and it's here, in secret, that most of the German U-boat fleet was surrendered. The scuttling of the 'grey wolves' that had caused so much damage to Allied shipping in the Atlantic was a pivotal moment at the end of the war.

The loch was nicknamed 'Lock 'orrible' by the British sailors whose boats were anchored on it, in response, no doubt, to the frequent wind and driving rain. Hamish Henderson is more approving. In the 1950s, he camped by the loch with the Stewarts of Remarstaig, an extended family of Gaelic-speaking Travellers who worked as tinsmiths and hawked their wares in the crofting townships of the North-west Highlands. Writing of that time, he compares the loch favourably to the Mediterranean: 'as though the Aegean were lovely as Loch Eriboll!' Hamish was travelling with the Stewarts so that he could record their traditional songs and stories for the School of Scottish Studies. He describes that summer on the road with them – with their horses, carts and bow tents – as the high point of his life. From Cranstackie's ridge in mid-October, the loch *was* lovely: grey-green, lustrous, with spindrift thrown from white-capped waves; a harsh, Scottish loveliness.

Unexpectedly, I found life on the ridge of Cranstackie. There was no soil or turf, but there were trees, extraordinary trees. They were an alpine form of juniper, a prostrate variety, with tight, flat growth, spreading horizontally, rooted in cracks and crevices in the rock. The largest of them were only the length of my arm, but their branches were vibrant with evergreen needles, and each bore a handful of small blue-black berries. Once I had an eye for it, I began to see a sparse forest on the ridge. Some of the trees had trunks that were as thick as my wrist, representing decades of growth, maybe hundreds of years; stunted but surviving, thriving even, on their terms.

The weather closed in as I approached the summit, with cloud and whipping rain. I turned back before reaching the cairn, spooked, aware that all around me, invisible in the mist, were crags that dropped away. I was glad to climb down below the cloud and feel the wind lessen in the lee of the ridge. Sitting in the relative quiet of a gully, I tried to figure out some kind of coherence between the mountain and its shattered stones and the green world of the strath below. I'd picked a sprig of juniper from the ridge, with three berries on it. I took it out of my pocket and put one of the berries in my mouth. The taste was bitter, resinous, intense.

Nowadays, Cranstackie is translated as though 'cran' is a misspelling of *carn*, for 'hill'; but older references clearly state the name as Crann Stacach, where *crann* is 'tree', and *stacach* is 'rugged' or 'rocky'. It seems the name might refer to the presence of the juniper trees. Either way, having climbed up into the stone world of the mountain, I was glad to find them there. Hugh MacDiarmid, brooding on Whalsay, self-absorbed and intellectually isolated, admired the indifference and 'barren but beautiful reality' of the stones. I preferred the juniper trees, their vulnerability and tenacity, their intense, compact aliveness; and I wondered about Valda, MacDiarmid's wife, how she had managed, bringing up their child in poverty, coping with her husband's solipsism.

*

Back down in the strath, I took off my boots and socks to ford the river, and kept them off to keep them dry, crossing the boggy moor barefoot. A snipe rose two yards in front of me and twisted away. It was well dressed for the moor, its feathers striped in shades of brown like patterned tweed.

I stopped and filled my water bottle from a stream fringed with bright green watercress. The cress tasted mild, earthy. With my knife, I carefully harvested a bunch – it would go well with oatcakes and cheese – and I thought of the words attributed to Suibhne Geilt, the medieval bush-mystic of Celtic folklore. Remembering his time wandering in the wilderness, he says: 'Though you like the fat and meat which are eaten in the drinking-halls, I like better to eat a head of clean watercress in a place without sorrow.'

The wind was at my back as I crossed the strath, bending the grass and reeds in great waves so that it seemed as though I was surfing back to the bothy.

Chapter 9

A' Mhòine

A large stone marks the start of the Moine Path. It sits like a squat, uneven pyramid, two feet high, with its point chipped off to form a narrow plinth. The path is an old drove road that links Strathmore with Kinloch to the east, at the head of the Kyle of Tongue. Nowadays, a single-track road takes what traffic there is out of Strathmore, joining the A838 and bisecting A' Mhòine, 'The Peat Moss', a few miles to the north. The road is so little used it has patches of turf colonising a strip down the middle of the tarmac.

Opposite the start of the Moine Path there is another stone, the size of a smallish suitcase, lying next to a willow tree. According to tradition, this is Strathmore's *clach neart*, its 'strength stone', that would once have been used as a trial of manhood. Rough handholds have been shaped at each end of the stone for lifting, the challenge being to pick it up and balance it on the plinth of the marker stone.

It was mid-afternoon, and three days of fierce wind had eased at last. I'd left Strabeg Bothy in the morning and climbed the bealach over the ridge between it and Strathmore, and then down to Strathmore River, hoping to cross at Cashel Dhu, the 'Dark Ford'. Steel shutters enclosed the windows of a handsome cottage that stood nearby. No one was at home, but there was firewood neatly stacked, a new shed at the side of the house and a rope swing in the garden. A remote holiday home, I guessed, nestled amongst birch and rowan, the river looping around its quiet, isolated beauty.

The river was rain-swollen and wide, but it was four miles upstream from the ford to the nearest bridge. I stopped for lunch and considered my options, then cut a birch stick for support, took off boots, socks and trousers, and followed the track into the water. I could feel the river's muscle against my thighs, and leaned into it, firming each foot before I lifted the other. A dozen steps forward, and I stopped as though snagged on something. My attention had been caught by the swirl of the surface of the water, and I stood and looked until looking made me dizzy and I was nearly couped over. To steady myself, I had to focus on the far shore, and when I eventually scrambled out, my legs shook, my teeth chittered, and my heart was pounding.

The risk-taking left me uneasy, as though I'd infringed my own code of conduct for the journey, and I realised I'd been rash to cross the river when it was running so high. I was also discomfited by the way that the water transfixed me. The dark pull of it, while my body was balanced halfway above, halfway below, made me think of hunters in tales being beguiled by singing deer-women, and of those other beings that are notorious for haunting the fords and rivers of the Highlands.

The River Conon, fed by the Black Water, which I'd sat next to, regaining my balance, after the hitch with the hatchback-driver, is the setting for one such tale.

At midday, the men working the field next to a ford in the river are interrupted by a black horse that stands up to its hocks in the Conon's dark water. 'The hour has come but not the man,' the horse booms, before plunging into deeper water and disappearing beneath the swirl of its surface.

The men, knowing a kelpie when they see one, vow to let no one cross the river for at least an hour; but soon another horse with a rider appears, galloping towards the ford. The rider, a man, is a stranger to them, but they block his way, and when he refuses to

*heed their warning, they pull him from his horse. Despite his angry
protests at being detained, they escort him to a nearby church and
lock him inside for his own safety.*

*The men resume their work in the field, and then, once the hour
has passed, return to release the man from the church. Inside, they
find him face down, drowned, in the shallow basin of water used
for washing hands. Who he was, and why the kelpie of the River
Conon was so determined to claim his soul, has never been told.*

Standing by the *clach neart* at the start of the Moine Path, I
looked at Ben Hope rising in front of me, the name an anglicisation of Beinn an Òba, 'Mountain of the Bay'. It's
Scotland's most northerly Munro but is often dismissed as a
rounded lump and compared unfavourably with Foinaven,
its smaller but more dramatic neighbour. From where I stood,
it was impressive enough, the broad west face wrinkled with
gullies and with buttresses that caught the sun; a singular
mountain, none the worse for being un-peaked. The way it
loomed straight up out of Strathmore, glowing in the afternoon light, reminded me of photographs I had seen of Uluru
in Australia.

With both hands, I could budge one end of the *clach neart*,
prising it a few inches off the ground, but there was no way I
could lift the whole thing, never mind carry it across the road
and set it on the plinth of the marker stone. When I let go, it
sank back firm into the turf that was growing up around it. As
I walked by, I touched the unburdened plinth, offering my
respect to the mighty folk of Strathmore's past.

The Moine Path is seven miles long and wide enough for a
horse and cart. I followed it up through spent bracken, with a
young birch wood, protected by deer fencing, thickening on
the hillside to my right. The path curves around the lower
slopes of Ben Hope and then stretches out across the moor,
skirting small lochs and knolls, banked up where the ground is

boggy – although its upkeep has long been neglected. In deep ruts, water gathers and colonies of moss expand, while elsewhere the heather has overtaken it. The only prints I found on the path were from deer.

A' Mhòine gives its name to the geological fault zone that runs from Loch Eriboll down through Assynt and all the way to the Sleat peninsula on Skye; the same fault zone that so dramatically twisted the quartzite flanks of Na Tuadhan, by Coire a' Mhadaidh.

The Moine Thrust Belt baffled the nineteenth-century geologists who first came to study it. The fault zone contains old layers of rock overlying younger layers, a pattern that undermined one of the basic assumptions of geology at that time: that the youngest rock always lies closest to the Earth's surface. Based on their field studies in the region, Victorian geologists Ben Peach and John Horne proposed that the older rock had been forced, or thrust, over the younger. Peach and Horne sounds like a comedy double-act; but several decades before the theory of plate tectonics was formalised and accepted, the duo were astute enough to surmise that this forcing was due to the intense pressure of what their contemporary, the German geologist Alfred Wegener, called 'continental drift'.

None of the turmoil in the rock beneath me was apparent on the surface of the moor. Moss, heather and deer grass stretched to the coast and the sea, the land rolling gently like the sea itself, or like a steppe, a wet Scottish steppe. After days of wind, the quiet on the moor was thick around me, with just the occasional *tseep tseep* of pipits and, once, a raven, who *craaked* at me as it slouched over Creag Riabhach, the 'Brindled Crag'. I settled into the rhythm of the afternoon's walk, pleased to be on a path that knew where it was going, but one that curved with the land as though it had nothing to prove. I was far north, deep in Sutherland, and there are no straight Roman roads here.

Half a dozen deer were walking ahead of me, following the lead hind. I was glad to see them so elegantly alive, threading a timeless line across the moor. According to tradition, they shouldn't be here at all.

MacIntyre of Clunamacre, known as An Dròbhair Bàn, 'The Fair-haired Drover', is on the moor. It's late in the eighteenth century, and change is being forced on Sutherland. Lord Reay has brought sheep farming to the region, and out on A' Mhòine, An Dròbhair Bàn encounters a marvel: a column of deer crossing the moor, over a thousand strong. They have gathered from all the straths and hills of Sutherland and are migrating to the mountains in the west, leaving the land in protest at the coming of the sheep and their shepherds and their dogs. The drover stands in silent witness as they pass him on the path.

Over a thousand strong. I tried to imagine so many deer filing past: their raised heads and dun-coloured haunches merging into a flow of bodies, the churn and drum of their hooves, their brown eyes seeing beyond me; and then the silence and amplified emptiness they would leave behind.

The deer and the people are intertwined. Hearing the tale, it is impossible not to think of the families exiled from the land during that same terrible period of 'clearance': columns of them, walking with their belongings on their backs to the coast and to the transportation ships. Ewen Robertson, a carpenter and composer of songs and poetry, who lived on the shores of the Kyle of Tongue during the second half of the nineteenth century, and who is known as the Bard of the Clearances, was unequivocal:

> *Mo mhallachd aig na caoraich mhòr,*
> *Càit bheil clann nan daoine còir*
> *Dhealaich rium nuair bha mi òg,*
> *Man robh Dùthaich 'ic Aoidh na fàsach?*

My curse upon the great sheep,
Where now are the children of the kindly folk
Who parted from me when I was young,
Before MacKay's Country became a desert?

Some of the most notorious clearances took place in Dùthaich Mhic Aoidh, 'MacKay's Country', the Gaelic name for Sutherland, with people burned out of their houses in Strath Naver, Strath Halladale and the Strath of Kildonan. Nowadays, we don't need to imagine what that might be like, because we see it happening on the newsfeed of our phones and on our TV screens: different circumstances, but the same desperate families, adults clutching children and carrier bags of belongings, forced from their homes in places like Idlib in Syria, Taiz in Yemen, the Donbas of Ukraine; the same smoke billowing from the houses, the same timeless line of the dispossessed.

The deer are still on the moor, though the people aren't. This remains a contested landscape. Some would see A' Mhòine rewilded, with deer numbers reduced and trees and scrub returning; others would put wind farms on the ridges, build power-lines to send the electricity south; others still would reverse the Clearances and bring people back to the land, placing ownership in the hands of the communities who live here. Meanwhile, planning permission has been granted to Space Hub Sutherland to begin constructing the UK's first spaceport. It will be built on a four-hectare site in the middle of the moor, creating a launch pad from which satellites will be rocketed into space.

In some places A' Mhòine's turf and moss had been eroded, exposing bedrock that glinted in the late-afternoon sun. Elsewhere, great squared boulders sat like gaming pieces, casting long shadows: glacial erratics, or stones dropped from the Cailleach's apron. Both accounts seem equally implausible.

Hugh MacDiarmid, brooding on Whalsay amongst his stones – 'detached intellectuals', he called them – insisted that 'it's necessary to make a stand and maintain it forever'. Perhaps that's what these boulders were doing: stubbornly making their stand; and yet, in the deep time of geology, or even the circular time of myth, only an instance has passed since they were plucked from who knows where and dropped on the moor. So much for immovability, so much for maintaining a stand forever; perhaps that's the kind of calcified thinking that has made so much of Sutherland a derelict landscape, one that is depopulated and ecologically denuded.

I camped next to a stream, pitching my tent on a flat bank by the path, midway across A' Mhòine. It was a cloudy night, and the sky and the moor merged into darkness. There were no lights or signs of human habitation. Without wood for a fire, I cooked supper on my Trangia then climbed into the tent and zipped myself into my sleeping bag. Stags were bellowing at each other in the corrie below Creag Riabhach. I had been glad of the shelter of thick walls and a slate roof in the storm, but after three nights at Strabeg Bothy, it was good to be camping again, to make my bed on the moor and feel the night settle around me.

A' Mhòine is deemed ideal for a spaceport because of its 'emptiness' and lack of light pollution. Lying in my tent in the dark, I thought about the difference between 'empty' and 'absent', about the loss of the settlements and homes that the Moine Path once linked, and about how loss is carried forward, is inter-generational, like a weight on the cultural consciousness, pressing down whether acknowledged or not.

*

Squalls of wind and rain scoured the moor through the night, testing the tent. It felt like being at sea, the tent a currach, prow to the waves, its skin keeping me dry and buoyant.

More rain, drumming against the flysheet, woke me in the morning, but it soon cleared, and by the time I had eaten breakfast, packed and started walking, the sun was breaking through the cloud. The Kyle of Tongue opened before me. The view was tremendous: curved sands and shallow water; shifting patterns of silver and blue; and a purple haze of birch on the far shore. At the head of the kyle, Ben Loyal was a lopsided jaw, jutting out of the moor.

Some say he was gifted the box by a lover while journeying on the continent, others that he got it from a witch, others still that he won it in a contest with the devil. No matter, it's a box made of black wood, studded with brass, and Donald, Laird of Tongue and Chief of Clan MacKay, has it hoisted on his shoulder as he strides across A' Mhòine towards home.

The Kyle of Tongue opens before him, and soon he's at its shore, bathing his feet in the salt water, taking his rest before walking the last few miles around the head of the kyle. The box on the grass beside him is a magnet for his attention, and despite a stern warning to leave it be until he's within the walls of his house, he can't resist a quick peek inside.

As soon as he unlocks the box, the lid bursts open, and a hundred tiny, winged fairies spill into the air. 'Obair, obair, obair,' they cry, 'work, work, work.' Like a cloud of midges around his head, they poke him and pull at his hair, and all the while they scream: 'Obair, obair, obair.'

Parched from a day's walk under the sun, Donald commands them: 'Fetch me water,' and in an instant the fairies swarm first to the shore of the kyle, then to a stream that flows from A' Mhòine, and then back to him, each with a tiny cowrie shell brimful with fresh water. Donald is delighted to have his thirst quenched by each fairy in turn pouring water from its shell onto his tongue. But as soon as the last drop is poured, up goes the cry: 'Obair, obair, obair.' Looking around for a task to distract them, he commands that they pull all the heather from a nearby hill – the hill is still remembered as Aon Streapan, 'One Single Stalk', which is all that re-grew after the fairies stripped it bare.

No sooner started than finished, the fairies are back at Donald, poking and pulling and screaming: 'Obair, obair, obair.' A torment in his ears as he racks his brain for a task to defeat them. Eventually, in desperation, he commands, 'Make me a rope of sand that will stretch from one shore of the kyle to the other, and don't come back till it's finished!'

The minutes pass, the silence is a balm. Out on the kyle, the fairies twist ropes of sand which crumble in their tiny fingers and are washed away by the tide. They're out there still, working and working, and sometimes, knowing that their task will never be done, you'll hear their sighs drifting across the sands of the kyle.

In the 1970s, three different versions of this story were recorded by pupils of Farr Secondary School, when they went out to gather local tales from the last of the Gaelic-speaking crofters between the Kyle of Tongue and Strath Halladale. It's a frivolous tale, but testament nonetheless to the ways that the people who lived here anchored their belonging through stories.

As I walked down into Kinloch, a curlew flew above me, its long beak like an insect's proboscis. The rising whirl of its call was answered by other curlews on the shores of the kyle, and I heard oystercatchers and, nearer, amongst trees, the *chink chink* of chaffinches. It was a joy to see woodland thriving here: a protected planting of young oaks, holding their spent leaves, mixed with thickets of birch and willow and alder.

Who owns the land? How might it best be stewarded? Has owning anything to do with love? These questions were never far from my mind on the walk as I witnessed the different ways that owners responded to their duty of care. The issue is as important today as it was in the time of the Clearances. Back

then, the changes in land-use enforced by the lairds, legiti-
mised in the courts, and sanctioned by the Kirk, led to the
mass displacement of people, many of whom were forced from
places that they had inhabited ancestrally. In Assynt alone,
forty-eight townships were cleared: forty-eight communities,
like Grianan, the 'sunny place' on the shore of Loch Glendhu,
where people had learned to live in accord with their environment. Some of the most poignant testimonies recorded at the
end of the nineteenth century by the Napier Commission, a
public inquiry into the conditions of crofting in the Highlands,
are from those who express dismay, not just at being cleared
from their land to make way for sheep, but at the consequences
for the land itself: that it would be neglected and degraded,
that the generations of stewardship they'd given to it would be
laid to waste.

More recently in Assynt, in the early 1990s, when the
North Assynt Estate was put on the market, the local crofters set up a trust to buy their land. It was a revolutionary
moment, a culture-shift in the history of, and attitude
towards, land ownership in Scotland; proof that stands need
not be maintained for ever. The success of the Assynt
Crofters' Trust has been followed elsewhere, in places like
Knoydart, the Isle of Eigg and the Isle of Ulva, off Mull – an
island which was once home to 600 people, but which was
extensively cleared and recently had a population that had
dropped to six.

Each community buy-out – a fine and growing litany of
places, one that counters the old Proclaimers song – marks
more than just a change of ownership: each is an act of redress,
shifting the weight of loss, a *clach neart* being slowly, and
collectively, lifted.

I followed the road from Kinloch past the farm at Ribigill,
looking for the memorial to Ewen Robertson, raised close to
the spot where he died. It stands by the side of the road, a

simple granite pillar, like a grave stone, five feet high, with his name and dates carved on it, and a prophetic, hopeful quote from one of his verses:

> *'N àit nan caorach*
> *bithidh tuath.*
> *Crodh-laoigh air airgh 'n*
> *'àit damh ruadh.*

> In place of the sheep
> there will be people.
> Cattle at the sheilings
> in place of stags.

Chapter 10

Diarmaid's Grave

It's a familiar story: an old, powerful man marries a young, beautiful woman. In this case, the old man is Fionn mac Cumhaill, high chieftain of the Fianna, a caste of aristocratic warriors, like Celtic Samurai. In old age, Fionn is irascible, brooding, a hero in decline. Gráinne, his new wife, elopes with her guileless lover, Diarmaid, and Fionn seeks revenge, compelling Diarmaid to hunt a monstrous boar. Diarmaid confronts and kills the boar, casting it from the summit of a mountain, but Fionn, in his treachery, insists that Diarmaid measures the corpse by pacing its length, and in doing so, the sole of one of his feet is pierced by the boar's poisonous bristles.

This is a much-compressed version of a well-known tale from the Fenian or Ossianic Cycle, that body of oral literature that relates to the legendary deeds of Fionn mac Cumhaill and his men – the name is sometimes anglicised to Finn McCool, or Fingal. It's a body of literature that was in circulation in Ireland and in Gaelic-speaking Scotland from the early medieval period onwards, and it remains imprinted on the topography of both countries, with tales attached to standing stones, hill forts, burial cairns and all manner of geological phenomena.

In Glen Roy, in Lochaber, for example, a geologist would tell you that the 'parallel roads' visible on the sides of the mountains are old shorelines from the end of the last glacial period, contouring the glen and marking successive levels of melt water as the ice receded. But the people who once lived in Glen Roy, who read the story of the land in a different way, knew otherwise. They would tell you, with as much conviction as any geologist, that the roads were made by Fionn mac Cumhaill and his warriors, as they raced their chariots round and round the sides of the glen.

Places layered with such stories are like deep memory-stores. One of those places is Cunside, at the foot of Ben Loyal. Here's what the Reverends William McKenzie and Hugh Ross had to say about it in their description of the Parish of Tongue, published in 1792 in the *Old Statistical Account of Scotland*:

> Ben Laoghal is famed, in the songs of the bards, as the scene of the death of Dermid, a young man of such extraordinary beauty, that no female heart, of that age, could resist; and withal of such powers, that even Fingal, whose wife he had seduced, would not himself attack him, but found means to get him slain by a boar. He and the lady, or the boar, (it is not yet determined which), lie buried at the foot of the mountain.

It was an afternoon of wind and showers and rainbows, golden birch leaves and rusted bog myrtle, and a faint, daytime moon risen above the moor. Ben Loyal was in shadow above me, its summit peaks jutting like fangs from the dark jaw of its ridge.

I'd followed the track from Ribigill out to Cunside: a semi-derelict cottage and byre, with a grass infield protected by a crumbling drystone dyke – a small field won from the moor by generations of digging, draining and fertilisation with seaweed carted up from the kyle. Next to Cunside on my OS map was the name Uaigh Dhiarmaid, 'Diarmaid's Grave', though there was no indication of where it lay. Thankfully, prior research had led me to the 1878 edition of the map, which pinpoints the exact location of the grave, just beyond the drystone dyke.

According to tradition, a rowan tree once grew on top of the grave, but there was no sign of it now. Instead, I found an unremarkable mound, elongated, like the upturned keel of a boat, twenty-five feet long and three feet high in the middle, its prow pointing towards the great spike of Sgòr Chaonasaid, Ben Loyal's northern spur. The mountain's name is anglicised from the Gaelic Beinn Laghail, 'Law Mountain'. The meaning of 'Chaonasaid' is unclear, though it gives its name, also anglicised, to the cottage and field.

Hamish Henderson visited Cunside in the summer of 1957. He was travelling with the Stewarts of Remarstaig, the same Traveller family with whom he'd camped on the shores of Loch Eriboll. Whilst the Stewarts were at Brae Tongue, at a place they called 'the king of campsites', Hamish walked over to Cunside, looking for Diarmaid's Grave. He'd have heard the tale from Alexander Stewart – Ailidh Dall, the old, blind patriarch of the family, and a piper and a storyteller without peer. Hamish had been told that the grave lay at the foot of Ben Loyal, but he didn't find it that day, and later expressed regret that he never had the chance to return and try again.

I didn't know Hamish Henderson well, but he was an honorary fellow at the School of Scottish Studies when I was an undergraduate there, and I was lucky enough to sit in a few times when he held court at Sandy Bell's bar. He was in his late seventies by then, somewhat dishevelled but still with a glint in his eye, and still, in his work, his politics, his gregarious humanity, an inspiration to so many of us. After reading his account of that summer with the Stewarts of Remarstaig, and of his failed search for Uaigh Dhiarmaid, I'd long wanted to make my own attempt to find the grave, and it seemed fitting to be doing so at the midpoint of my month of tracking tales, and at the turning point, now that I'd reached the north coast.

I walked around the mound three times, sunwise, like a pilgrim, thinking about Hamish, and about Diarmaid. I realised that it didn't matter whether I believed that he was buried here or not – there are many sites throughout Scotland and Ireland that claim to be his final resting place. What mattered is that the people who lived at Cunside *knew* it to be so, and if further evidence was required, they could simply point to the great scar on Ben Loyal's northern face, gouged by the tusks of the monstrous boar as it fell – a scar that geologists might give a different explanation for, but which is still known today as Sgrìob an Tuirc, the 'Furrow of the Boar'.

My presence at the grave honoured the knowledge of those whose stories were rooted in this landscape, and while part of me craved a different kind of knowing – a proper, archaeological excavation of the mound – I recognised that such an act would be a violation, a contract broken between place and story.

For many traditional cultures, the idea of a story – or indeed a life – *not* being rooted in place would seem preposterous, disquieting. 'Everything that happens must happen somewhere,' Keith Basso explains, in *Wisdom Sits in Places*, his book about the world-view of the Western Apache of Arizona in North America. For the Apache, their stories, and therefore their culture, would not exist without being entangled in the landscape. It's a challenge for those of us who've grown up in modern, globally homogenised cultures to grasp such groundedness.

When Hamish Henderson failed to find Diarmaid's Grave, he went for a nap in the shade of the birch wood that surrounds the east side of the infield at Cunside, escaping the heat of the summer afternoon. In his essay, included in Timothy Neat's book, *The Summer Walkers*, Hamish writes that when he awoke a young deer was watching him from just a few feet away: 'It showed not the slightest fear. For some time we looked at each other and then, half playfully, it scampered off. By its size it must have been a roe deer fawn, not a red deer calf. I remember the broken sunlight on its spots.'

Yellow hawkbit was in flower amongst the turf on the mound, cupping the last of the day's sun. I turned my attention to practical concerns. The cottage at Cunside was uninviting, the door open but rubbish strewn inside, the roof collapsing in places; so I made my camp in a clearing in the birch wood instead.

That evening, my fire down to a glow of embers, I sipped the last of the whisky from the bottle I'd bought in Fort Augustus and raised a toast to Hamish, who, sixty years earlier, had taken his nap amongst these birches. I thought of the epigraph to Sorley MacLean's haunting, unforgettable poem 'Hallaig', written for another birch wood: '*Tha tìm, am fiadh, an coille Hallaig*' – 'Time, the deer, is in the wood of Hallaig'. I spoke the words aloud, let them resonate out beyond the clearing, then crawled into the tent to bed. In the night, I dreamt of being chased, of looking back as I ran, and I woke myself up shouting: 'Who are you?'

*

The sky was clear, and the birch wood was frosted in the morning. After breakfast, I packed my gear and went to fill my water bottle from the stream that runs past Diarmaid's Grave, marking the boundary between the farm and the moor – the narrow stream that flows from Sgrìob an Tuirc, the 'Furrow of the Boar'.

Diarmaid is lying pale and cold, the boar's poison in his veins. Fionn, full of remorse for what he has done, is scooping water in his healing hands. He rushes back from the stream to tend to Diarmaid, but when he sees him there, the grace of youth and beauty on his brow, jealousy is a great spike in Fionn's heart. His hands loosen, and the water slips away. He tries again, and a third time, finally returning with the water unspilt. Too late. Diarmaid, bright flower of the Gael, is dead.

There's a notion that stories are eternally present in the landscape, that Diarmaid is always hunting the boar on the hill, that a roe deer fawn is always slipping into the birch wood and finding Hamish Henderson asleep there. Looking up at Sgòr Chaonasaid, the sun glinting off its summit, I visualised in my head a hunter in dun-coloured plaid, with bright shield and spear, agile on the crags, facing down the frenzy of the great tusked boar; but I couldn't quite flip the hunter and the boar out of my head and onto the mountain. No matter how hard I tried, nothing moved on Sgòr Chaonasaid.

The attempt was clumsy, but I sensed that with the right attitude and practice, it might be possible to loosen and project my attention, to develop the flexibility required to *see* in that way. It was similar to when I was camped on the lip of Coire a' Mhadaidh, below Conival, trying to look at the land with the intense concentration of a wolf. I doubt I came close, and it was a strain to even try – like working a muscle in the brain that had not been used for a very long time, but which was there nonetheless. Perhaps it was that same brain-muscle that Spiridon the Yukaghir hunter used, when he saw the *ayibii* of the elk as a young woman dancing and singing to him, or that San Bushmen used, or Aboriginal Australians – maybe some still do, allowing them to properly witness their Dreamtime ancestors going about sacred business on the land.

Shaped by modernity, I'm an outsider to myth, and the truth of the turf mound as Diarmaid's grave is an affront to my rationalism. But there it was, between the dyke and the stream on a bright, cold morning, berthed in the landscape according to a mythic truth, exercising that atrophied muscle in my brain; and it felt right and necessary to grant it the same respect that I would grant the sacred places of any traditional culture. I might not be able to recover the experience of those who once sat around a hearth at Cunside, weaving the narrative of their tales into places they knew intimately, so that their lives were entangled with the lives of ancestors both real and mythic; but I could begin to attune myself to elements of that experience.

Which is when it struck me, looking up at the spiked ridge of Ben Loyal, culminating in Sgòr Chaonasaid, that the mountain itself takes the form – of course – of a boar, crouched at bay, hackles and snout raised in defiance. Perhaps more than chance linked the tale of the death of Diarmaid to Ben Loyal; perhaps long before the Gaels pitched up, it was a sacred mountain, a 'boar mountain', and that whoever imprinted Diarmaid's tale, naming Sgrìob an Tuirc and assigning meaning to the stone mound at Cunside, did so knowing that they were overlaying an older story, like a palimpsest, and that their story-layer simply continued an association that began when the first people sailed into the Kyle of Tongue and settled beneath the mountain.

I made ready to leave, but something held me, snagging my attention, as though I had unfinished business, as though a response was required of me before the place would let me go. I'd felt it the previous evening, a tugging at the edge of my awareness, an instinct to stick around. So I sat for a while, enjoying the silence, and then went to gather an armful of stones from the rubble of a tumbled section of the dyke. I used them to make a small circle on top of the mound, amongst the turf and the hawkbit flowers, and placed a rough, heart-shaped stone in the centre, for Diarmaid, for Hamish. Then I hoisted my rucksack and, without looking back, followed the stream up onto the slopes of Ben Loyal.

Scattered across the mountain's north-eastern slope, mostly submerged now amongst the turf and moss, lies the wreckage of yet another RAF aeroplane, a Handley-Page Hampden bomber, which crashed in August 1943 as it was returning to Wick airport. Caught in a lightning storm while flying above

Tongue, it hit Ben Loyal at 150 mph. Of the four crew members, remarkably, one man survived: Flying Officer Faulks, who was thrown clear of the wreckage and lay injured for six hours before being rescued by a party led by a shepherd from Ribigill farm.

In a shallow pool, I found a large piece of fuselage, unrusted – the alloy it was formed from keeping it true, despite over seventy years of Scottish weathering. I veered east and followed another stream, the Allt Chaonasaide, up towards the bealach between Ben Loyal and Ben Heil. The bealach is a watershed, though some of the water is not for shedding: a soupy bog fills a dip, with an island of bright green sphagnum moss in its middle. I skirted the bog and climbed grass slopes onto the ridge of Ben Loyal, ignoring the summit, An Caisteal, and walking north instead to the granite tors of Sgòr Chaonasaid, where Diarmaid slew the great boar. The views were tremendous: A' Mhòine and the mountains of Assynt, and the Kyle of Tongue, where the fairies still try to shape their ropes of sand. The wind was building and pulling a blanket of cloud in from the west. Below me, Cunside had become a small green patch on the moor, with the mound of Uaigh Dhiarmaid an indistinct bump.

In most versions of the tale, Gráinne, Diarmaid's lover, gets a bad press, as though their elopement is all her fault, whereas throughout, Diarmaid appears to keep faith with his chief – so much so that one day, fording a stream, a splash of water wets Gráinne's thigh, and she comments, archly, 'Though your courage in battle is great, Diarmaid O' Duibhne, it seems to me that that splash of water has more boldness in it than you.'

Yet before we're too quick to judge Gráinne, it's worth remembering how the elopement begins.

Fionn attends some feast or other with his new wife, Gráinne. Many heroes are present and the table heaves with haunches of venison, whole braised salmon, and pitchers of ale. The great deerhounds of the Fianna lie at the warriors' feet, beneath the table. Two of the dogs begin to fight over a scrap of food, and Diarmaid leans down to separate them, just as Gráinne looks to see what's caused the commotion.

Now Diarmaid has a mark on his forehead, a freckle, that has a kind of enchantment to it; and if any woman glimpses it, she will fall utterly, heartsick in love with him. That's just how it is. To guard against this, Diarmaid wears a specially fitted cap that sits low over his forehead and hides what's known as his 'love-spot'.

At the feast, he's leaning down to separate the fighting dogs, and Gráinne is looking on, and the cap slips. From that moment, from just the briefest glimpse of the love-spot, Gráinne is infatuated. In the days and weeks that follow, she pesters Diarmaid, begging him to go away with her, and eventually lays a 'geas' upon him – a kind of bond or taboo that cannot be refused. The cap has slipped; their fate is sealed.

The tale of Diarmaid and Gráinne is associated in my mind with another story of two lovers, though in this case, the love-spot has transferred to the woman's forehead. The story is a true encounter, a moment when the boundary between this world and the other, adjacent world loosened.

One summer at a folk festival in Wales, on a farm in the foothills of the Cambrian mountains, I sat at the Bardic Fire – the story-fire that was kept lit throughout the festival, and where anyone could contribute a tale, a song, a tune. I spent most of the weekend there, enjoying the conviviality and unpredictability: ancient Welsh myths told with solemn dignity, contemporary performance poetry, bawdy folksongs.

It was the Saturday night and late, or early: that pre-dawn time when the sky begins to brighten. The fire was low, and a fiddler was playing an air, her fiddle hoarse, throaty. She told us the bow lacked rosin, having been played all night, but it sounded just right to the few of us who were still there.

In that quiet hour, a young woman joined us, dark-haired, and on her forehead, a small red heart, painted, I suppose, in the carnival spirit of Saturday night at the festival. She sat down and said: 'I'm looking for a clean-shaven Irish man. We were on the hill together, with the horses. Have you seen him?'

We thought this might be the start of a story, but she was in earnest. 'He told me he loved me,' she said, 'and I think, maybe, I love him.' She looked directly at each of us in turn, as though to impress the importance of her request: 'If you see him, will you tell him, and that I'm looking for him?' Then she walked away, across the stream, into the dawn.

It was a liminal moment for those of us at the fire, simple and strange, and true: we'd been telling folktales all night, but she was living one; she was inside its unfolding.

I've been back to the festival a few times since, and I always stay up late at the Bardic Fire on the Saturday night, half-hoping that, eventually, in that timeless way of myth, a clean-shaven Irish lad, who's been up on the hill with the horses, will sit down and ask us if we've seen a dark-haired girl with a small red heart painted on her forehead.

Chapter 11

Welcoming the Stranger

Loch Loyal is four miles long. Without woodland on its banks to leaven the monotony, it looks drab, like a slab of grey slate embedded in the moor. I was climbing down towards it, following a stream from the bealach on the shoulder of Ben Loyal, twin of the stream I'd followed up: dark, peaty water stepping down the mountain in falls and pools, with the odd scrawny birch or rowan clinging to the sides of gullies. Above me, the clouds that rolled over Sgòr Chaonasaid and An Caisteal were orange-tinged. It was late morning, but the sky was already late-afternoonish, as though a partial solar eclipse were underway. It made the day otherworldly and the hillside sullen. The few deer that I saw in the distance were indistinct, furtive – *crodh-sìthe* for sure. By the time I reached the road that skirts the shore of Loch Loyal, the wind was whipping rain onto the tarmac, and the long fetch of the loch brought a surge of grey waves.

As I walked south on the verge of the road, only one car passed me in fifteen minutes, and it was travelling in the opposite direction. Hitching is a test of faith, especially in the wind and rain on an empty road in Sutherland, in mid-October, and it would serve me right, given that I'd dismissed the loch as drab, if I had to spend a stormy night camped on its shore.

Eventually, an American couple stopped. They were in their late sixties, I guessed, but sprightly, both wearing jeans and checked shirts. I was grateful that they were willing to risk a lift to a stranger, especially one who climbed into the back seat of their small, clean hire-car wearing soaked waterproofs and muddy boots.

It was their first visit to Scotland, and the first time they'd crossed the Atlantic. There was the usual ancestry to be traced, but also a desire to engage with the country as it was now. They were interested in Devolution, Brexit, the ongoing debate over land ownership, and I liked their lack of reserve: straight away they apologised for Trump, as though they had been personally remiss and hadn't done enough to thwart his election. They were the first people I'd spoken to in over a week, since my hitch from Ullapool to Creag nan Uamh. When I told them so, they were delighted and replied that it was an honour. Their sincerity humbled me.

'That would be plenty of time for thinking,' the man said.

'Or not thinking at all,' the woman countered, and they both laughed.

They were from rural Iowa; they understood space and solitude and were completely authentic in their slow-spoken homeliness. I was surprised by how much I was affected by their company. It wasn't that I'd been lonely on my walk; rather, having spent days alone, absorbing the spaciousness of the landscape I was walking through, I was wide-open to their warmth and lack of cynicism.

The Americans told me about Storm Ophelia, how it was bringing warm air and dust from Africa, as well as ash that had been thrown up into the atmosphere from wildfires raging in Southern Europe. That's what was making the day-time sky so gloomy and orange-tinged. The winds would be strongest in the evening, they said, and they had heard warnings on the radio of expected structural damage to buildings.

The Flow Country, from Old Norse *flói* meaning 'wet', straddles Sutherland and Caithness. At 400,000 hectares, it's the largest area of blanket bog in Europe, and for thousands of years it lay largely untouched, building up layers of peat, drawing carbon out of the atmosphere and storing around 400 million tonnes of it – more than double the amount of carbon stored by all of the UK's woodlands. In the 1970s, however, Government tax incentives for forestry encouraged estate owners to drain large areas of the Flow Country and plant them up with fast-growing conifers. The trees never thrived, the depth of the peat unsuitable for them, and over the last couple of decades some of the estates, working with NatureScot and Forestry and Land Scotland, and with major funding from the EU, have begun to undo the damage done, removing plantations and blocking up drains. So far, around 2,500 hectares planted with forestry has been restored to blanket bog – an increasingly rare habitat that is home to threatened bird species such as greenshank and golden plover, as well as myriad species of insect and peat-bog flora.

The Americans were used to open spaces, but as we drove across the swell and dip of bog and moor, on a single-track road empty of traffic, they said it felt more isolated than back home, more desolate, although we agreed that the rain lashing the windscreen didn't help.

We stopped in the village of Lairg, where the Americans had booked a B&B. When I climbed out of the car, we shook hands and exchanged good wishes. My thanks were heartfelt. The man offered their phone number in case I was ever in Iowa. 'He won't be,' the woman said, smiling and waving me off. The sky was strange and orange, and I was mostly out of food. I bought a sandwich and a cup of tea in the village shop, but I wanted to stock up properly for the days ahead. From Lairg, the A836 would take me south to Inverness, or else I could follow the A839 as it wound west through Strath Oykel, back towards Assynt and Ullapool.

Finding Diarmaid's Grave and climbing Ben Loyal, I felt like I had completed my journey to the far north, and I was ready now to swing back down to the West Highlands, to pick up the trail of the Cailleach and those shape-shifting deer-women. The traffic confirmed my decision: what little of it passed was heading south on the A836.

A local drove me the few miles to Invershin, and the conversation in the car quickly turned to politics. He was a man who gave his opinion freely and with certainty, and who assumed that I would agree with everything he said. As suspicious of Holyrood as he was of Westminster, he told me: 'You just can't trust these Scots, they're all in it for the money.'

I was struck by the shifting nature of identity. Despite the fact that spoken Gaelic is all but lost in Sutherland, my lift-giver considered himself a Gael, and to him a Scot was someone from the Lowlands. Whereas in the 1950s, when Hamish Henderson asked the Stewarts of Remarstaig why they never went further east, into Caithness, Essie Stewart, demonstrating an accurate folk-knowledge of origins, explained, 'Up to here, the people are Scots like us, and speak Gaelic.'

The driver continued with his rant: 'Where were they when we were actually fighting for our independence, eh? Do you ever think about that?'

It was an odd, one-way conversation, but there was at least, I suppose, something fraternal in the way he considered me to be a fellow Gael – though he never asked where I was from – rather than one of those cowardly, money-grabbing Scots. If I'd had time to gather my thoughts before his next pronouncement, I might have pointed out that during the Jacobite Rising he was referring to, the clans of Sutherland, under the leadership of the Mackays, mostly remained loyal to King George, fighting on the side of the British Government; but I suspect he would have given short shrift to my reply.

From Invershin, a young German couple gave me a lift all the way to Inverness. Their English was good, but they didn't have much to say, and I was happy to sit quietly in the back.

Their iPod, which was plugged into the car stereo, played a medley of Beatles songs by a covers band with a drum-machine. For over an hour, this was the soundtrack to our journey. I was grateful, as always, for the lift, but the music pushed me to the edge of endurance. Along the way, we stopped at viewpoints so they could jump out and take photos of the Kyle of Sutherland and the Dornoch Firth. I fantasised about cutting the iPod cable with my knife while they were out of the car.

The light was alien as we drove from Ardgay up and over the Struie Road and down to the Cromarty Firth. There were black pillars of cloud in the orange sky and sheets of rain. Trees along the side of the road shook in the wind as though they were convulsing.

*

Inverness booms. It's one of the fastest-growing cities in the UK, with new business parks and housing developments expanding its girth. Looking down on it as we crossed the Kessock Bridge, high above the Beauly Firth, I could see warehouses and builders' yards, the glass-fronted showrooms of car dealerships; and although I've never been, I imagined it was like somewhere in America, maybe in Iowa, some regional city that, for all its size and sprawl and shiny newness, is dwarfed by the landscape around it. That's how Inverness appears: incidental compared to the breadth and brawn of the Beauly Firth, or to the mountains rising to its west.

The Germans dropped me on the outskirts. They were continuing south to Edinburgh, and I was tempted to travel with them down the A9. I could return to Speyside, find shelter from Storm Ophelia in a pine forest, then hitch west via Laggan. But I wasn't quite ready to be south and east of the Great Glen Fault, and I didn't think I could cope with another half-hour of the drum-machine Beatles, so I walked into the centre of Inverness instead, just as the shops were closing and the street lamps flickering on. I was resigned to spending the night in a hostel or a B&B, to taking stock and deciding what to do in the morning, but as I passed the bus station, I spotted that there was a bus heading west to Fort William, leaving in five minutes. Without a second thought, I bought a ticket and jumped aboard.

Travelling on the A82 along Glen Mor, somewhere between Drumnadrochit and Fort Augustus, I passed my other self in the dark, the one who had hitched north along the same road two weeks previously, blistered, limping, demoralised. I knew what was ahead of him: Glen Affric, Creag nan Uamh, Coire a' Mhadaidh and Bealach Horn, Strabeg Bothy and Cranstackie, Uaigh Dhiarmaid. If we'd stopped and met each other on the road, what tidings and encouragement I could have shared.

Fort William was quiet, with just a few folk scurrying down the High Street in the rain, the town bracing itself for the storm. I booked into Ossian's Hotel and enjoyed my first hot shower since Ullapool, then went out for a late dinner. In the pub nearby, a surly waitress served me fish and chips and a pint. She was just as surly to a group of Asian tourists who were doing their best with the language. Instead of helping out, she glared at them and repeated her questions more quickly and forcefully, disregarding her duty of care. I thought of the two Americans who'd picked me up by Loch Loyal, their openness and generosity, their curiosity about Scottish culture and society. I wondered what they'd make of this pub and its staff, and I reminded myself that in the Highlands, as in many cultures, there was once a tradition of hospitality that was sacrosanct, and that would be extended even to an enemy if they should come to the door.

Back along the A82, at the foot of Glen Moriston, Invermoriston House sits on the shore of Loch Ness. It's a modern building, but it rests on the site of the fortified house that was once the stronghold of the Grants of Glen Moriston.

A quarrel arises between young Grant and a contemporary of his from a neighbouring clan. Fierce words are spoken, dirks are drawn, and in the fight that ensues, young Grant is slain. The killer flees the wrath of the dead man's clansmen, but with nowhere to hide, and with the Grants in hot pursuit, he finds himself hammering at the oak door of Invermoriston House. The clan chief, old Grant, answers the door, and the young man asks only that he might have bread and water to slake his hunger and thirst. Old Grant welcomes the stranger and sits him down at his table, offering food and drink, and whatever else his guest might need.

Soon after, Grant's kinsmen appear at the door, and to his horror and despair, explain that they are pursuing the murderer of his son and heir, and that he was last seen running towards the house.

Without hesitation, the old man draws his sword and guards the door: 'No hair of his head shall be harmed while he is under my roof-tree. I have pledged hospitality, and never shall it be said that a Grant broke that pledge.'

Later, the bereaved clan chief escorts the young man out of Glen Moriston, telling him: 'I will protect you no further. Keep away from my people, and may God forgive you for what you have done.'

Witnessing the waitress's rudeness, the man who placed a stone heart on Diarmaid's Grave would have crossed to the Asians' table and apologised to them on behalf of a culture. In the glare and din of the pub, beneath a giant screen broadcasting football, I was and wasn't that man. I ate my cooked-from-frozen fish and chips and left, returning to the hotel room where I lay in bed and watched television. The storm battered the roof of the building, interfering with the reception.

Chapter 12

Rubh' Arisaig

Fort William withstood Storm Ophelia, and by morning the sky had cleared and the wind was reduced to bluster. I bought food for a week and boarded the Mallaig train. A group of pensioners filled the carriage, their excitement palpable, like children on a school trip. The conversation that rippled down the aisle was all about the 'Harry Potter Viaduct', which we would be crossing at Glenfinnan. It was a useful reminder that the lore of a landscape isn't fixed: it flows. In a hundred years, Glenfinnan might be better known for wizards than for being the place, at the head of Loch Shiel, where Charles Edward Stuart first raised his standard on Scottish soil.

For my part, I was excited to be travelling west to the Atlantic coast, and to the oak woods of Moidart.

Mac Mhic Ailein of Arisaig, chief of Clan MacDonald of Clanranald, Lord of Moidart, is hunting in his woods when he encounters a stag with wide-branched antlers. He raises his gun to shoot, and, of course, the stag takes the form of a woman, more beautiful than any he has met. He lowers the gun, and it's a stag, but in that first glimpse young Mac Mhic Ailein is smitten. He raises the gun and keeps it raised, so that the deer retains her human form, and he steps towards her until the barrel is at her breast. Then he drops the gun and catches her in his arms. 'You will not be separated from me,' he says. 'I will marry no one but you.'

'You have no business with me,' she warns. 'I won't suit you, and there will never be a day goes by but that you will need to kill a cow for me.'

Mac Mhic Ailein is heedless, infatuated. 'You will get that,' he says, 'though you should ask for two.'

Soon Mac Mhic Ailein's herd begins to grow thin as, each night, when they sit down to supper, his beloved devours every part of a slaughtered cow and is still hungry for more. A chief's wealth is in his cattle, and financial ruin is a sore test for infatuation. Eventually, Mac Mhic Ailein wishes only to be rid of the deer-woman, but no matter what he says or does, she will not be sent away.

I stepped off the train at Arisaig and walked down through the village to the bay, thinking about Mac Mhic Ailein's deer-woman and her insatiability. In Scottish folk tradition it's a sign of 'otherness', of something being out of kilter. When the fairies steal a newborn child and replace it with a changeling, the first indication of the swap is that the child, till then content to be nourished at the mother's breast, becomes ravenous, eating everything placed in front of it until the family's cupboards are bare, and still the changeling screams for more.

Other cultures have similar traditions. In North America, in Algonquian myth, the wétiko is an avaricious spirit that possesses people, so that no matter how gluttonous they become, they remain emaciated and dissatisfied. The Native American writer and activist, Jack D. Forbes, suggests that the myth of the wétiko is analogous to the story of Western civilisation's excess and insatiable greed. In his book, *Columbus and Other Cannibals*, he explores the terrible consequences of that greed, particularly for indigenous peoples and the lands they live on, arguing that 'the history of the world for the past 2,000 years is, in great part, the story of the epidemiology of the wétiko disease'.

None of us are immune. I'd spent a fortnight immersed in the landscape of the North-west Highlands, my body thriving on the rigour of walking and camping, eating when hungry, sleeping when tired; and the pace of my days brought spaciousness, clarity, balance. But in Fort William, I had sought the glare and din of the pub, processed fish and chips, the lure of the television, as though such things were a 'treat', as though I had convinced myself they were what I needed.

The twentieth-century Scottish psychiatrist R.D. Laing worked with people suffering from acute psychosis. In films of his talks and lectures, Laing strikes a curious figure, like a cross between Alex Fergusson and Ivor Cutler: sharp, formidable, but also a little shambolic; and funny, in that deadpan, Glaswegian way that leaves you unsure whether the humour is intentional or not.

But he was also a profound thinker who challenged the methodologies of modern science – he describes laboratories as the 'torture chambers of nature' – and who, in his talks and his writing, lays bare the damage and alienation caused by modernity. In *The Politics of Experience,* he writes: 'Only by the most outrageous violation of ourselves have we achieved our capacity to live in relative adjustment to a civilisation apparently driven to its own destruction.'

Whatever it was – this violation of ourselves, this wétiko infection – it had flared in me in Fort William, where it seemed that the balance I'd gained after two weeks of immersion in the living world was being traded for cheap food and crap TV.

An old man in the village advises Mac Mhic Ailein that if he wishes to be free of the deer-woman, there's only one person who might be skilly enough to help him. A summons is sent to MacPhie of Colonsay, and soon his boat arrives in the bay of Arisaig.

'What business is this you have with me, Mac Mhic Ailein?' asks MacPhie, and the Lord of Moidart explains his predicament.

'Slaughter her a cow for supper as usual,' says MacPhie, 'and set me a place opposite her at the table.'

They sit down to dine without speaking, the woman devouring every part of the cow. When the meal is finished, MacPhie looks directly at her.

'What's your news today, Sianach?' he asks; and she replies: 'What's that to you, Brian Boru?'

'I saw you, Sianach,' says he, 'when you consorted with the Fianna. When you went with Diarmaid O' Duibhne, and accompanied him from covert to covert.'

'And I saw you,' she says, 'when you rode on an old black horse, the lover of the slim fairy woman, ever chasing her from brugh to brugh.'

'Dogs and men after her,' cries MacPhie, 'long have I known her!' And with that, the woman flees, chased by every available man and dog, out towards Rubh' Arisaig, the 'Promontory of Arisaig'. She takes back the form of a deer, and they lose her in the landscape, and she is never seen again by Mac Mhic Ailein, Lord of Moidart.

It's five miles out to the beach at Port nam Murrach, 'Port of the Sailor', on the southern tip of Rubh' Arisaig. The single-track road passes through oak woodland as it leaves the village. Sheltered by the promontory and enjoying the mildness of the coast, the leaves on the trees were still green. I walked beneath the oaks, grateful to be in their vibrant world again, with the sun filtering through the branches and the birds singing – as though this was a day that had been kept back from summer, a borrowed day of warmth and growth.

It was low tide, and where the road skirted the coast, I could smell the iodine of bladderwrack and kelp on the shore. Looking back across the bay, the white cottages of Arisaig gleamed in the sun. There were so many herons. I counted six, each stationed a good distance apart along the shore, hunched in on themselves, patient for fish or frogs; and there were oystercatchers too, with bright traffic-cone beaks, high-strung compared to the herons, their calls a constant, anxious *kleep kleep kleep*.

In the tale of Mac Mhic Ailein, the conversation between MacPhie and the deer-woman is like a border crossing, a stepping over into a different country, one where time is torn and where identities are confused and conflated. She is Sianach, which means 'enchanted one', and at the same time she is Gráinne, who seduces Diarmaid and flees with him from the wrath of Fionn mac Cumhaill, while MacPhie is Brian Boru, High King of Ireland in the tenth century; and then, finally, the pair become their timeless, archetypal selves: the lover on his horse, ever chasing 'the slim fairy woman'.

The image made me think again of Spiridon, the old Yukaghir hunter in the Siberian Forest, how he saw and heard the elk-woman dancing and singing, enticing him to follow her; and of Dòmhnall Donn-shùileach on Beinn a' Bhric, stalking the dun-coloured hind, moving in time with her on the mountain. In the otherworld of myth, age seeks youth on an old black horse; the past dances with the ever-elusive present.

*

I've walked the road to Rubh' Arisaig many times. For several years, from my mid-twenties onwards, I came here at midsummer, sometimes with two or three others; sometimes there were a dozen of us. Initially, it was a gathering in remembrance of a friend of a friend who had died in a motorcycle crash, and whose ashes were scattered off the point. Later, it became a chance for a wider circle of friends to meet, and the gathering became the high point of my year, looked forward to with more anticipation than Christmas or Hogmanay: to be on the beach in June in fine company, to be astonished again by the midsummer light.

A white horse stood on a knoll in a field, practicing heraldic poses as though it expected to be photographed. I smiled and waved and took no pictures. At the road end I followed the track and then the familiar footpath across the bog and over the rocky rise. Below me, Port nam Murrach was a perfect scoop of white sand, held between two rocky arms, and sheltered from rough seas by its own tiny island, Eilean Port nam Murrach, lying just offshore. By the time I reached the beach, I had walked back more than twenty years.

I dumped my rucksack on the sand, took off my boots and socks, and then my clothes, and stepped into the sea. It was cold, but not as cold as Loch Beinn a' Mheadhoin, and the water was clear so that I could see as well as feel my toes gripping the sand. It was good to swim in the salt sea, to rinse myself clear of the evening in Fort William. Afterwards, the sun was full on my face when I climbed the crag to where we used to sit and watch it set. The Isle of Eigg, ten miles off the coast, loomed large, and the sea in between was still corrugated after the storm.

The long ridge and sheer crags of Beinn Bhuidhe tilt the northern end of Eigg upwards out of the waves, so that it looks like a breaching whale, with An Sgùrr as its dorsal fin and the Isle of Muck, to the south, like the flukes of its tail – Eigg that has risen since I first looked across to it from Rubh' Arisaig.

After decades of neglect and instability, the island was bought by the Isle of Eigg Heritage Trust in 1997. It wasn't the first community buy-out, but it has been one of the most high-profile and inspiring, in part because of the circumstances leading up to its sale: the toxic ownership of Keith Schellenberg; the weird sideshow of Maruma, the German 'artist' with dubious credentials who briefly took possession of the island; and then there was the public campaign to raise funds for the buy-out, which itself raised the profile of the debate about land ownership in Scotland. In the last twenty or so years, the islanders have provided a dynamic example of how small, remote communities can come together and figure out best practice for housing, power generation, job creation, land stewardship. The island is now thriving, its population growing. With the air so sharp, from my look-out on the crag I could see the white gleam of houses at Kildonan.

One summer, a group of us spent a fortnight at Port nam Murrach, our numbers swelling and ebbing as others arrived and left. The sun shone, and we passed the days swimming or lazing in the shade of our tents. We built a table and benches from driftwood, played vigorous rounds of backgammon, talked late into the night by the fire. After the first few days, no one wanted to leave the beach, and we had to draw straws to see who would go to Arisaig to collect supplies. Another time, I walked in off the last train having travelled up from Edinburgh with my flatmate Jane. We were there to surprise two friends who had driven up from the south to camp for a few days at the end of summer, having missed the June gathering. Jane and I walked out from Arisaig in the dark. The sky was clear, and there were thousands of tiny frogs on the road. It was after midnight when we arrived at Port nam Murrach, and the tide was low. We walked down barefoot to the sea, and when we reached the water's edge, every step we took sparkled. It was unexpected, bewildering, until I remembered the boat trip across Loch Crinan, years earlier, with my friend Alastair. The wet sand at Port nam Murrach was impregnated with phosphorescent plankton. We ran along the tideline leaving a trail of sparks, and when we waded into the water, it was alive with light.

I climbed down off the crag and sat next to where our fire had been set; bright grass now, but once a circle of hearthstones with all the years layered in ash. The place was familiar, intimate to me. I knew the best spot to pitch a tent and alternative sites for a fire if the wind was blowing too hard from the south-west. I knew where the nearest stream was for fresh water and where to find an overhang of rock that was almost a cave, hidden at the back of the crag – we stored firewood there for the following year, as well as driftwood planks for benches, fish boxes for storage, an old lobster creel to stock with beer bottles and sink offshore as a fridge. And although I struggled to remember which year it was that we enjoyed a fortnight of sunshine, and which year I walked in with Jane at midnight, and where those visits sat in the chronology of gatherings, the images themselves were vivid, as though they were imprinted on the beach before me.

Being at Port nam Murrach was like standing at Uaigh Dhiarmaid and looking up at Ben Loyal, and trying to *see* Diarmaid and the boar on the mountain. The beach, the flat patch of machair grass, the fireplace – all were there in front of me, and when I closed my eyes, I could see friends feasting, swimming, climbing the crag to watch the sunset, with only the flicker of my eyelids separating us. If I was Spiridon hunting in the taiga or an Aboriginal Australian walking the Dreamtime paths of their people, or Dòmhnall Donnshùileach on Beinn a' Bhric, there might be no separation at all: the past, whether my own or that of the ancestors, fully present.

*

The sun was on my shoulder when I walked away from Port nam Murrach. I would have relished camping there for the night, relighting the fire at our hearth, but the wind was picking up, and I'd heard in Fort William that it would rise to gale force by the evening, so I set out instead for the shelter of a bothy.

I might have walked two miles or twelve miles that afternoon, following the coast north back to Arisaig and then skirting the white sands of Morar towards Mallaig, or else south along the coast of Loch nan Uamh, and on towards Ardnish. Either way, I can't tell, not because I don't remember, but because the bothy was one of those marked as secret on my map – an 'unofficial bothy', its location only to be shared person to person, just as the old man at Carnmore Bothy had shared it with me.

I passed a bay with a seal bobbing its Labrador head above the water, watching me, and yet another heron guarding the pebble beach. A robin was singing amongst straggly oaks that hugged the crags set back from the shore – the old coast as was. Raised beaches and coastlines are common in Scotland, the land rising, and continuing to rise, after the end of the last glacial period and the release of its immense weight of ice; while consequently, like a see-saw, the southern half of the landmass of the British Isles tilts back downwards. It's the same geological process, known as isostatic rebound, that accounts for the decompression of Rannoch Moor and for the raised beaches of West Linga in the Shetland Isles, so forensically described by Hugh MacDiarmid in his poetry.

The strip of ground between the crags and the pebble beach was strewn with plastic. Stumps of flag iris poked up amongst plastic bottles, crates, nylon rope, old training shoes, wedges of polystyrene, fish netting, fish boxes, creels, broken bits of fibre-glass boat: a rubbish tip of plastic in this one small bay, all the colours of a garish rainbow. Fifty years ago, what was washed ashore would mostly have been composed of natural or non-toxic materials: wooden crates and boxes, glass bottles, hemp rope; all of it re-usable or biodegradable. Now, amongst all the plastic, there were only a few pieces of driftwood, bleached by the sun.

Some say that we shouldn't separate the two, that plastic products are also part of nature, and that words like 'natural' and 'man-made' are no longer useful. I'm not so interested in that argument; I'm not sure what purpose it serves. A piece of wood, whether branch or timber, will break down quickly, becoming food for insects and mycelium, eventually becoming soil. It won't choke the throat of a guillemot in the process, and if it should lodge in the gut of a whale, it won't leach toxins into the animal's nervous system. Recently, a sperm whale was stranded and died on the Isle of Harris in the Outer Hebrides. In the post mortem, over a hundred kilogrammes of plastic – bottles and bags, fish netting, rope – was found entwined in its intestines. Globally, it's been estimated that the total mass of plastics now exceeds the total mass of all living mammals: a shocking truth that can't be intellectually argued away.

I sat down amongst the rubbish, perching on a stone. Next to me, the feathery leaves of silverweed poked through the perforations of a plastic lid, entangling the lid in growth, overthrowing it. There's a long game being played. In a few thousand years, where I was sitting would almost certainly be underwater, but silverweed would still be throwing out runners to carpet the shoreline, whatever its raised level, and all the plastic scattered around me would be broken down into smaller and smaller pieces, becoming a thin layer of sediment marking our brief Anthropocene.

The names have their own poetry, a catalogue of compound words describing strange alchemies with terrible consequences: polyethylene terephthalate, used to make packaging and containers, which can leach antimony, a toxin; polyvinyl chloride, known to us as PVC and considered the most hazardous plastic, with a cocktail of hormone-disrupting phthalates and carcinogenic dioxins – we use it to make windows and doors and furniture; polystyrene, whose styrene component is a neurotoxin; and good old polycarbonate, staple plastic for the manufacture of cups and plates and toys. The bisphenol A it contains has been linked in animal studies to numerous health problems, including chromosome damage, altered immune function, increased risk of breast cancer, prostate cancer, infertility and metabolic disorders. Until recently, this was the favoured plastic for making baby bottles.

It would take a lifetime to clear the plastic strewn along this small stretch of coast. Meanwhile it carries on leaching chemicals into the water and the atmosphere, carries on ending the lives of birds and other creatures, choked by the bright scraps they have ingested. This is the material evidence of our psychosis, the effluvia of our wétiko infection: we throw it all away, and it comes back, creating new raised beaches of plastic.

Walking here once with a friend, he was horrified to see how strewn the bays and beaches were. Jack is a native of Northumbria on the East Coast, where currents and prevailing winds ensure that most of the North Sea's rubbish drifts towards Scandinavia. He knows all about the scale of waste we produce, the destruction it causes – he's seen the films, read the books – but it was a shock nonetheless, to be so vividly confronted. If it was happening in a city, we agreed, in a public park or square, there would be uproar at the mess; but the West Coast, our beautiful West Coast, the one that the tourist industry projects only pristine images of, has become, in places, little more than a dump.

What do we hope for? Meaningful lives, not defined by materialism? An earth inhabitable for us and other species? From my perch on a stone, somewhere on the coast of Moidart, the tideline of plastic around me seemed like a truer measure of our aspirations.

*

I climbed out of the bay and followed a path along the coast, well-trodden by deer. Sure enough, when I looked up, a handful of hinds was silhouetted on the ridge ahead, watching me. Between us, on the slope below the ridge, lay the remains of a township: half a dozen ruined cottages, tumbled dykes, abandoned *feannagan* – 'lazy-beds' for crops – and a stream running close by; the deer and the people intertwined.

I imagined the hinds as the first people populating this coast – Mesolithic hunter-gatherers, wrapped in dun-coloured skins and furs, making their camp some 8,000 years ago, and watching me, the intruder, approaching from the future. They did well to turn their backs on me, to disappear over the ridge and lose themselves in the landscape, to secure a few thousand years of grace before we would meet again.

Rounding a knoll, I surprised a stag, close enough that I could see its haunch muscles ripple as it sprang into movement. It ran off across the hollow we were in with a funny high step, as though it was trying to keep its shins clear of the boggy ground. It was large, wide-antlered, and I was glad that it ran away from rather than towards me. Once it established a more appropriate distance, it stopped and turned, and uttered a muted half-grunt, half-bellow. If a stag could look sheepish, it did.

One moment I was walking through heather on gently sloping ground, the next I was on the edge of a crag, clinging to the roots of a rowan tree so I could lower myself into a gully. The bay below was the quickest way to reach the bothy, and I had spotted what seemed to be a suitable route. I'd been careful, after my scare crossing the ford in Strathmore below Ben Hope, but here I was, snagged again. The roots were strong, like rope, and hanging from them, I had been able to stand on the ledge below. So far so good, but my rucksack made me top-heavy, imbalanced, so that I had to press against the rock to stop myself teetering. After considering what might break, I unclipped my rucksack and dropped it twenty feet down the gully, hoping that the bottle of meths for the Trangia, and bottle of whisky for me, would be padded enough by the spare clothing they were wrapped in. The rucksack bounced a couple of times and landed in a bog at the bottom. I shimmied and scrambled down after it, glad no one was around to see my foolishness, then set off across the bay, imagining the censure of my family, feeling as sheepish as the stag I'd surprised earlier. An inevitable heron, standing on one leg on the shore, practising its avian yoga, objected to my presence with a loud *skraak*.

Chapter 13

Carlotta's Eyrie

The bothy is perched on a crag above the sea, and there is only one way up; a knotted length of rope helps you climb the steepest section. Carlotta's Eyrie was built in the 1950s by student friends of the woman it's named after, whose family at the time owned that stretch of the coast as part of their estate. It has all the odd beauty of a thing handmade, using mostly foraged materials: the low walls constructed with stones carried up from the shore, mortared into the solid rock of the crag; the arched tin roof nailed in place and now lashed with lorry straps against the wind. It's a small space inside, maybe ten by fifteen feet, with a wooden tongue-and-groove ceiling, a sleeping platform for two and planked benches that have been smoothed by over sixty years of use. An old Calor Gas bottle has been fashioned into a wood-burning stove, with a flue pipe welded on. Various 'useful' things litter the shelves and windowsills: old bottles for candle sticks, broken lighters, a selection of mismatched Tupperware, and there is a small library of books, the kind you would find in a charity box at the supermarket: thrillers, out-of-date travel guides, an introduction to Buddhist practice, a guide to seashells. The large main window looks straight out to sea, like the window of a ship's bridge, facing into the prevailing winds. It's a fine place to be in a storm.

On another visit early one January, with Jack, my Northumbrian friend, we arrived at the bothy late in the day. Walking in, we met someone walking out who told us there had been seven people staying on Hogmanay. It would have been a cosy way to welcome in the year.

I fired up the stove, feeding it with driftwood that I'd gathered on the shore, then unpacked my rucksack and cooked my evening meal. The day faded, and looking out of the window, I could no longer distinguish between headlands, sea or sky. The wind gathered its strength, rattling the flue of the stove; waves boomed at the foot of the crag; and I was glad of stout walls and a tin roof raised like a shield. When I curled into my sleeping bag and blew out the candles I'd lit, the window was a black screen lashed by rain.

*

In the morning, gulls scudded across the sky, and the sea flexed its grey-green muscle between the headlands, throwing up flecks of white spray from broken waves. When I went outside to see the day, the wind scooped the breath from my lungs.

A pebble beach sits to one side of the bothy's crag. In the afternoon, during a break in the weather, I scrambled down and sat amongst the pebbles, watching the waves climb the shore and fall back again. The vagaries of wind and tide meant that this small beach was mostly free of plastic. Here, there were just round, shining pebbles and a tideline of bladderwrack and leathery straps of kelp; despite the presence, no doubt, of microplastics and other pollutants, the water offshore looked clean and clear.

The sea conceals its sickness. We convince ourselves that it can absorb and dissolve our waste and that we can carry on with our polluting industries, our malignant economies. That afternoon, I was glad of the deception and that I had no microscope to show me otherwise, glad that the cormorant swimming offshore was sleek and glossy, despite what might be tangled in its intestines, glad that the ebb and flow of the waves held the possibility of return. The wind rose again, and rain arrived in squalls. I donned waterproofs and followed the coast to the next bay to collect an armful of driftwood and then climbed back up to my eyrie for the night.

Most evenings on my journey, especially if the day's walk was long, I'd be able for little more than cooking dinner then sitting quiet and tending to the fire. It was a good time to think about the stories I was tracking, to recite a tale and wrap its layers of meaning around my tired body and drowsy head.

MacPhie has left the hunting hill where he trysted with his fairy lover, vowing not to return. He marries instead a woman from his own township, and soon they are expecting their first child. When his wife's lying-in time is upon her, the labour is prolonged, and the baby will not be born. In desperation, MacPhie goes back to the hunting hill.

'What news today, MacPhie?' asks the fairy woman.

Affecting nonchalance, MacPhie says, 'There is a goat in my paddock that cannot birth its kid.'

The fairy woman is surprised, and replies: 'What, even with the white-flowered pearlwort beneath its feet?'

Having gained the required information, MacPhie doesn't conceal his pleasure, and the fairy woman realises she has been tricked, that it's no goat but MacPhie's wife whose labour is prolonged. Pretending concern, she hands him a thick leather belt and instructs him to take it home and wrap it around his wife's belly, 'For it will surely help the passing.'

MacPhie leaves the hunting hill, but before he reaches home, suspecting the ill-will of the fairy woman, he winds the belt around a boulder that stands by the side of the path. As soon as it's buckled, the belt tightens and tightens, until, with a crack like gunshot, the force of its tightening splits the boulder in two.

Back home, MacPhie picks the white-flowered pearlwort from his paddock and rubs it on the soles of his wife's feet, and soon the healing virtue in the plant helps ease the birthing of their child.

In Gaelic tradition it was widely known that hunters, who spent many nights or even weeks in the forest or on the hill, were susceptible to the charms of a *leannan sìthe*, or 'fairy lover', a figure who is synonymous with shape-shifting deer-women. In the case of our old friend MacPhie of Colonsay, the correlation between the two is only implied – MacPhie trysts with her on the hunting hill – but in other tales, such as that of Mac Mhic Ailein of Moidart, it is made clear.

For the Yukaghir of Northern Siberia, it is also understood that hunters run the risk of being seduced by the *ayibii* of the elk that they hunt. Should he be so, a hunter will sicken and die, and his own *ayibii* will be reincarnated in the body of an elk. Which is why, when the Yukaghir encounter an elk behaving strangely, perhaps one that wanders into the midst of their encampment, they say that the elk has a hunter's *ayibii*, and that it yearns for the conviviality of its former companions.

In another account, one of Rane Willerslev's informants describes an experience he had as a young man, during a period when elk were scarce and the Yukaghir were forced to hunt reindeer instead. He had spent a fruitless day tracking a large herd. The next morning, hungry and weary after a sleepless night, he saw an old man ahead of him, dressed in the 'old fashion' and gesturing for him to follow – which he did, despite noticing that the old man seemed to leave reindeer footprints in the snow. Eventually, they reached a large encampment with people of all ages going about their business. The old man took him to his tent, where his wife served them each a bowl of food. The hunter noticed that rather than speaking to each other with words, the old man and his wife grunted like reindeer, and that instead of the expected meat, the bowl the wife served was full of lichen.

Willerslev's informant claimed that, being so hungry, he ate the lichen and found that it tasted fine, and that, being so weary, he lay down on the bed they provided. In the night, he dreamt that he was surrounded by reindeer, and in the morning, he realised that, already, he could scarcely remember the name of his own wife, and that if he didn't escape, he would be lost forever. Sneaking out of the tent before the old couple awoke, he found his way back home, much to the surprise of the people in his village, who thought he must have perished: "'What do you mean?' I asked them, 'I have only been away for a week.' 'No,' they said. 'We have not seen you for more than a month.'"

Once again, the parallels between this account, vouched for as a true experience remembered from youth, and stories from Highland tradition are uncanny. There are many well-known tales in the Highlands of men and women who have been lured into *sitheanan*, 'fairy hills', where they find people going about lives that mirror the drama and domesticity of human lives – a slanted mirror, similar but different, like the reindeer people that Willerslev's informant encountered. And like the informant, if a human should escape from a fairy hill, they soon find that time there is not consistent with time here: the usual postscript to such tales is the discovery that a day passed in the otherworld of the *sithean* equates to a year and a day in this one.

Of course, folktales of the Scottish Highlands are not only comparable to the stories told by the Yukaghir of Siberia. After reading Willerslev's book, I began to research widely and found, again and again, in anthropological texts, similar stories and experiences, particularly amongst the hunter-gatherer cultures of North America and the Arctic and sub-Arctic regions of Europe. At the heart of all these cultures there's a common world-view, one that is embedded in specific landscapes and that is intensely local in the way that it's expressed, but which is universal in its founding principle. I have no doubt, now, that the tales I was tracking are rooted in the same archaic consciousness: a way of seeing and being in the world that has come to be known as Animism.

How far back might we look? How far forwards? Australian Aboriginal peoples are reckoned to be practitioners of the oldest continuous culture in the world, having been around for over 60,000 years, making them custodians of the deepest memories of our species. Their culture is based on the notion that all things have spirit or 'personhood', and that even the land is alive; it's the same for the Yukaghir and the Inuit, and the San Bushmen. What prickles the hair on the back of my neck is that here in the Highlands, within living memory, there is an oral tradition that takes us back to a time and a culture where a similar belief held sway.

We struggle to recognise this now, but the evidence is there in the stories and in the place-names that anchor the stories. If you told an elder of the Warlpiri people from the Northern Territories of Australia about Cailleach an t-Sniomha, the 'Spinning Old Woman' on the ridge north of Corrie a' Mhadaidh, or about Sgrìob an Tuirc, the scarring carved by the tusks of the boar as it fell from the summit of Sgòr Chaonasaid, they would likely have no trouble in recognising what they might call a Highland Dreaming or, to use the Warlpiri term, Jukurrpa.

Before bed, I went outside and perched on the edge of the crag. The sky was black with cloud, the wind was blowing up to gale-force, and the sea bellowed beneath me as it pounded the rocks. Back inside, the stove belched smoke, and the bothy's roof creaked and strained as though the wind was trying to peel it open.

*

The wind blew out in the night, and at dawn I was woken by a bird scratching on the tin of the roof with its claws. A raven dropped onto the window ledge, folded its wings, and peered in at me. The bothy was gloomy and cold. I packed, swept the floor, and left, clutching the knotted rope for balance as I climbed down off the crag, my head cloudy, sleep-deprived. The storm was over, but there was no colour in the day, and the sea was a furrowed grey field. I followed a path inland from the coast.

Chapter 14

Rois-bheinn

Even in the sullen damp of a grey morning, the land I was walking through lifted my spirits. It was old land: craggy hills and hollows, wooded with oak, birch and hazel; hunter-gatherers' land. Four ducks flew up from a reeded loch, wheeling away above the trees, and I met a Highland cow on the path that was doing her best impression of an aurochs. A small herd of cattle was grazing by the side of the loch, shaggy, aboriginal, the plastic identity tags clipped to their ears the only sign of their domestication. The one I met stood on her own on the path, blocking my way but not deliberately: she was just there, solid in herself, considering her next move in that unhurried way that cows have. I sidled past, giving a wide berth to her horns. When I rested my hand on the broad warmth of her back, she swung her head and looked at me from under her fringe, without much interest, as though her thoughts were elsewhere. The morning, through her small brown eyes, was timeless.

I gathered sticks as I walked and found a flat spot on the bank of a stream to set a cooking fire for tea and porridge. The stones that curbed the bank were thatched with moss, and the previous night's wind had shaken leaves over everything. After breakfast, I shouldered my pack and forded the stream.

Stepping out of the oak woods onto the tarmac of the A830 was like crossing time zones, the difference measured in centuries, not hours. I followed the road south and east as it wound through Moidart, careless as to whether I would gain a hitch or not. A pair of buzzards kept ahead of me, playing tag between the telegraph poles. Eventually, a local man stopped and gave me a lift. He spoke quietly, unhurriedly, easing into words in the same way that he negotiated the bends in the road. We talked about the autumn colour in the trees and the storms of the last few days. I noticed a fishing rod in sections, in the back of the car, along with nets, reels and a pair of waders, and I asked him how the fishing was. The vehemence of his response surprised me.

We were driving towards Loch Ailort, which has been used for fish farming since the 1960s. The driver told me that the continual application of pesticides and other chemicals has had a devastating effect on the ecology of the sea loch, with a severe decline in wild fish as well as lobster, crab and other wildlife. He was angry with the Norwegian company that operates the fish farm, and with the Scottish Government who grant its license.

'They would never get away with what they do here, in Norway,' he said. 'The legislation for environmental protection is much stricter over there.'

The driver told me about a group of local fishermen who were working together, voluntarily, to improve wild spawning on the River Ailort, a once famous salmon river that flows into the loch. Their measures were having some success, despite the fish farm, and it struck me as a useful example of the way that people will apply themselves to finding solutions to environmental problems when the impact is direct and personal. I was curious about the bigger picture. Given the decline in wild fish stocks, but the importance of fish as a source of protein for an ever-growing human population, I asked him what the alternative was to yet more fish farming.

'It's simple,' he said, 'build fish farms, but not in the sea.' He explained that the netted marine cages could easily be replaced by large, onshore tanks, and that it was already happening in Norway and in North America. The technology is there, he told me, but the infrastructure costs are high. Once up and running, however, because it is a closed environment, it's so much easier to control disease or parasite infestation, and it ends the contamination of the sea and the damage to marine life.

'But it will never happen here,' he said. 'Our government is in bed with the fish-farm companies, and they don't want to spend the money.'

His anger made him drive faster. When he dropped me off at the head of Loch Ailort, the damp of the morning deadened the sound of his car's engine as he drove on towards Glenfinnan and Fort William. It was still early, and there were no other cars on the road, and no sign of life in the Lochailort Inn as I walked past. Following the single-track road that skirts the south shore of the loch, I thought about what the driver had said.

The notion of a salmon, with all the wonder of its life cycle, being contained from egg to harvest in vast tanks with tens of thousands of others, possibly hundreds of miles from the sea, was abhorrent to me; and yet the current system of marine farming is no better. I've seen the photographs of salmon in those farms, packed into cages, their scales eaten away by sea lice until the flesh is exposed; and what cost to the health of humans, eating fish that are so regularly bathed in pesticides?

Rain was falling into the loch and into the floating cages of the fish farm. I passed Inverailort House, catching a glimpse of its boarded-up windows through the trees. The owner, Lucretia Cameron-Head, died in 1994. Her hospitality and eccentricity were legendary. After her death, her friend and chatelaine, Barbara Mackintosh, continued to run the local post office from the parlour of the house. She also sold Calor Gas bottles to locals and to holiday-makers from the nearby Forsay caravan site; but there was no money for essential repairs, and the house, which is almost a castle, crumbled around her and her menagerie of pets.

I was one of those holiday-makers, visiting Forsay regularly with my wife and daughters, when they were younger, staying in a friend's caravan on the site. The girls loved our holidays there. The trip to the post office for stamps and gas was always a treat, but Barbara died in 2015, and Inverailort House is now derelict and probably beyond repair.

Few cars passed me on the road, and none stopped, but I was in no hurry, and it was fine to be following the shore of the loch in the rain.

*

The hind was sprawled awkwardly amongst the birch trees and bracken, a few feet down from the verge on the shore side of the road. She'd likely been hit at night: the glare of headlights, the bump against the body, the driver braking hard; or perhaps, if there was no serious damage to the car, just driving on. One of her legs was almost torn away, and she'd been lying dead a few days: congealed blood plugged her ears, and the jelly of her eyes had thickened; in her opened belly, beetles crawled amongst the sludge.

Barry Lopez, the American writer and ecologist, wrote an essay called *Apolagia* in which he gives an account of a year he spent stopping his car whenever he passed a dead creature on the road. Animal, bird, reptile, he picked them up – sometimes he had to scrape them up – and carried them away from the road to be buried and honoured. When asked why he bothered, he said, 'You never know [. . .] the ones you give some semblance of burial, to whom you offer an apology, may have been like seers in a parallel culture. It is an act of respect, a technique of awareness.'

When I first read the essay, the idea gripped me, and in the years since, I've tried to follow Lopez's example. Not so comprehensively or with such dedication, but I have stopped for fox and badger, roe deer and hare, and numerous birds. The notion of 'seers from a parallel culture' is beyond my experience, but I like that he says 'you never know'. Practicing that uncertainty, accepting the discomfort of it, feels useful, like working a muscle to loosen it, like learning to see the way that Spiridon or Dòmhnall Donn-shùileach might.

The smell of the hind was like a septic tank, and her coat was loose on her back, the skin unstitching from the muscle, the wet fur pulling away easily. Hoodie crows, buzzards and foxes would continue to feed off her carcass, and eventually what was left would seep into the soil, nourishing the roots of the birch trees. Although I had no connection to the hind, I felt remorse, and my enthusiasm for the day was in danger of being blunted. In 'Frontier Country', the Canadian poet Karen Solie writes that 'our separateness amongst separate things unites us: a violent wonder at convergence'. But there was no wonder here, only violence. I hoped that the car, at least, was efficient, killing the hind quickly rather than leaving it injured on the verge.

It was late morning, and I hadn't far to walk – I planned to stay at my friend's caravan at Forsay, a mile or so along the road – but the hind was dead at my feet, and the rain had eased, and Rois-bheinn rose above me, a mountain I'd never climbed. I thought of Barry Lopez and his acts of respect and plucked a clump of fur from the hind's coat, wrapping it in a plastic bag and tucking it into the zip pocket of my waterproof.

I followed the track that had been built to service a small hydro system on the Irine Burn. Irine is the old name for the settlement at Roshven Farm and appears to be an anglicisation of *uileann*, 'elbow' or 'angle', referring to the way the land there protrudes into Loch Ailort. The farm is named after the mountain which dominates the south side of Loch Ailort. The most plausible, and appropriate, interpretation of Rois-bheinn is

'Hill of Showers'. Today, despite it living up to its name, I was hoping it would clear by the time I reached the top.

It was an unfamiliar pleasure to be walking without the weight of my rucksack, having stashed it amongst trees at the foot of the track. I tried to climb with an awareness of my body and surroundings, tried to stay present to each step and to use my senses as though they'd been augmented by the encounter with the hind, as though I was climbing for both of us. I mostly failed, but it was fun to try, and the view as I gained height was tremendous. Between rain squalls, shafts of sunlight picked out the rocky islands at the entrance to Loch Ailort, burnishing them. The tidal race between the islands, out into the Sound of Arisaig, created contoured patterns on the surface of the water.

After climbing beyond the track, up onto the shoulder of Rois-bheinn, I noticed a large orange digger below me, clearing a second track: another hydro system, I guessed, this time on the Allt Lagan a' Challtuinne, 'Stream of the Hazel Hollow'. The driver must have been on a tea break, but now he'd started the engine again, and my attention was challenged by the bump and grind of the digger.

Rois-bheinn is the tallest and shapeliest of Moidart's mountains, and I was troubled by the thought of hydro-schemes on its flanks. But there's no shortage of water flowing from the 'Hill of Showers', and maybe it's irrelevant whether that water completes its journey to the sea via dams and pipes, or via the streams that have worn their courses over thousands of years; and surely harnessing the falling water's latent energy is better than the alternatives: a nuclear plant at the head of the loch? A coal-fired power station?

The digger was making a mess of the slope, piling turf to the side and gouging out mud and rock, but in a few seasons, the mud would re-seed, and the track would settle into the folds of the hillside. As for the streams, the Allt Lagan a' Challtuinne and the Irine Burn, both were too small and steep for migrating fish to use for spawning, so the overall impact could be said to be minimal, and in return there would be an endless supply of renewable energy, powering local homes.

But what if the question wasn't just one of ecology: what if you threw theology into the mix? Like a deer killed and left without honour by the verge of a road, is it a sacrilege to stop the flow of a mountain's streams? I think I know what Barry Lopez would say.

As I gained height, the digger and its noise diminished. The land opened, with bands of cloud shadowing the ridges and mountains. Across Loch Ailort, I could see Peanmeanach bay on the Ardnish peninsula, with its row of ruined houses – another cleared township. One of the cottages there was re-roofed in the sixties and is now a well-maintained and popular bothy. To the north, I could see Sleat on Skye and the Cuillin ridge. Inland, I looked down over a rugged landscape towards Meall a' Mhadaidh Mòr and Lochan na Caillich, which sits above Glen Uig; the names of wolf and Cailleach, as they are in so many places, still ringing in the land.

It was a steep haul to the summit of Rois-bheinn, and I was higher now than the peaks around me. Southwards, I could see as far as the Isle of Mull, its mountains rising above Ardnamurchan. The cloud was thickening west and north, so that Skye and Rum had disappeared, and even Eigg was beginning to be smudged out. Below me, Roshven Farm sat on its elbow of land. It was clear why it would have been an attractive place to make home: sheltered from south-westerlies, and with a gravel shore for launching boats; the bounty of fish available from the sea, and the bounty of game from the wooded slopes around it. I wondered how long people have lived on the shores of Loch Ailort, how many thousands of years passed before hydro-electricity troubled the streams that flow into it.

The wind had gathered strength as I climbed and was now flaying the slopes and quivering the deer grass until the mountain seemed to vibrate. Butterwort plants were anchored in the turf, their flower stalks and seed heads long since blown, but the five basal leaves still open, still hungry. Butterwort is one of Scotland's few carnivorous plants, attracting insects to its sticky leaves, which trap and slowly dissolve them, ingesting the remains through pores on the surface of the leaves. The plants looked like small, green starfish, as though they'd been scooped up out of the sea by the wind and scattered onto the slopes of the mountain.

Whatever remorse I'd felt for the dead hind had been sharpened into purpose. I stood on the summit and dug out from my pocket the little patch of dun-coloured fur, plucked from her back. I thought about the other dead deer I'd encountered: the carcass of the stag I saw hanging from a hook in the estate-yard shed, the sodden stag that lolled in the back of the 4x4, its head bumping against the wheel arch, as I crossed the Corrieyairack Pass; and I thought again of my encounter with the stag at the mouth of Bone Cave, and of all the other living deer I'd met on my journey.

There was little weight or substance to the clump of fur. When I held it up above my head, the wind cast it away, and I had a sense, then, that although I'm no Animist, although I don't see or sing the Dreamtime, sometimes a practice is more important than adherence to the belief that underpins it. Thinking about the killing of the hind, the process of her disintegration, and about the fish farms polluting the loch, and the rubbish on the beaches, and the sperm whale on Harris with a hundred kilos of plastic in its belly – thinking about all of that, I didn't believe that my action offered redress or amelioration. But, as Barry Lopez says, you never know, and if nothing else, the hind had led me to the top of a fine mountain, one that I hadn't climbed before and that I would likely have walked past otherwise, preferring to reach the comfort of the caravan early.

I left the summit in the rain. On the way down I disturbed what, at a distance, I took to be a pigeon, until I noticed that its wings were turning winter white. Then there were four of them: ptarmigan. They'd had enough of my intrusion and cast themselves off the mountain, plotting a bright arc through the air below me, crossing between Rois-bheinn and the black crags of Sgùrr a' Mheadhain.

The rain was still falling when I reached a stretch of woodland on Rois-bheinn's lower slopes. The deer fence that sheltered it looked new, only in place for a few seasons, but the transformation was profound, the older trees now surrounded by young birch and rowan. Regeneration requires little effort: you just need to keep out the deer and the sheep. When I climbed down into the woods, the noise of the digger was muted by the sound of the wind in the leaves and the gurgle of water from a nearby, non-hydro stream. From beneath the trees, the view was more selective than from the bare slopes, Loch Ailort revealing itself in glimpses through veils of birch and rowan. I crouched by the mossy bank of the free-flowing stream and filled my water bottle. There were seedling oaks growing on the bank, and the water tasted like the mountain.

*

Forsay, from Old Norse *fors*, meaning 'waterfall', sits between Roshven Farm and Glen Uig, six miles from Inverailort. The name applies to a field of pasture that slopes down to the shore and is skirted by the Forsay Burn, which tumbles over a series of falls before it flows into the loch. According to tradition, Forsay was where Charles Edward Stuart first set foot on the Scottish mainland before advancing to Glenfinnan to raise his standard in 1745. True or not, in the aftermath of Culloden, the settlement there was razed to the ground in punishment against those of the inhabitants who took up arms with Charlie. There is no trace now of any buildings.

Post-Culloden, as a fugitive being hunted by redcoat soldiers through the Highlands, his plans in tatters, the Young Pretender may well have acted with fortitude, but when he first landed in Moidart, greedy for power and careless of the lives of others, he set in play a sequence of events that led to the state-sanctioned assault of a civilian population, with all its attendant atrocities. While he sailed back to France, in the Highlands, the British Government, supported by Scots and English alike, imposed the same brutal social and economic suppression, and cultural deracination, that it was imposing wherever people found themselves under the boot of its Empire.

I've not much patience for those who get misty-eyed about the Bonnie Prince, but then I'm not from Moidart. Years ago, hitching from Fort William to Arisaig, on my way to Port nam Murrach for midsummer, I was given a lift by a retired priest who spoke fondly about Charles Edward Stuart, as though remembering a relative, and who talked about local incidents during the Rising as though they'd happened early in his own life. His knowledge and depth of feeling shames my lack of patience: his attitude to the prince had nothing to do with the rights and wrongs of monarchs, and everything to do with honour, tradition, loyalty. The old priest, native of Moidart, Gaelic-speaker, Jacobite, shook my hand when he dropped me off, and I felt as though I'd received a benediction from someone who existed outside of time.

In the 1960s, my friend Neil's parents asked the farmer if they might place a caravan in a corner of the field at Forsay. Since then, the field has evolved into a small, official, though unconventional, caravan site. There are no neat lines of mobile homes on level plots, with gravel paths and electric plug-ins. It's just a sloped field with caravans, some of them relics from those early days; but the view of the Sound of Arisaig and out to the Small Isles is spectacular, and the site has been cherished by generations of families. Plots remain sought-after and rarely relinquished.

The site would soon be closed for the season, but the toilet block was open, the showers had hot water, and Neil's family's caravan was comfortable and familiar. There was no one else on site, and the other caravans sat vacant, curtains drawn, deck chairs stowed away for winter. By six o'clock it was raining heavily. I went to bed soon after dinner and fell asleep listening to the rain rattle the roof.

*

When my dad was in his early seventies, he and I stayed at the caravan with Neil and his dad. Our relationship had long been repaired – by the time I reached my twenties, I had realised that my teenage strategy of self-containment was unfit for adulthood, and I didn't want to be numb anymore. So after twelve years of estrangement, I'd written my dad a letter, and he'd replied, and slowly we began to find a way back into each other's lives.

There's a photo of the four of us, setting out from the caravan the next morning to walk in and spend the night at Peanmeanach Bothy. It was a special and poignant journey: both Neil and I sensed that it was the last time either of our fathers would manage such a strenuous walk.

*

Rain fell all the next day, swelling streams on the slopes of Rois-bheinn and spinning full-tilt the turbines of hydro systems. I looked out from the caravan window at a reduced world, one that had no islands in the sound, no mountains, no oakwoods of Moidart. All I could see were a few drab caravans and a concrete toilet block in a saturated field. The days were running down – I had only a week of walkabout still to go.

The following morning, the world expanded to its former self. A brisk wind blew high clouds across the summits of the mountains. I locked up the caravan and walked down to the shore, to the pebble beach where my children used to play on summer holidays. Bordering the beach, a great table of igneous rock, riven with cracks, tilted down to the sea. The tide was low, and the rock was studded with limpets and whelks, while muscles clustered in its crevices. I climbed onto the rock and sat listening to the burble of the sea. Out in the sound, a bird rose above the water. Cormorants and shags tend to fly low over the waves, but this one kept rising, its wings huge, ungainly at first: a sea eagle. I could see the white flash of its tail as it flew north, and I watched it until it became a dark speck against the headland on the far side of the sound. The poetry of its name in Gaelic is elegant and evocative: *iolair sùil na grèine*, the 'eagle with the sunlit eye'.

I shouldered my rucksack, left the beach at Forsay, and stepped back onto the road. The birch trees along the verges were casting the last of their leaves, and by the time I reached Glenuig village, only two cars had passed, and neither of them stopped. The road curved inland, and I looked across for the last time to the Isle of Eigg, out beyond the sound. It had been ever present as I walked the coast from Arisaig, a beacon at sea, in so many ways. I waved in gratitude and respect, and then turned south, heading towards another, bigger island.

The A861 is mostly single-track from Lochailort all the way to Strontian at the head of Loch Sunart. From there, the A884, also single-track, passes through Morvern to Lochaline, where a ferry crosses to the Isle of Mull. The first section of the road is one of the finest stretches in Scotland — if you like roads that are almost empty of traffic in October, and that flit between the coast and the interior, weaving through oak and birch woods, cresting hills to give expansive views of mountains and lochs and islands.

Almost empty of traffic in October. The hitching test was upon me: to trust that someone would eventually stop, but to also accept that I might not travel far that day. The quietness of the road, at least, made walking on it easy, and allowed me to stop in the middle of it and appreciate the view when I climbed up and out of Glen Uig to Bealach Carach – a lazy, diminished version of the original Bealach Aon Achadh na h-Airidhe, 'Pass of the One Field of the Shieling'. As the road crested the pass, Loch Moidart opened below me, and in the distance, I could see Loch Shiel with the peak of Beinn Resipol rising behind it.

A horned sheep, crouched on the verge ahead, watched me approach with almond eyes. '*You* would pick me up, wouldn't you?' I asked. The sheep, impassive, fluffed with its winter coat, didn't even bother to rise as I walked past. No lift, and the rain beginning to fall. A pair of great tits flitted along the birch that lined the road, chirping companionably, while a small flock of fieldfares flew overhead.

Hitching on a quiet road encourages eye contact with every driver that passes. They can't pretend not to see you, though for many it's simple: they would never dream of picking up a hitcher. Maybe for some there's regret: 'He looks decent enough, but you just never know.' Maybe for others, self-satisfaction. And maybe I was just over-thinking the lack of a lift.

My faith was restored by an elderly English couple on holiday. They took me to Acharacle, and then a nurse gave me a lift to the Lochaline turn-off at the head of Loch Sunart. She was in her twenties and had been working in Australia but had returned home to look after an infirm parent. She told me she would go back to Australia as soon as she could. She didn't elaborate, as though there was no need to, as though, driving through Moidart in October in the rain, the reason was self-evident.

Eight geese flew above Loch Sunart in single file, their calls disturbing a heron on the shore which sprawled into the air, pretending to be a pterodactyl. The loch is a long, deep fjord that opens out to the west into the Sound of Mull. As I skirted its shore, walking along the A884, a sea otter kept pace with me, swimming just offshore, its head up, checking me out. It wasn't too long before a car stopped at my raised thumb and offered me a lift to Lochaline.

Chapter 15

The Post Road

The MV *Lochinvar* plies its trade between Lochaline on the mainland and Fishnish on the Isle of Mull. The main, larger ferry, the MV *Isle of Mull*, sails from Oban, transporting the bulk of the island's traffic, but the *Lochinvar* caters for those travelling to Mull from Morvern and the north. It's a short sail across fairly sheltered waters, and sometimes, when poor weather has cancelled the Oban ferry, the *Lochinvar* will still be in service.

With the days running down, my attention became more focused on a few specific story-places. When I had boarded the bus from Inverness to Fort William, I already had in mind Mac Mhic Ailein's encounter with the deer-woman in the oak woods of Moidart. I also knew that, from there, it would be easy enough to hitch south and then cross to the Isle of Mull, an island particularly associated with the Cailleach. There's Beinn na Caillich on Skye, of course, and Cailleach na Mointeach on Lewis, and there are tales connecting her to other Hebridean islands, but on Mull there is a concentration of stories, clustered around a few key locations, suggesting that her presence in the landscape was once an important part of the island's cultural ecology. The most significant story-place is Loch Bà, a freshwater loch lying in the pinched middle of Mull, between the Sound of Mull and Loch Na Keal, a sea loch that opens out to the west.

The settlement of Gruline sits on the isthmus between Loch Bà and Loch na Keal, three miles south-west of the village of

Salen. Two hitches from the ferry took me there. The couple who dropped me at Gruline were both natives of the island, *Muilich*, and crofters, though he had also worked on the mainland for a while in his younger days. Their car was an extension of the croft, with a boot full of waterproofs, hand tools, rolls of baler twine, a five-gallon petrol can. I sat in the back seat next to two sacks of pelleted hen food and a black and white collie, who eyed me suspiciously from where it was crouched in the footwell. The couple looked to be in their seventies, at least, and held the years between them graciously. When they spoke, it was in a single, lilting voice, with only the timbre changing as one responded to the other, neither of them rushing to fill the pauses. After I explained that I was walking south from Loch Bà over the pass on the shoulder of Ben More, they told me I would be following the old post road.

Before the new pier was built at Craignure, the mailboat from Oban would call in at Salen as it sailed to Tobermory. Up until early in the twentieth century, a post-runner from Salen would then carry the satchel of mail for the post office at Bunessan on the Ross of Mull, via Loch Bà and Màm Clachaig, the 'Stony Pass', and down to Kinloch on the shore of Loch Scridain, the 'Scree-sided Loch'. There they would exchange satchels with the post-runner bringing the mail from Bunessan, each completing a round trip of over thirty miles. The old couple thought the post road would be in a poor state. 'You used to be able to ride a pony over it,' they told me. 'You wouldn't manage that these days, but maybe a quad bike could.' They smiled at each other, as though relishing the idea of attempting such a feat. When they dropped me off, both reached back and shook my hand as I climbed out of the car, wishing me luck.

Loch Bà, 'Loch of the Cow', didn't stint on its beauty. Birch and oak were thick on the surrounding slopes, and alder lined its banks. On a knoll amongst Scots pine, Benmore Lodge had a fine view across the water, though no one was living there to appreciate it. After days of rain, streams pouring down the flanks of Beinn a' Ghràig were like white braids untangling themselves into the loch. As I followed the estate track, I looked out for a pool in one of the streams.

Before setting out on my walk, I'd researched as best I could the places I hoped I might visit. At Loch Bà, I was principally interested in traditions relating to the Cailleach, but I also found out about a well, Tobar nan Ceann, 'Well of the Heads', that was marked on a nineteenth-century map and shown as a pool next to the track that skirts the shore of the loch. Intrigued by the name, I rooted around for an explanation.

A feud simmers between Maclean of Duart on Mull and MacDonald of Sleat on Skye, with periodic raids and repercussions, each bringing fire and sword to some district owned by the other. A party of MacDonalds, along with other clans allied to them, sails towards Gruline at the head of Loch na Keal. The boats are landed, and the clansmen stop to sharpen their swords on a stone by the shore — you can still see the marks today. The Macleans, warned of their arrival, retreat to the mountains, where they hope to hold at bay the superior numbers of their enemy. But young John Maclean of Inverscardale can't bear to witness the advance of the MacDonalds across his land without challenge, and leading a handful of men, he engages them on the banks of Loch Bà. It's a rout, and the impetuous young Maclean is slain, along with all his followers. The MacDonalds sever the heads of their fallen enemies and throw them into the pool of a well by the shore of the loch, known ever after as Tobar nan Ceann.

The skirmish took place in the late sixteenth century, one of many in the internecine wars between the Macleans and the MacDonalds. As for the tradition of the heads being thrown into the well, curiously, I had heard of another Tobar nan

Ceann, over by Loch Spelvie on the south side of Mull. The claim there is that the wife of Maclean of Lochbuie murdered the two young sons of Maclean of Duart, and tossed their heads into that well. There is also a Tobar nan Ceann on the Isle of Canna, and one at Vatersay on Skye, as well as several on the mainland, including, most famously, one by Loch Oich in Glen Mor. There, in the late seventeenth century, the heads of seven men, who were caught and killed for their part in the assassination of Alexander MacDonell of Keppoch, were washed before being presented to the clan chief, MacDonell of Glengarry, as evidence of justice having been served.

You'd be forgiven for thinking that wells throughout the Highlands and Islands were regularly being clogged by severed heads. But what's really going on here? Is it just another example of a story-meme being adapted and localised, like the many Diarmaid's Graves dotted around Scotland and Ireland?

A clue to the answer can be found in Torridon in Wester Ross. In the 1960s, the folklorist Dr Anne Ross visited a township there and met a man who was hereditary keeper of yet another Tobar nan Ceann. The whereabouts of the well was a guarded secret, but Dr Ross was taken to it on condition that she wouldn't disclose its location. Near the well, a small stone cist contained a human skull, one that, according to tradition, belonged to a woman who had committed suicide. Water from the well, scooped in the skull and drunk in the name of the Holy Trinity, was a known cure for epilepsy, and faith in its efficacy persisted through the twentieth century. The keeper, whose family had guarded the skull since it was first put to use hundreds of years previously, told Dr Ross that epilepsy sufferers came from far and wide, and that the treatment had never been known to fail.

Whether aware of it or not, the Torridon well-keeper was continuing a practice and a belief that takes us back to when the people we call Celts first arrived in the British Isles, sometime around the fifth century BCE. Those people brought with them their veneration of the human skull, regarding it as a talisman and source of wisdom and healing, and Celtic mythology is rich in tales of severed heads and their magical powers – most famously, that of Brân the Blessed, whose head is said to be buried beneath the Tower of London. Two thousand years ago, Livy, the Roman historian, wrote about a 'head cult' amongst the Celtic tribes, as did his Greek contemporary, Strabo, while a few centuries later, the medieval Celtic Church – that assiduous preserver of veiled pagan rituals and beliefs – promoted numerous instances of the heads of saints being used at wells to heal the sick. Such was the case, for example, with St Marnan's skull in Aberchirder in Aberdeenshire, and Saint Teilo's at Llandeilo in Pembrokeshire in Wales.

As for Tobar nan Ceann by Loch Bà, perhaps a lingering tradition connecting heads to the well persisted, but once knowledge of its significance had lapsed – once the memory of skulls used as part of a healing ritual had been forgotten – the origin of the name still had to be accounted for.

It's difficult for us who read and write to appreciate the way that patterns and repetitions are used by non-literate cultures. In the case of place-names, stories are applied, and re-applied, as a memory fixative, and what better than a familiar, oft-repeated tale of a fight between the Macleans and the MacDonalds, especially when the tale is embellished with the shocking detail of the beheading of the corpses of local clansmen, thus providing a memorable explanation for the name of the well.

Finding the well's stream, I discovered that it had recently been widened and straightened by a digger, presumably in order to stop it flooding the estate track. The ground on either side was churned by the digger, the banks had been lined with excavated boulders, and there was no longer any sign of the pool that is so clearly marked on the nineteenth-century OS map. By altering the flow and course of the stream, presumably under the instructions of the estate owners, the digger operator had completely removed Tobar nan Ceann from the landscape.

I followed the stream back uphill, to where it flowed out from a copse of trees, and sat by a small pool with a birch tree leaning over it, woven through with honeysuckle. The main stem of the honeysuckle, arm-thick, was twisted around the birch's trunk.

Maybe a skirmish did happen on the shore of Loch Bà – it seems as though every inch of Mull has been fought over at one time or another – and maybe the MacDonalds did throw the gory trophies of their victory into the pool by the track, but I think it more likely that the original naming and significance of Tobar nan Ceann is archaic, stretching back into pre-history. In any case, the well is now unmade: the stream is straight and no longer carries, and I was left disturbed by how easily a place that holds such meaning could be scoured out by a JCB and its bucket in the course of a morning's work.

This is the way of modernity. In Australia, the mining company Rio Tinto was recently fined for dynamiting a cave that contained Aboriginal rock art dating back tens of thousands of years. Routine work for Rio Tinto, the fine they received a minor setback in their ongoing extractive industry. Meanwhile, elsewhere, smaller acts of destruction are happening all the time. On the Isle of Mull, a well that once offered the possibility of healing is now a ghost well, an otherworld well, adrift in time and place – *there was a well, there wasn't a well*. I dropped a fifty pence piece into the small pool beneath the birch tree as a token of remembrance: substitute silver in a substitute pool. The water was so clear, it wasn't there.

*

It's said that there are three great ages: the age of the eagle, the age of the yew tree and the age of the Cailleach. These are not spans of time as we moderns perceive them; this is big, deep, ancestor time, and the Cailleach is the oldest of all. But even so, according to one island tradition, the Cailleach does eventually meet her end. Following the estate track along the shore of Loch Bà, I reached the spot where this is said to have taken place.

On being asked how old she is, the Cailleach casts her gaze south from the Ross of Mull and points to the stretch of sea between there and the Torran Rocks, declaring that in her youth, a forest grew where the waves now foam. Such is her great age.

To sustain herself, once every century, at Beltane, on the morning of the first of May, she washes in Loch Bà at the centre of the island and is renewed. It must be done at dawn, before dogs bark or birds greet the day with song.

A hundred years have passed, and the Cailleach walks to the shore of the loch, worn and withered, leaning on her stick as she goes. The sun is on the edge of rising, but before she sets foot in the water, a shepherd's dog barks in the distance, the noise of its bark echoing off the crags of Beinn a' Ghràig, and the Cailleach cries:

> It is early the dog spoke, in advance of me;
> the dog, in advance of me.
> It is early the dog spoke, in advance of me,
> in the quiet of the morning, across Loch Bà.

The rite has been broken, time shrivels the Cailleach's body, and she falls to the ground as dust and bones.

The sheepdog's bark at dawn on the shore of Loch Bà, like the ball of blue worsted yarn found in the belly of Dòmhnall Donn-shùileach's stag, signals a shift in culture and cosmology.

The Cailleach, mistress of the deer, who gives her approval and blessing for the hunt, is superfluous to the needs of the shepherds and farmers who now claim the land.

There's a small gravel beach by Sròn a' Chrann-lithe, the 'Promontory of the Carpenter'. I stood at the water's edge and watched a handful of mallard ducks paddling out from the shore. The sky was clearing, and the loch sparkled in the afternoon sun. Sheep grazed amongst the birch trees behind me, and two white vans drove past, bumping along the estate track. When I rounded the promontory, I saw that they were there to attend to fish cages moored close to the shore. A farm for trout, I guessed. Men were at work on pumps and pipes, and I wondered if the impact of fish farming on the ecology of freshwater lochs was as bad as it was on sea lochs.

I had thought to spend the night camped by Loch Bà, on the shore where the Cailleach sought her rejuvenation, but the fish farm on the loch discouraged me, so I followed the old post road instead, up into Glen Clachaig. The 'road' becomes a rough path as it climbs away from the shore, running parallel with the river that flows down the glen. As I looked out for a spot to camp, a flock of fieldfares or perhaps redwings swooped past, and then a sparrowhawk spluttered up from amongst reeds by the river, to give chase to the flock, not caring whether they were fieldfares or redwings, glad only that they would keep her in meat through the winter.

The glen became a corrie, walled in by mountains, with the east ridge of Ben More dominating. Chutes of scree spilled down into the corrie, and I could trace the post road as it climbed the southern wall, up to a notch in the ridge at Màm Clachaig. The corrie was gloomy beneath the mountains, my feet were wet, trudging through bog and surface water on the path, and there was nowhere dry to pitch my tent. I kept walking, even though it was late in the afternoon and would be dark by the time I reached the pass. I reasoned that, if I was lucky, the moon would be up and I would be able to make a careful descent to Glen More on the other side, where I'd find a dry place to camp.

The post road was well defined, even in the gloom, and on the higher section I could see how carefully it had once been maintained, with stonework shoring up its banks and edges. I was committed now, so late in the day, and strangely elated, just as I'd been on Conival in Assynt, when I wanted to stay high, to walk the ridge in the cloud to the summit of Ben More Assynt, to grapple with the mountain's intractability.

Màm Clachaig was in use long before the postal service, and the cairn that guards the pass has an old name, Carn Cul Righ Albainn, which means literally 'Cairn with its Back to Scotland' – though it's important to remember that, up until at least the tenth century, the name Albainn, or Alba, referred only to the Pictish kingdom of the north and central Highlands. Thus, the cairn is said to mark what was once a border-pass between the kingdom of the Picts to the north and Dalriada, the kingdom of the Gaelic-speaking Scots, to the south; according to tradition, from the sixth century onwards, pilgrims and missionaries regularly used the pass after Saint Columba established his monastery on the Isle of Iona, which lies off the tip of the Ross of Mull.

Iona is the only place I've lived where, on any given day, stepping out of your front door means stepping into an immoderate measure of beauty. It never became familiar and never ceased to nourish me. You could shield yourself – your mind could be wrapped in other things, in the same way that you would wrap up against the wind – but then you'd turn down a path onto the village street that ran along the shore and be unwrapped by the angle of an artic tern diving for sand eels in the turquoise water of the sound. It's the fault of the light, I suppose, and how it scrapes everything clean – crags and pebbles, machair and sand, the sea's blue fields. Little wonder that so many artists make pilgrimage to Iona to paint its landscapes over and over. When

I left the island, I understood that it was likely I would never again live anywhere so radiant.

Living in Edinburgh, attending university, provided a different kind of illumination, a different source of nourishment. As an undergraduate at the School of Scottish Studies, exposed for the first time to my country's depth-culture, I began to understand that the culture I'd grown up with was thin gruel in comparison. Slowly, twenty-years slowly, I have reached, not backwards, but towards — towards an appreciation of traditional story and song, and to a realisation that the carrying stream of those traditions still flows, still matters.

*

Night settled on the ridge. To my right, the summit peak of Ben More rose into darkness, and at the crest of the pass, the silhouette of the cairn looked like a hunched, crony figure, waiting. I picked up a stone from the path, placed it on the cairn, and then slipped between kingdoms.

To be on a mountain on Mull at night was thrilling, but this wasn't like midsummer on Slioch in Torridon; it was late October and the clouds were spilling rain. I found myself exposed, unwrapped in a different way to the weather and the isolation, and the uncanniness of place — as well as to an irrational conviction that I wasn't alone, that there was something *other* with me on the ridge. Thrilled, spooked, I was gripped by two compulsions, neither of them helpful: the first was to start running, to descend from the pass as quickly as I could, no matter the risk of fall or injury; the second, inexplicably, was to follow the ridge upwards, to climb towards the dark mass of Ben More's summit.

Panic is rarely handy. I resisted both options, turning away from the summit's strange pull, focusing instead on the solid ground beneath my boots — solid but slippy, and the path hard to see, though there were puddles reflecting enough of the moon's clouded light to mark the way. I was reluctant to use my head torch; its beam would poke a hole in the dark, picking out each step immediately in front of me, but beyond it, the night would be even darker, and I didn't fancy that. Slowly, carefully, I climbed down the mountain. Glen More and Loch Scridain lay below, and I could see lights glowing in the windows of houses at Kinloch and at Pennyghael.

A large shadow-creature scuffled away from me: a deer, I told my racing heart. I had lost the path but could see a black block of forestry plantation not far below, and I knew that it bordered the far side of the Glen More road. The ground levelled into a bog, and I tried and failed to step from grass clump to grass clump, like a drunk staggering his way home after a night out.

For once, it was a relief to stand on tarmac. I was soaked, filthy, but safely down, and I knew a good place to camp at the head of Loch Scridain, two miles along the road. Halfway there, the noise of a car's engine broke the silence behind me, and it occurred to me that the driver might stop to check if I was okay, walking so late at night. Unsure of myself, my senses reeling in the same way that they were when the stag's roar woke me in Bone Cave, and unsure of what words might spill out if I attempted conversation, I stepped off the road and crouched below the bank. Headlights glared, and the car passed with its human sealed inside, music playing, his or her foot on the accelerator.

The Coladoir River flows beneath a humpbacked stone bridge before it opens out into the salt marshes at the head of Loch Scridain. Nearby, a metal bridge takes the road and its traffic. I pitched my tent on flat ground by the old, redundant bridge. Layered in dry thermals, zipped in a goose-down sleeping bag, I curled around my gratitude – thankful to be there and not still up on the ridge at Màm Clachaig.

*

Before dawn, I was standing at the bus stop at the Kinloch crossroads, hoping to catch the early bus. I had friends on Iona and on the Ross of Mull that I would've been glad to catch up with, and there was Cailleach lore to track there, including the whereabouts of a site on Erraid, a tidal island off the Ross that, according to tradition, holds the ruins of her house. But I was aware that the past few weeks had led me to some peculiar places in myself, not least the previous evening on the ridge, and that if the old trope was true, if civilisation was only three days deep, then I'd spent enough time alone and away to loosen, or at least unsettle, my civilised, socialised self. A meeting with friends might, initially, be awkward, or might break the journey's spell before I was ready for it to be broken.

A car approached, Craignure-bound; the bus was due in ten minutes, but a hitch would save the fare. There'd be other times for visiting friends and finding the ruined house of the Cailleach.

Chapter 16

Poison in the Poet's House

The Great Glen Fault, when it reaches the West Coast at Fort William, at the head of Loch Linnhe, carries on out into the Firth of Lorne, so that the Isle of Mull sits to the north and west of it. Sailing on the ferry from Craignure to Oban, I crossed back over the fault for the first time since I set out from Speyside and limped down into Fort Augustus. Looked at on a map of the Highlands, my journey was shaping a figure of eight, looping either side of the Great Glen. Now it was time to close the lower loop and to return to where I first began to track the Cailleach and her deer-women in the land.

Out in the Firth of Lorne, the MV *Isle of Mull* is proportionate: a large ferry negotiating a wide stretch of sea. It's only as it approaches Oban that it becomes too big for its surroundings, squeezing through the kyle between the Isle of Kerrera and the mainland, towering above the houses along the Gavanan Road, and dwarfing the yachts that are moored offshore. Standing on the ferry's top passenger deck, I felt as though I was being borne into the bay on the back of a leviathan.

This was the reverse of the journey I first made thirty years ago, when I boarded the same ferry en route to Iona. The memory is vivid: the bustle of the port on a bright, spring day; half a dozen fishing boats tied up along the pier, hulls painted in primary colours, decks busy with crates and coils of rope and chain; bellicose herring gulls perched on masts and derricks; and me, casting off from the mainland, my orange rucksack packed with everything I owned, leaving behind a life in Glasgow that had soured.

The ferry's tannoy returned me to the present, announcing that it was time to disembark. My older self looked down on the pier, grateful to the young man who, despite his shyness, despite having no idea what he was reaching for, had been bold enough to make the leap.

Oban is a handsome town when approached from the sea, with its grand Victorian architecture along the waterfront, whitewashed guesthouses tucked amongst wooded slopes and, above them all, McCaig's Tower, a late-nineteenth-century folly built to emulate the Colosseum in Rome.

The town is the main hub through which people travel to and from the Hebrides. It's invariably busy, not just with tourists but also with islanders over on business, or for the fortnightly shop, or to visit their children who weekly-board there through the school term.

During my first winter on Iona, travelling back to the island after a trip to Glasgow, I was stuck for a night in the port. Storm-force winds had cancelled the ferry, so I booked into a B&B and went for a pint in the Oban Inn. It might have been Friday night – in any case, hard drink was being consumed, and the pub was raucous, brightly lit, thick with cigarette smoke and Hebridean accents. On the way to the toilets, I was accosted by a fisherman who had lost one of his arms from below the elbow; he was wearing a checked shirt with rolled-up sleeves so you could see the stump. The fisherman pinned me up against the wall with his good arm and growled, 'You're no' a Campbell are ye?' After assuring him that I wasn't, he patted me on the back and sent me on my way. For the rest of the evening, whenever I caught his eye, he grinned and waved as though we were the best of friends.

Around that same time, a bus driver in Argyll, a MacDonald, made the local news for being sacked from his job after repeatedly failing to stop for those that he knew to be Campbells. He would drive past them at bus stops, pretending he hadn't seen them.

The past intrudes the present. For the one-armed fisherman and the bus driver MacDonald, the Massacre of Glencoe in 1692 – when the MacDonalds of Glencoe were 'murdered under trust' by soldiers whose commanding officer was a Campbell – had not been forgotten and would never be atoned. If I had been a Campbell, that night in the Oban Inn, I doubt that if the fisherman had blackened my eye or bloodied my nose it would have been enough to salve the anger in his heart.

I know that kind of anger, and how quickly it turns to violence. The young man in the bashed hatchback radiated it, two weeks previously, when I was hitching to Ullapool; and as an apprentice in the garage in Partick, I knew men who carried it into work every day. One colleague's moods flared like the acne that scarred his face, so that his jaw was an open wound, another sneered and snarled his way around the workshop, and for all the wit and generosity of the many good men who worked there, every morning my stomach clenched like a fist when I walked into the garage.

Living and working on the Isle of Iona, and then studying at the University of Edinburgh, distanced me from that world, but never completely. One night in the city, walking home, a couple approached, middle-aged and pissed. He fell off the pavement onto the road, taking her down with him. A car skidded to a halt to avoid them, and the two young women who were in the car jumped out. The man gripped my hand firm like a handshake as I helped him to his feet. The woman was on her knees, tights ripped, one shoe off. He'd cracked his forehead and blood was flowing freely down the side of his nose, but when I mentioned an ambulance, he tensed his shoulders and said, 'No fuckin' ambulance.' The mess of blood on his shirt and coat was impressive.

The woman tried to stench the flow with a sanitary towel out of her bag, but he was reeling, punch-drunk, his anger rising, reaching for something in his pocket. I urged the two women from the car to leave and then walked away quickly myself, crossing the road. When I looked over my shoulder, he was coming for me, heedless of cars. Booze-addled, he must have deflected blame for his split head to me, or else by helping him up, I had somehow humiliated him – and there was only one way to respond to that. Younger and sober, I was quick enough to leave him behind, but I remember the shame I felt for running, as though I'd unmanned myself, and there's a shadow-voice in me, still, that jeers at the shy young man who didn't stay to fight.

*

I didn't need anything from Oban, and after my encounter with Fort William, I was keen to pass through the town quickly. Waiting in the station next to the pier was a Glasgow-bound train which would take me the four stops to Tyndrum. Along the way, the train passed beneath Ben Cruachan and its famous hydropower station and skirted the shores of Loch Awe, a loch created, as many will tell – for the story is widely known – by the Cailleach herself.

Near the summit of Ben Cruachan, a spring bubbles up from the core of the mountain to a well that is capped by a great stone slab. The Cailleach, guardian of the well, removes the slab each morning, and the water gushes forth, irrigating the land below. Then at dusk, each evening, she replaces the slab, staunching the flow of water.

One evening, over-weary from herding goats across her stepping stones, the 'Cailleach's Clacharan', at the mouth of Loch Etive, she falls asleep and forgets to replace the slab. By morning, the water has flooded the land and drowned the people and their cattle.

What was once a fertile glen is now Loch Awe, and the Cailleach, mortified by her neglect and the destruction it has caused, is turned to stone. She stands still, a stony penitent, overlooking the Pass of Brander.

Stepping off the train at Tyndrum, I stopped at the local shop, which is well-stocked for the needs of walkers and campers. After buying enough supplies for the rest of my journey, I followed the route of the West Highland Way along the old military road that runs north towards Bridge of Orchy, parallel to the railway line and to the busy A82.

I was walking inland, away from the coast and the islands, feeling the pull of Rannoch Moor, the elevated bowl, Scotland's centre of gravity, its *omphalos*, and place-source of so much deer and Cailleach lore.

As you approach the railway viaduct at the foot of Auch Gleann, Beinn Dòrain dominates the view. The name is disputed: it might be 'Otter Mountain', or 'Mountain of the Small Streams'. In the late nineteenth century, local Gaelic speakers knew it as 'Mountain of Storms'. Swooping up in a great curve, it's one of the outlying mountains that form the rim around Rannoch Moor; it's also the subject and setting of Duncan Ban MacIntyre's celebrated long poem *Moladh Beinn Dòbhrain* – 'In Praise of Ben Dòrain'.

Composed in the 1760s, the poem celebrates the mountain's flora and fauna, and in particular the deer that graze on it; but unlike much of the English-language nature poetry of the period, this is no pastoral reverie. MacIntyre lived and worked as a deer-stalker in Auch Gleann, and his poem is grounded in the lived reality of hunting in a harsh landscape.

Moladh Beinn Dòbhrain famously mimics the structure of pibroch, the *ceòl mòr*, or 'big music', of Highland bagpipe tradition, beginning with a main theme, the *ùrlar*, and then weaving variations, *siubhal*, onto that theme. My beginner's

Gaelic doesn't equip me to appreciate the way that the original poem echoes the music of pibroch, but I've read enough translations to at least gain a sense of it, if not to catch the grace notes.

Beinn Dòrain is also the setting for an older kind of poetry. According to tradition, a smith by the name of Lon mac Liobhunn lived on the mountain, and 'Duan na Ceàrdaich', 'The Lay of the Smithy', tells of events that took place long before Duncan Ban MacIntyre's time. Or more correctly, it tells of events that happen within a different reckoning of time altogether.

The sword of Fionn mac Cumhaill has lost its virtue, owing to the misdeeds of certain of his men. To restore it, the blade must be retempered, and only one smith has the skill for the task: Lon mac Liobhunn of Beinn Dòrain.

The smith is tall and one-legged, and wears a cloak of blackened hides and an apron of the same. He instructs Fionn's men, the Fianna, to follow him as best they can, then leaps in single bounds across the glens and mountains. Eventually they reach the smithy below Beinn Dòrain, and Daor-ghlas, one of the Fianna, assists Lon mac Liobhunn by working the bellows. The blade is retempered, the sword's virtue restored, but Daor-ghlas, in his enthusiasm, works the bellows so hard that the heat turns his face redder than oak embers, and warps the iron of the anvil.

The smith sends the Fianna on their way, complaining that 'the thin fearless man has wrecked my anvil'. And from that day forth, Daor-ghlas, one of Fionn mac Cumhaill's chief companions, is called Caoilte, 'the thin one'.

The tale has echoes of other lame smiths, like Wayland from Germanic myth and Hephaestus, smith to the Greek gods. As I walked beneath the great upward sweep of the mountain, I thought about the meaning of the lay and the spoiling of the sword's virtue; about the reckless enthusiasm of young men and how, without guidance, such enthusiasm can so easily go awry. I thought about the one-armed fisherman and the man in the bashed hatchback. I thought about violence passed down and the challenge, as a parent, to break the cycle, to be a better conduit between generations.

Leaving the West Highland Way and the noise of cars and lorries on the A82, I turned east into Auch Gleann, the name a lazy shortening of Gleann Achadh-Innis Chailein; 'Glen of Colin's Meadow Field'. The ridge behind Beinn Dòrain's summit forms a craggy north-western wall, and the glen was as remote and rugged as any that I had walked through in the previous three weeks, with the Allt Kinglass flowing down it – a fine Highland river, sparsely lined with alder. I met no one on the track but passed an ugly modern bungalow that looked like the winters would soon get the better of it. Beyond the bungalow, I removed my boots and socks to cross the ford over the Allt Coralan, which flows fast into the Allt Kinglass.

Near the head of Auch Gleann sits a semi-derelict stone building. It's called Ais-an t-Sìthean, after the two prominent mounds, Sìthean Mòr and Sìthean Beag, that sit just below it in the glen. The house is partially roofed in tin, but in the 1860s it was recorded as being a thatched shepherd's cottage. A hundred years before that, it was where Duncan Ban MacIntyre lived when he was keeper in the glen, and where he composed his poetry.

MacIntyre was illiterate, his poems transcribed to memory and held in his head until eventually they were written down by a friend, Rev. Donald MacNicol of Lismore, in advance of publication. I peeked inside Ais-an t-Sìthean to see if it might be a place to sleep for the night but found that it was being used as a fank for treating and sheering sheep. The floor was strewn with clumps of wool, empty plastic sacks, pesticide cans. The mess in the poet's house depressed me; the pesticides, no matter how practical, seemed like a desecration, as though the poison might be seeping down into the *sìtheanan* in the glen below.

A story tells that MacIntyre's favourite spring on the flanks of Beinn Dòrain, where he often stopped to drink, has been blocked: a Lowlander, walking the hill, rammed his staff into the spout of the spring. Thus, the well of Gaelic poetry has been quelled by the near domination of the English language. One day, the story promises, the staff will be found and removed, and the spring will flow free.

Chapter 17

Tigh nam Bodach

Numbered stretches of tarmac delineate the connections we make between different parts of the country: we cross the M8, head up the A9, down the M74. On foot, different connections are made, and in mountain country it's all about the passes: as I crossed from the head of Auch Gleann into Srath Tarabhan, I stepped out of Argyll and into Perthshire.

The strath leads down to Loch Lyon at the head of Glen Lyon – a name which seems to be a corruption of the Gaelic *lòn*, a 'marshy meadow', and which may be linked to Lon mac Liobhunn, the lame smith of Beinn Dòrain. I followed the estate track as it contoured the lower slopes of Beinn Mhanach, above the north shore of the loch. Beinn Sheasgarnaich rose above the opposite shore, its massive flank wrinkled with gullies. Trudging along the track in soft rain, late in the afternoon, my shoulders were hunched beneath my rucksack, my legs and my body were tired, my head was tired, and I slipped back to the childhood memory of trudging behind my father on a mountain path, the red of his gaiters guiding me on through the gloom.

I stopped to rest and drink some water, and the land imposed its own perspective on me, the bulk of the mountains diminishing the distance I'd walked; not just that day, but all the days of my month's journey, so that they became trivial, immaterial. I packed away my water bottle and carried on along the track, my lungs breathing against the tension of my rucksack's chest-strap, the present sharp and corporeal.

Loch Lyon is ugly. It's a large body of water with eroded, treeless shores, its depth regulated by the hydro dam that spans its eastern end. Built in the 1950s, the dam doubled the length of the loch, flooding meadows and settlements, erasing their names – Lubheasgarnich, Invermeran, Tullich, Sheanvore – and drowning the river that once flowed through them, if a river can be drowned.

The day was ending, and the likeliest place to find a level pitch for my tent would be on the shore of the loch, where I could also harvest firewood from the washed-up stumps of submerged trees. But it was too bleak down there, too haunted. I followed the track north instead, into Gleann Meurain, which forks west at its head into Gleann Cailliche. Walking towards that upper glen at twilight, I was apprehensive, preoccupied, not with fear, but with conflicting expectations of what I would find there.

*

Gleann Cailliche was another waypoint on the route I'd loosely imagined before setting out, somewhere I knew I *ought* to visit if I found myself nearby. It's the location, some say, of the oldest site of continuous ritual practice in Europe, which is quite the claim to be making.

Following the track up Gleann Meurain, looking out for a flat, dry spot to camp, I noticed two owls quartering the slope of the hill. Soon, four others joined them, so that there were six owls above the hillside, noiselessly wheeling around each other, their wing beats irregular, like the flittering of bats – large, blunt-faced bats. They were ale-brown with streaked wings, either short- or long-eared owls – I hadn't the skill to tell which.

We think of owls as solitary birds, solo hunters, but short- and long-eared owls will sometimes gather in small flocks in the autumn. This bunch accompanied me up the glen, wielding their silence like ghosts in the last of the day's light. I was spooked and mesmerised; the owls seemed curious. At one point I stopped and stood on the track, looking up, arms spread, while all six owls circled above me. Eventually, they widened their circles and dispersed over the glen.

It was dark by the time I walked on, and I had to use my head torch to find a place to pitch my tent. Curled in my sleeping bag in the quiet of the night, I was free of the sense of diminishment I'd felt earlier, when I was trudging along the track, and of the conflicting expectations I'd held about visiting Gleann Cailliche. Both had been dislodged by the wonder of being escorted to the entrance of the glen by a dusk patrol of *cailleachan-oidhche*.

*

My campsite was more sloped than I thought, and I slept poorly. In the morning, when I crawled out of the tent, a hoodie crow was mooching around on the hillside, and the track below me was puddled with the night's rain. I left the tent pitched with my gear zipped inside and entered Gleann Cailliche quietly, before the sun had risen above the ridges to the south.

A man and a woman come down from the mountains in a snowstorm, seeking shelter in the glen. They are very old and larger than human, but the people of the glen are hospitable. This pleases the man and woman, and they stay, and the people build a house big enough to accommodate them. The woman, despite her great age, gives birth to a daughter.

The glen flourishes like never before: meadows are lush with grass for cattle, birdsong is loud in the trees. The years pass. A day arrives when the old man and woman, and their daughter, make ready to leave, but they give word that, if the people remember them, and if they tend to the land as they themselves have done, the glen will know peace and plenty.

The people build a small stone house and thatch it with turf. They choose shaped river stones to stand as the old man and woman and their daughter, so that they won't forget. In autumn, the house is re-thatched and bedded with straw, the stones are placed inside for winter, and the entrance blocked. In spring, the entrance is unblocked and the old man and woman and their daughter are brought out into the sun.

There's not much to distinguish Gleann Cailliche, no lush glades or tree-thick slopes – it's as stripped as any that is over-grazed by sheep and deer, though the Allt Cailliche is lively enough, tumbling over rocks and into pools, singing its way down the glen to join the Allt Meurain. I followed the river upstream, stopping to dunk my head in a pool and shock myself out of sleep-deprived grogginess. As I did so, I spotted a piece of white quartz on the riverbed and fished it out. It was flat, semi-translucent and angular, although the sharp of its edges had been blunted by time spent in the welter of the river. It sat in the palm of my hand like a wedge of fossilised snow.

Researching stories and places relating to the Cailleach, you soon find mention of Tigh nam Bodach, 'House of the Old Man', also known as Tigh na Cailliche, and you learn, according to various blogs, that the people of Glen Lyon have been tending the stones at Tigh nam Bodach for thousands of years, bringing out the old couple and their daughter at Beltane, on 1 May, and putting them back into the house at Samhain, on 31 October.

The folklorist and archaeologist Dr Anne Ross, author of *Folklore of the Scottish Highlands* and *Pagan Celtic Britain*, and the same Dr Ross who visited Tobar nan Ceann – the 'Well of the Heads' – in Torridon, was one of the first proponents of the site's antiquity. The version I know of the tale of the old man and woman is based on the one written in her books, which itself was gathered from the oral tradition of Glen Lyon, most likely from the telling of Bob Bissett, head gamekeeper at Invermearan Estate.

Anne Ross met Bob Bissett when she visited Glen Lyon in the 1960s. He was by all accounts a remarkable man: deer-stalker, leather-worker, shoe- and fiddlemaker, scholar of Burns poetry; and for many years, the unofficial custodian of Tigh nam Bodach. In old age he requested that, when he died, his body be buried in Gleann Cailliche, but the estate's owner refused, so he arranged to be cremated instead, and his ashes now lie beneath a small cairn in the glen. Bob Bissett also arranged for the duty of tending to Tigh nam Bodach to be passed on to the next generation of Glen Lyon's gamekeepers and ghillies.

If you didn't know what to look for, you might pass the 'wee house' without noticing it. It's not really a house at all and could barely shelter a sheep; it's more like a cairn or a stone cist, nestled on a slope above the Allt Cailliche. I liked the modesty of it. It's the kind of shrine that would be familiar to the members of any aboriginal culture. Invite to Tigh nam Bodach an elder of the Warlpiri people, invite Spiridon of the Yukaghirs; both would recognise the shrine and its stones as sacred business and would find the story of the old man and woman and their daughter analogous to their own stories of the ancestors.

Which is to say that, whether through genuine unbroken transmission, or from a reconstitution of that transmission, Tigh nam Bodach has an antediluvian, a stone-age, sensibility. I don't use the terms pejoratively. Quite the opposite. That there are cultures still practicing ways of being on the Earth that have been sustainable for, in some cases, tens of thousands of years, is remarkable to me, and worthy of deep respect and admiration, even more so given the oppression, deracination and in many cases deliberate extermination that those cultures have endured.

There were lots of pieces of quartz tucked in the turf of the roof of Tigh nam Bodach – so that *is* what you give as a gift to the Cailleach. I added the piece I'd found in the river and then sat down on the grass next to the collection of shaped river stones in front of the shelter. The family had grown, and there were now half a dozen stones standing in a huddle, out in the open for a few more days before they would be placed inside and blocked up for winter. Each stone was no more than a foot high, and they were all, to some degree, anthropomorphic, like miniature Henry Moore sculptures. I wanted to pick one up and feel its weight in my hands, feel the river-worn grain of it, but I didn't. Perhaps, in earlier times, they were handled regularly, passed around in the belief that something essential to them, some power they possessed, might be porous, might bring good fortune, but since I didn't know how to approach the stones – was unsure what I thought of them – it seemed best to leave them be, to observe but not participate. The stones themselves were like those that Hugh MacDiarmid encountered on West Linga, off Whalsay: 'imperturbable, inscrutable, in the world and yet not in it'.

Dr Anne Ross and her books introduced Tigh nam Bodach to the wider public, and it has become a pilgrimage site for neo-pagans, Celtic revivalists and devotees of New Age mysticism, as well as for the simply curious. Inevitably, as with all such sites, a process of modern myth-making has occurred.

A decade ago, Tigh nam Bodach's existence was threatened when the then owner of Auch and Invermearan Estate sought planning permission to dam the Allt Cailliche, flood the glen and install a hydro-electric system. The plan was opposed by local people and eventually shelved, not because of the opposition, but because the estate's owner, a man in his fifties, was struck by illness. He withdrew the planning application in 2011, only a few weeks before he died, his untimely death provoking dark mutterings from those keen to apportion cause and effect.

A story about Dr Ross herself seems to provide further proof that the stones shouldn't be meddled with. It was told to me by a colleague of hers, and I have heard it affirmed by others who knew both her and Bob Bissett, the gamekeeper.

In the 1970s, Anne Ross returned to Gleann Cailliche with a small group of academics from the University of Edinburgh. Bob Bissett was, of course, their guide, and they spent the afternoon examining the site and the stones. As the group set off back down the glen, led by the gamekeeper, Ross lingered, claiming that she wanted to take just a few more photographs and would catch them up. Two days later she turned up at Bob Bissett's house, alone, agitated and upset. He understood right away that she had taken one of the stones. Temporarily, she explained, to further study it; but the stone, dislocated from Tigh nam Bodach, had preyed on her mind, so much so that she now needed his help to return it and to make right her misdeed.

I don't know what to make of Tigh nam Bodach. Nearby shieling sites confirm that transhumance, the practice of moving livestock up to higher grazing grounds in the summer as part of a seasonal cycle, took place in Gleann Cailliche for at least hundreds, if not thousands of years, continuing up until the end of the eighteenth century; and very recently, an archaeological dig at another shieling site in Perthshire has unearthed similarly enclosed stones, suggesting a pattern of practice more widespread than previously thought.

In his book *Wisdom of the Mythtellers*, Sean Kane writes that the sacred is best defined as 'something that prefers not to be talked about'. I like that, and it fits well with local attitudes towards Tigh nam Bodach. The people charged with tending to the 'wee house', with putting the stones to bed at Samhain and bringing them out at Beltane, do so privately, without fanfare, retaining the integrity and mystery of the act, asserting that even now, in the twenty-first century, the severance between culture and nature is not quite complete.

Meanwhile, Historic Environment Scotland, the public body appointed to protect our ancient sites, has declined to give Tigh nam Bodach any historic status whatsoever, and suspicion remains that the shrine and its ritual are a twentieth-century reinvention, propagated, no matter how sincerely, by a charismatic gamekeeper and an over-enthusiastic folklorist.

The ambiguity and lack of official status means that there are no signposts or information boards in Gleann Cailliche, no agencies mediating the experience. This allows Tigh nam Bodach to remain part of a living, evolving culture, caught in the carrying stream, validated by its keepers and its visitors, whatever their persuasion, and irreverent, as the best of folk culture often is, in a way that the standing stones at Callanish, or at the Ring of Brodgar on Orkney, could never be. The current structure has a sheet of plywood underneath the turf roof, holding it up, and when I visited, the Cailleach stone had a cheap plastic necklace wrapped around it. The necklace was to me an affront, but for someone else, the placing of it might have had as much meaning and value as throwing coins in a pool to mark the loss of a well on the Isle of Mull or tossing to the wind on the summit of Rois-bheinn a patch of fur plucked from the back of a road-killed deer.

The pity of Tigh nam Bodach is not the plastic tat or the unverifiable claims for its antiquity; it's the state of the glen around it: no trees, few wildflowers, just thin turf and reed bog, and no chance of regeneration. In that deeper sense, the ritual of the stones has been hollowed of meaning, the duty of care to the land entrusted to the people by the Bodach and the Cailleach forgotten. Recently, for the second time in five years, Invermearan and Auch Estate was put up for sale; its 11,500 hectares, along with farms, cottages and tenants, just another commodity to be traded on the open market. Perhaps the new owners will see fit not only to encourage the tradition of tending to the stones but also to honour the injunction implicit in the practice.

Chapter 18

Campbell Generosity

The concrete wall of the Loch Lyon dam is like the facade of a dystopian government building, perhaps a Ministry for the Regulation of Water. It dwarfs the cottage at Lubreoch on the slopes below, which was once home to Bob Bissett and his wife. It must have been strange to live in the shadow of the dam and to remember the upper part of the glen, catching glimpses of it in dry summers, when the loch's level dropped enough to expose old roads and the ruins of houses.

I'd left Gleann Cailliche, returned to my tent, packed my gear and followed the estate track east along the length of the loch. The only woodland to break the monotony of its banks was at Eas Eoghannan, 'Adomnán's Waterfall', where a deer fence protected young trees growing on the hillside around the waterfall. An EU symbol on a sign on the nearby gate, with its twelve gold stars and blue backdrop, was a poignant reminder that when we were members of the European Parliament, we had access to funding for such regeneration schemes.

Glen Lyon is the longest enclosed glen in Scotland, running for thirty-four miles from the loch to the village of Fortingall in the east; in Gaelic it's also known as An Crom Ghleann, 'The Bent Glen'. For several hundred years it was Campbell territory, and it was Robert Campbell, 5th Laird of Glenlyon, who brought infamy to his clan – as well as the forever enmity of a one-armed fisherman – by acting as commanding officer at the Massacre of Glencoe.

The 5th Laird ticks all the boxes if you were looking for an example of the way that the ideal of the clan chief had degenerated in the early modern period.

Born from notions of sacred sovereignty, clan chiefs were given authority by their kinsmen to act as leader, protector and steward of the clan's *dùthaich* – a complex word denoting land and the collective claim to it, as well as a shared culture of belonging. By the late seventeenth century, such a role, and its responsibilities, had been displaced by a more plutocratic system of lairds and proprietors.

When Robert Campbell became laird, he frittered away his inheritance on gambling and booze, as well as on extensions to Meggernie Castle, the family pile. Deep in debt and breaking faith with any idea of good stewardship, he sold the woods of Glen Lyon for timber, inviting Lowland foresters to come and fell the ancient Scots pines. It wasn't enough, and by 1689 he had also sold most of his land and tenancies to the Earl of Tullibardine, and had enlisted as an officer in the Earl of Argyll's Regiment of Foot. After Glencoe, and his part in the 'murder under trust', Campbell fought with the Argylls at Flanders and died in poverty in Bruges in 1696.

Not all Campbells of Glen Lyon were so ignoble. My favourite is the 2nd Laird, renowned not for martial skill, nor for participation in blood feuds or betrayals, but for something else entirely.

A sixteenth-century Irish bard, living under the patronage of Gorrie, an Irish chief, is passing through Glen Lyon with his band of harpers and poets. Duncan Campbell, laird of the glen, known as Donnachadh Ruadh na Feileachd, 'Red Duncan the Hospitable', welcomes the bard and his retinue with typical generosity. A fat bullock and six wethers, alongside venison and other game, are served at the feasting table, and similar fare is provided for the guests every day of their stay.

When the bard of Gorrie eventually takes his leave, Red Duncan accompanies him part of the way up the glen. The bard happens to mention that his own linen undershirt is threadbare, and, without hesitation, Red Duncan strips and insists the bard takes his. Thus, naked, he bids the bard farewell and strides home.

Back at the castle and dressed once more, Red Duncan orders his cooks to prepare a feast twice as elaborate as the previous day's. 'For,' he says, 'the bard suspects I have furnished my table for his sake only, in order to impress him; his departure is a trick to test me, and he will soon be back.'

As predicted, the bard of Gorrie finds some excuse to explain the necessity of his return, and to his astonishment, when they sit down to dine, the laird's table is more lavishly furnished with food than before.

After further days of feasting and poetry, the bard departs in earnest and returns to Ireland. When his own chief, Gorrie, inquires after Red Duncan and suggests that surely guests fare better at Gorrie's table, the bard promptly replies:

> Let Gorrie be praised over the sea,
> and each man in his own country;
> but let none of the race of men
> be compared to Red Duncan but himself.

Indignant at the faint praise given to him in comparison to the elevated praise for Red Duncan, Gorrie dismisses his bard who, nonplussed, makes his way back to Scotland and Glen Lyon, where the 2nd Laird gifts him a patch of land.

The generosity of Donnachadh Ruadh na Feileachd has long been a byword in the glen, carried through story and inscribed in the landscape: woodland growing on the patch of land that he gifted is still called Coille a' Bhàird, 'The Bard's Wood'.

I was glad to leave the dam behind and take the road which follows the river downstream, passing the settlement of Pubil, a strange, dead place of empty and dishevelled holiday cottages. A mile on from Pubil there's a memorial to another Robert Campbell, who was born in 1808 at nearby Dalchiorlich, and who became an explorer and fur trader for the Hudson Bay Company in the Yukon territory of north-western Canada. The plaque on the memorial declares that he'd walked 3,000 miles in 104 days in order to catch the boat back to Scotland to find himself a wife, his journey putting my own month of walking into useful perspective.

The upper reaches of Glen Lyon are mostly denuded since the days of the earlier, ignoble Robert Campbell, but on the slopes above Meggernie there is a significant remnant of Caledonian pine forest. Spared from the clear-felling of the Lowland foresters, the slopes are believed to have been continuously wooded since the end of the last glacial period. It was a joy to encounter proper woodland again, a taste of the forest I hoped to reach that night.

Few cars passed as I walked the road, but I stuck my thumb at one and gained a short hitch to Innerwick, halfway down the glen. The church there was built in 1828 on the site of an older church and is based on a design by the ubiquitous Thomas Telford, who was commissioned to build over forty such churches in the Highlands and Islands. Telford churches are compact and unfussy, with whitewashed stone walls and a grey slate roof. Inside the one at Innerwick, you'll find an iron bell, known as Adomnán's Bell, which dates from the eighth century. It used to sit in a nearby graveyard and was moved to the church for security and to protect it from the elements. The graveyard dates back to the early medieval period and once had an adjoining chapel dedicated to St Adomnán, 9th Abbot of Iona and author of the *Vita Columbae*.

Along with the chapel and the bell, and the waterfall on the banks of Loch Lyon, Adomnán's name is linked to a nearby standing stone, which has been inscribed on both sides with a cross. The saint, it seems, had much to do with Innerwick and upper Glen Lyon, visiting often and performing miraculous deeds, as when he saved the lives of those who lived there by holding at bay an outbreak of the plague that had killed all but one of the inhabitants of the village of Fortingall, at the foot of the glen. The association with Adomnán and the abundance of nearby Christian sites and artefacts suggests that this remote settlement was an important centre for the early Celtic Church. The old path which leads from Innerwick over the hills to Loch Rannoch is still known locally as the Kirk Road, and for hundreds of years, the people who lived along the shores of the loch used it to walk the sixteen-mile round trip to attend holy days and fairs.

A handful of rooks were blethering in the sycamore trees when I stepped off the tarmac road opposite the church and followed the Kirk Road up into the Lairig Ghallabhaich, the steep pass between Meall a' Muich and Meall Glas. The name seems to be a distortion of *Lairig Calbh Àth,* 'Pass of the Rushing Ford'. Having spent the previous two days walking eastwards, I was now heading north, curving up towards Rannoch Moor, completing my journey's almost-figure-of-eight.

The path followed the course of the Allt Ghallabhaich, passing the clustered ruins of shielings on its banks. As I approached the height of the pass, I disturbed four hinds and their followers. They vaulted gracefully away, disappearing over the brow of the hill. The sun had dropped below the mountains, and the watershed was gloomy and empty. A mile ahead, I could see a dark line of trees, marking the southern edge of Coille Dubh Raineach, the 'Black Wood of Rannoch'.

Chapter 19

In the Black Wood

The southern stretch of the Black Wood is mostly plantation forestry, but with the wind gathering strength and the rain lashing my back, I was happy to reach the shelter of trees, whether domestic or wild.

In a forest of evergreens, the transition from summer to winter is not nearly so marked, and self-seeded saplings on the verges of the track were vibrant green, the young pines and spruce thriving on poor, stony soil. I made camp in a clearing, my routine honed, like a ritual: pitch tent, roll out mat and sleeping bag, stow gear, gather dead wood. By the time it was dark, I was sitting by the glow of the cooking fire, wearing a warm fleece and dry socks, my evening meal bubbling in its pot.

The wind swung through the trees in the night, and I swung too, between wakefulness and a light sleep of vivid dreams. By early morning the wind had calmed, and curled in the warmth of my sleeping bag, I listened to birdsong, picking out the wheezy twitter of siskins.

After breakfast, I packed and left the first of my Black Wood camps. The land sloped steadily down towards the shore of Loch Rannoch, and the track passed under the shade of tall plantation conifers, with clear-fell patches where timber had been extracted, leaving behind grey stumps and scarred soil. This wasn't the old-growth forest I had expected: there were no granny pines with billowing skirts of drooping branches, no rowan or birch, nor understory of juniper and blaeberry. In part, my expectation was fuelled by the name itself – evocative, chthonic, primordial – but the truth of the Black Wood of Rannoch is more prosaic: today it is a remnant patchwork of Caledonian pine forest, hemmed in by plantations.

When, through the trees, I spotted a couple with a dog ahead of me on a track that converged with mine, I slowed and waited for them to pass, preferring not to break the solitude of my morning. The dog barked a couple of times, having seen or smelt me, but the couple shushed it and called it away. I chose the opposite direction to them, walking with a steady attention to the sound and movement of birds, tasting forest air on the roof of my mouth. The plantations broke out into mixed, semi-natural woodland, and shafts of sunlight lanced the cloud. I stood still to enjoy their warmth on my face.

After lunch, I left the track and walked into the woods, careless of direction, eventually stopping to make camp in a level clearing amongst young and old pine, the ground carpeted with needles and surrounded by mossy humps and clumps of blaeberry. I found two large wood-ant nests nearby and left them both a sprinkling of oats as an offering, hoping it would stop them raiding my camp. The few ants on the surface of the nests seemed sluggish, and I guessed the colonies were tucked in for winter.

My afternoon was one of simple pleasures. I gathered firewood, harvesting branches that had snapped off but that were still tangled in the other branches of their tree – they were wind-dried and seasoned to perfection. Returning to camp, I sat and watched a gang of long-tailed tits flit from tree to tree, animating each one in turn with colour and movement, filling the air with the scratchy texture of their call: *tsee, tsee, tsee*.

In 1439, Rannoch Estate and its forest was gifted by the crown to the Robertsons of Struan, in thanks for the part they played in capturing the men who assassinated King James I of

Scotland. For several hundred years, the Black Wood fell in and out of the hands of the Robertsons, and during that time it was increasingly exploited for timber. By the 1750s, 1,200 trees a year were being felled, and during the Napoleonic Wars, at the start of the nineteenth century, that rate increased, so much so that canals were dug through the forest to float timber down to the loch and then away to be sold.

For all the steady extraction, up until the eighteenth century the Black Wood was still a wildwood, and it was known to be wolf-infested. So dense were their numbers, reports claimed, that the wood and the moors around were almost impassable because of the danger of attack. Wolf numbers are often exaggerated in historical texts, but it is also true that the great pine forest would have been an ideal habitat for them, and there are plenty of tales and traditions relating to their invariably malign presence, and to the heroics of those who despatched them.

It's midwinter, and wolves steal out from the Black Wood, converging on Cladh Mhìcheil, 'St Michael's Graveyard', attracted by the smell of fresh corpses. The Robertson brothers of Struan are on guard when three wolves of great stature attempt a raid. Donald, youngest brother, bends his bow, sends up a prayer to St Michael, and lets fly an arrow, which finds the heart of the first wolf. He bends his bow again, sends up his prayer and kills the second wolf. A third time he bends his bow but neglects to recite the prayer, and the arrow only wounds the third wolf, spurring it to a furious attack. Donald stands firm, prays for the intervention of St Michael and grapples with the wolf, finding strength and speed enough to plunge his dirk into its heart.

Celebrations are held and thanks given to St Michael. Tàillear Dubh na Tuaighe, the 'Black-haired Tailor of the Battle-axe', a renowned Cameron warrior, inspects the carcasses of the three wolves and praises the Robertsons thus:

O companions from Lochaber,
Great is the honour now to Rannoch,
That Struan has such valiant men
As these heroes from Auchtarsin;
And may they long be spared alive
'Neath coat of arms of three wolves' heads;
And may St. Michael's graveyard, too,
Be guarded long by men as brave!

Donald Robertson killed his wolves towards the end of the sixteenth century. A hundred and fifty years later, the Black Wood gave refuge to a different kind of persecuted creature. In the aftermath of the Jacobite Risings, the forest hid many of those who came out for the Stuarts, and whose lands and property were subsequently forfeited, including Donald's descendants, the Robertsons of Struan.

The animals and the people are intertwined. In the eyes of the British Government, Jacobite clansmen, with their archaic lifestyles and allegiances, had to be brought to heel, or else hunted down and killed, like wolves.

Since its acquisition by the Forestry Commission in 1947, this patch of 'wildwood' has been protected and is now designated a Site of Special Scientific Interest. Public access is limited, with few car parks or marked trails, and despite being relatively accessible to the Central Belt, the footfall of visitors is low, as though the Black Wood exists more in the cultural imagination than it does in lived encounters. Whilst there, I saw no one apart from the couple with their dog on that first morning. Maybe that's all to the good, allowing the flora and fauna of the forest to go about its business with minimum disturbance, but it's important to remember that people once lived and worked here, as herdsmen and woodsmen, charcoal-makers, berry-pickers, and that we are as much a part of its biomass as pine marten, wildcat and wood ant.

That night, I fell asleep thinking of those who had moved through the forest before me, and whose presence haunt the woods. So it is, over and over, wherever you walk or camp in the Highlands: you find evidence of belonging, of an enduring intimacy with place.

A deer hunter lives at Tigh na Coille, 'House of the Wood', where the Black Wood meets the shore of Loch Rannoch. One evening, he is making his way home through the forest, when he sees in a clearing a red deer hind and her calf. He raises his gun to shoot, and the deer take the form of a woman and her daughter. Startled, fearful, the hunter lowers his gun and turns away from the clearing, anxious to reach home. The mother and daughter follow in the form of deer, and when he reaches Tigh na Coille, he turns to look and sees them, standing on the edge of the forest, waiting for him.

It's said that the hunter recognised the woman as someone with whom he'd been intimate. It's said that he was so shaken by the encounter that he left his home in the Black Wood, took passage on a ship to America, and never returned.

Once again, a story that matches the experience of Spiridon the Yukaghir hunter, when he encountered the *ayibii* of the elk and her calf in the Siberian taiga. Once again, an example of an Animist world-view preserved within a Scottish folktale, a world-view which understands that the animals of the hunt are ancestral beings who need to be treated with reverence, and that there are taboos which should not be transgressed. Unlike in Spiridon's account with the elk, the hunter of Tigh na Coille has been unable to resist the charms of the deer-woman – it's said that she was 'someone with whom he'd been intimate', even implying that, perhaps, the calf was his daughter – and now she stalks him, a *leannan sìth*, drawing him to the otherworld. The tale doesn't tell whether the Atlantic Ocean was wide enough to throw her off his trail.

*

I spent four nights in the Black Wood, just as I had in the forest of Glen Affric at the start of my journey. The days were quiet and lucid, and I gave my attention away to the trees. One afternoon I sat down in a clearing with my back against the trunk of a pine and listened to the bright trill of a wren, watching as it fossicked amongst the moss of old tree stumps, darting so close I could almost touch it. I was far from any paths, and knowing that wrens tend to stick within their own limited territories, it struck me that I might have been the first human that this one had encountered. Charged with the responsibility of being ambassador for my species, I sat very still and praised the wren's fine chequered wings, the little kingdom of its clearing, the *ceòl mòr* of its voice.

On my last night, the sky was clear, and a river of stars spilled above the canopy of the forest. After dinner I sat till late, enjoying the warmth of the fire as the temperature dropped. It was nearing the end of October, approaching Hallowe'en, or Samhain, the old Celtic turning of the year – the moment when the Cailleach, as winter crone, comes into her own. There's a song that evokes this transition point, this time when the living and the dead might congregate. I used to know it well, and it didn't take long to remember the pattern of the words, so that I could sing it quietly to the fire.

'Hallowe'en' was written by Violet Jacob, poet and laird's daughter from Angus, born in 1863. It's a lament for those who were killed during World War I, including Jacob's only son, Harry, who died from his wounds in the aftermath of the Battle of the Somme in France, aged twenty. Jim Reid, Dundee-born folksinger and musician, put a tune to the rich Scots words of Jacob's poem, a poem which celebrates the bothy life of Angus farm workers and contrasts the high-jinks of Hallowe'en customs with the intense sorrow of remembrance for the dead. One verse speaks directly to that sorrow, and to the longing that it leaves:

> But gin the auld fowks' tales are richt
> An ghaists come hame on Hallow nicht,
> O freend o' freends! what wad I gie
> To feel ye rax yer hand to me
> Atween the dark an' caun'le licht?

Four years after his death, I thought about my father and how he would have enjoyed this fire with its good heart and drying branches cradled around the hearth. I regretted the years that we didn't sit around fires, missed the camps we might have had if he hadn't left my mother, or if I hadn't shut him out when he did; but I also knew that I'd been lucky, that we had the time to re-connect and rebuild our relationship before he died.

At seventy-six, my dad managed to outlive the life expectancy of a working-class Glaswegian male, and although he would have enjoyed more years, his death was timely, his life complete. There's been no need for me to wish him back, and I never dream him alive in the way that I do my friend Mo, regularly, even though she died more than twenty years ago.

Mo was one of a group of friends centred around a large flat many of us shared in Edinburgh, where I lived when I first left Iona. We were a tight bunch through our twenties, until, our lives in flux, we loosened, moved away, coupled up. Mo had moved to Oxford and was struggling in ways we didn't understand, her behaviour becoming ever more erratic. I visited her in London, where she was staying in a friend's flat, and she told me that a van parked outside in the street was MI5, spying on her. Swinging between depression and manic instability, she refused medical help and was clever at presenting as 'normal' when she needed to. Her desperate mother – and theirs was a tough relationship – tried to get her hospitalised, fearing the harm she might cause to herself or to others.

Mo moved back to Edinburgh, putting distance between herself and family, and the intervention of doctors. I saw her, though not often enough, and on our last meeting, sitting in sunshine on the grass of the Meadows, she was fragile but seemed at ease. A week later, when the police forced open the door of her flat, she had already been three days dead.

My dream is always the same, and strikingly vivid: that her suicide was an elaborate hoax and that she turns up years later, alive and well. It takes a while after waking for the truth to re-assert itself.

In the note that Mo wrote before killing herself, she bequeathed me her camping gear, newly bought during a manic spending spree and unused: tent, sleeping bag, rucksack, and she asked that I say hello to the hills for her. Over the years, I've done so again and again.

Hallowe'en is the time for tending to the dead, for gathering them to the fire. In remembering my dad, the grief that rose was like the smoke from seasoned pine: it was clean, astringent. Thinking about Mo was more complicated, with guilt smouldering amongst the grief – guilt that we, her friends, were not there for her enough, and that she might have pulled through if we had been.

Whisky goes down easily by firelight in a clearing in a forest on a still night, with just the trees breathing around you. I poured an extra dram on behalf of those who had gone beyond the ability to hold a cup. The Cailleach, as crone, would mock my sentimentality: 'Gathering the dead to the fire. Ha! There's no conjuring back, no second chance to speak your gratitude or placate your guilt, no *raxing*, or reaching, of hands *atween the dark an' caun'le licht*. Speak to the living while you can: the rest is ashes and bones and the fire burnt out.'

On my last night in the Black Wood I'd drunk enough whisky to be blethering nonsense, but I kept faith with the fire until the glow of its embers faded. When I stood up, unsteadily, to go to bed, stars plugged the gaps between the branches above the clearing.

*

Birch trees stood between me and the early sun, their branches dripping with dew and spooled by spiderwebs. The morning gleamed. I was walking north, downhill, following a path that led to old-growth forest. In amongst the granny pines and juniper, the hummocks of heather and blaeberry, I was at home to myself and to place in a way that I rarely am. Water glittered between the trunks of trees, and all at once Loch Rannoch opened before me like an inland sea.

A single-track, unmarked road skirts the ten-mile shore of the south side of the loch. I followed it west, passing Tigh na Coille, the house of the hunter who fled the deer-woman and her deer-calf daughter. The road brought me back to the concrete present, but Tigh na Coille, derelict, collapsing into itself – *there, not there* – declared a different, more fluid reckoning of time.

Loch Rannoch passes the 'interesting loch test', even though it's hydro-dammed at one end. Wooded promontories variegate the shoreline, with bays scalloped in between, and mixed woodland covers the slopes that rise above both sides of the loch. I walked the road with the sun on my shoulder and with birch leaves scattered like coins beneath my feet.

Towards the head of the loch, a tiny island with a small square tower lies half a mile offshore. Eilean nam Faoileag, 'Island of Gulls', is a crannog built on a sandbank that curves out from the south shore. The tower is a nineteenth-century folly, modelled on the older keep built by the Robertsons of Struan that once stood there. According to tradition, when the

Robertsons were outnumbered and being chased by enemies, they would run out along a submerged walkway on the sandbank to the crannog. Anyone who followed, not knowing the curve of the sand, would flounder and be drowned or forced to swim to shore. When the hydro-dam was built, Loch Rannoch's water-level rose, and Eilean nam Faoileag almost disappeared. Now only the tower and a few feet of stony ground remain visible, and even if you knew its route, the walkway on the sandbank is too deep beneath the surface of the loch to be used.

A chainsaw buzzed in the woods and broke the morning's quiet. Walking to Bridge of Gaur at the head of the loch, I was reminded that this is prosperous Perthshire: the houses along the way were either renovated and extended cottages, or large, larch-clad new-builds, with floor-to-ceiling triple-glazed windows. Many had the look of second homes, and although the handsome Braes of Rannoch kirk still advertised a Sunday service, I wondered how long it would be before that building too was tastefully converted.

By the turn-off to the old drove road to Bridge of Orchy, I passed a ramshackle cabin and, sitting outside it, a white-bearded, bonneted, weather-creased man, who smiled from behind his whiskers and nodded to me as I passed. Leaning back on a canvas deckchair in the sunny spot of an unruly garden, he too looked entirely at home to himself and to place, and I was glad, amongst the prosperity, that there was room, still, for such a cabin and its keeper.

After Culloden, redcoat soldiers were stationed at Rannoch Barracks at Bridge of Gaur and given orders to show no mercy as they burned houses, destroyed crops and seized cattle. Duncan Cameron, Dhonnacha Dhuibh a' Mhonaidh, 'Black Duncan of the Moor', was a renowned Jacobite who hid for months from the soldiers in the hills above Gaur, watching out for them from a rocky ledge known as Leaba Dhonnacha

Dhuibh, 'Black Duncan's Bed'. He and a companion are said to have been the protagonists who gave rise to the well-known tale of 'The Lone Highlander'.

A platoon of redcoat soldiers is on patrol west of Rannoch Barracks when they see a figure on top of a hill, gesturing with his sword and taunting them in Gaelic. A corporal and two privates are sent up to deal with the renegade. As they disappear over the top, the remaining soldiers hear shouts and cries and the sound of fighting, then silence. Soon, the figure appears again, gesturing and taunting, and an officer is sent with a troop up the hill to teach him a lesson. As they disappear over the top, the remaining soldiers hear shouts and cries and the sound of fighting, then silence. Once again, the figure appears, gesturing and taunting.

Finally, enraged, the colonel in command orders an all-out attack, and what is left of the platoon charges up the hill. As they approach the top, a wounded soldier limps down towards them, shouting frantically, 'Get back, get back, it's a trap. There are two of them.'

The story is more poignant to me than humorous, salvaging pride through its tall-tale bravado – a defeated people with 'wha's like us' defiance. The Barracks are now owned by Baron Pearson of Rannoch, along with the 8,000-hectare Rannoch Estate, and as I walked past his private driveway, two stone eagles glared at me from their gate-post pedestals.

Malcolm Everard MacLaren Pearson is a hereditary peer who sits in the House of Lords and lives for most of the year in London, although a decade ago he was found to have falsely claimed over £100,000 in expenses by pretending that his London address was only a second home. The baron is a former leader of the UK Independence Party and is known for his anti-Islamic proclamations. I found myself sympathising with the whiskered old man in his ramshackle cabin who had to contend with such an unseemly neighbour, even if the baron was only in residence during the shooting season.

The River Gaur flows deep and peat-dark beneath the bridge. Having crossed it, the unmarked road joins the B846 and continues west, parallel to the river. The day was quiet for hitching, but it's fine country to walk through, a patchwork of fields and mixed woodland and, south of the river, an expanse of young trees repopulating the hillside – birch mostly, ethereal against the sun, their branches catching and filtering the light.

As I climbed past the Gaur hydro-electric plant, Loch Eigheach opened before me, the green spears of a spruce plantation mustered around its southern shore. The land was bumpy with glacial moraine, and as I walked towards the loch, I passed drumlins that were like scaled-down models of the Glencoe mountains that lay to the west. To the east, Schiehallion, 'Fairy Hill of the Caledonians', was a dark beacon at the far end of Loch Rannoch. The weather was changing, cloud shrouded the sky, and the wind off the moor blew cold in my face.

Chapter 20

On the Road to the Isles

Rannoch Moor, from Mòinteach Raineach, 'Bracken Moor', sits on a bedrock of granite. Five thousand years ago, mid-Holocene, long after the last ice of the last Ice Age had melted, Scotland's climate turned milder and wetter, and increased rainfall on a landscape with an impermeable granite base transformed Rannoch Moor into bog and lochan. The pine forest that grew there, ancestor to the Black Wood, became waterlogged, and the majority of the trees died. Sphagnum moss, flourishing in the bogs, compressed into peat around the bones of the trees. Now the moor is a rare habitat: the largest area of unbroken blanket peat bog in the UK, and home to uncommon botanic treasures.

Like the Flow Country of Sutherland, Rannoch Moor is often described as a 'wilderness', but for all its status as a Special Area of Conservation, centuries of over-grazing by deer and sheep means that it is very much a managed and denuded landscape, another 'green desert' with no mosaic of willow and alder amongst the bogs and moss, no stands of birch or pine on drier ground.

The West Highland Railway opened in 1894, connecting Glasgow to Fort William via Rannoch Moor. To cross it, track was laid on thousands of tons of earth and ash, banked on a floating mattress of tree roots and brushwood. The first stop on the moor is at Rannoch Station, where the B846 ends.

A mile before the station, I left the tarmac road and stepped onto the 'Road to the Isles', the old drove road that was used to cross the moor before the railway arrived, and which was a major artery in the network of drove roads that led from the Highlands and Islands to the cattle markets of Crieff and Falkirk.

Walking the drove road, now metalled with gravel for estate vehicles, I passed a section of hillside that had been fenced to keep the deer out. The young woodland inside was all the evidence required to show that trees could, if given the chance, flourish here.

I spent the night in the shelter of a small square of plantation spruce. I had walked twelve miles from the Black Wood, mostly on tarmac, and my feet tingled with pleasure when I removed my boots and socks and stepped onto the cushioned moss of the plantation floor. After dinner I sat by the fire, my palisade of drying branches shielding the flames from gusts of wind. In the dark, a rumble like thunder grew louder and settled into a recognisable rhythm: the *clickety-clack* of a train's wheels on the West Highland Line, echoing across the moor.

*

The morning was brittle with ground frost and fractured sunlight through the trees. Back on the Road to the Isles, I watched another train trundle north along the dark line of the railway, like a noisy toy with three stubby carriages. I was walking north and west towards Beinn a' Bhric, where I had climbed and camped in spring, and as I walked, I looked out for a particular stone, one of countless glacial erratics strewn across the moor.

Clach an Fuaran, 'Stone of the Well', is a large table-like boulder lying a few yards below the Road to the Isles. There was no sign of a spring or well, but I found a crow's feather pinned into thick lichen on the side of the boulder, which seemed appropriate, whether it had been deliberately placed or not. Clach an Fuaran is also known as the Witch's Stone and is associated with the Cailleach of Beinn a' Bhric.

Tucked at the base of the boulder, I found a small parcel wrapped in a black bin bag and weighted down with stones. Curiosity prevailed over my concern that, given the boulder's name, the bag might contain some kind of occult offering: animal bones, or worse; but inside I found a Tupperware box with a note explaining that this was a Geocache site – part of a global treasure-hunt for GPS users. The treasure took the form of plastic bric-a-brac: a little toy car, a Homer Simpson badge, a vampire bat.

The ground around the boulder was rough and indented, but a shallow oblong depression was more defined than the other scrapes and folds. I was careful not to step into it.

The Cailleach of Beinn a' Bhric is a witch who sours the milk of dairy cattle and withers the crops of those who attempt to farm on the moor, stealing the goodness from the grain. One day she spirits away the best milk-cow of the crofter at Cruaiche, by Loch Laidon, and after days of searching, he finds the cow miles from home, held in an enclosure at Clach an Fuaran. The cow is emaciated after ill-use by the Cailleach. Furious, armed with his gun, the crofter confronts the Cailleach and shoots her dead, burying her body next to the stone.

The crofter, who should have known better, places her face upwards in the grave. At the next waxing of the moon, the Cailleach of Beinn a' Bhric shrugs off her death like a shroud and claws herself up and out of the grave, as would never have happened if she had been placed correctly, face down, able only to scrabble ever deeper into the ground.

The Cailleach has been demoted here from deer-goddess to witch, and it's a crofter who kills her on the moor, just as it's a shepherd's dog, barking, that causes her death on the shore of

Loch Bà on the Isle of Mull. Farming and herding are anathema to the Cailleach; she is a hunters' god, presiding over wild places, redundant in a domesticated world.

The Cailleach's grave is different to Uaigh Dhiarmaid by Cunside in Sutherland. The mound there seems plausible, and respectful, its size and position at the foot of Ben Loyal appropriate to the myth of the warrior buried beneath it. The grave at Clach an Fuaran is less likely but somehow more unsettling: it lies open and empty, and unresolved; its shallowness suggests a contemporary murder. Looking down into the grave, I had no offering to give, no heart-shaped stone to bring closure. Instead, I imagined a bony, crony figure rising up at night under the sliver of a new moon. I was glad to be there in daylight.

Climbing back up towards the track, I stopped to investigate a patch of willow scrub and found that it overhung and obscured a rock cleft, like a mini grotto. Leaning in, I discovered a pool: silted, stagnant, but a pool nonetheless – the *fuaran* that gave the boulder its name. The silt was rusty, ferrous, the pool fed by a spring that filtered through a seam of bog iron.

The story of the Cailleach's grave and the clear line of vision from Clach an Fuaran to Beinn a' Bhric, the Cailleach's mountain, confirms an old association, as do the two wells: the one just below the mountain's summit, and this one, overgrown, forgotten, sacred – a chalybeate spring, the bog iron giving it the taste of blood, connecting a witch's tale to ancient rituals of death and renewal.

Out on Rannoch Moor you will find traces of peat banks that have been worked by generations of families, cutting the peats each summer to dry and then store for winter fuel – just as the strange folk on the moor were doing in the story of Dòmhnall Mòr Òg, when they invited him to share their lunch. Peat-cutting is still practised in Scotland, but mostly now only on Skye and the Outer Hebrides. On a fresh-cut peat bank you can see most clearly the different strata: from the turf on top to the first spongy layers and then down to what is known in Gaelic as the *fàd a' chaorain*, or 'bottom layer'. This is where you find the darkest, densest peat.

The Cailleach inhabits the deepest layer, the *fàd a' chaorain*, of myth in this land, and Clach an Fuaran is like a waymark or an entry point. It's here that the focus shifts away from Schiehallion, that other sacred mountain to the east, towards Beinn a' Bhric, the Cailleach's mountain. It's here that her territory begins: the hunting lands, far from the settlements dotted around the shores of Loch Rannoch, and it's here, on Rannoch Moor, that the Cailleach is most deeply remembered in folklore and tradition.

There are modern stories too. In 1917, a gamekeeper at Corrour Lodge claimed that he had witnessed the Cailleach climbing Beinn a' Bhric to clean her well at Beltane; and in 1927, J.G. McKay, author of the 'Deer Cult' essay, interviewed a doctor in Fort William who confirmed that her presence on the mountain was still widely known and accepted. The reports continued, and in the 1990s, the journalist Rennie McOwan spoke to a stalker employed by Corrour Estate who was convinced he had seen the Cailleach, caught in the headlights of his Land Rover, as she flew through the air on a wild night of weather.

Myth degrades to superstition, the Cailleach becomes a witch haunting the moor, and the stories continue to swirl around the gyre of Beinn a' Bhric, adding to the volume of tales and references, and reaching back towards their archaic significance.

In many traditional hunter-gatherer cultures, prominent features in the landscape are believed to be the source-place of specific animals. They're a kind of spirit-reservoir where the original ancestor dwells, and from which the souls or spirits, the *ayibii*, of the animals emerge into material form, and to which they return after death.

I think it's likely that the people who lived around the rim of Rannoch Moor, who for thousands of years stalked red deer during the great autumn hunts, regarded Beinn a' Bhric as the source-place of their prey, with the Cailleach present there as the original deer-ancestor, a kind of *genius loci* and *genius cervorum* combined, analogous to what the Yukaghir call *khoziain*, the 'animal-master' who must be propitiated in order to secure success in the hunt. I think that the stories passed down to us of the Cailleach and of shape-shifting deer-women are a perception memory, a reminder of a way of seeing without separation, where literal and mythic truths are both articulated in the landscape.

*

I settled into the day's walk but was uneasy, disquieted by the Cailleach's grave in a way that I'd rarely been on my month's journey. There was no one on the old drove road and nothing moved on the moor other than the shadows of clouds. I imagined a camera, eagle-high, taking a picture once every hundred years of the land that lay below, for thousands of millennia. A stop-motion film of those pictures would show the land restless: tectonic plates shifting like muscle and bone, flexing and fracturing; a beast whose back bore pelts of ice then shrugged them off, then pelts of forest, thickening, scalped, thickening again.

A mouse caught my attention in the verge, and I stopped to watch as, instead of scurrying off at the sight of me, it climbed a stem of bog asphodel. It shimmied up the stem like an acrobat, its white belly exposed, chewed the asphodel's tip so that the seed head fell and then climbed back down. Little round mouse, hunched against the wind, chomping the fallen seed head, unfazed by my presence. Little witch's familiar.

The walls of Corrour Old Lodge are built from stone hewn out of the granite crags of Carn Dearg, a long-ridged mountain that stretches north towards Loch Ossian. The Road to the Isles contours the lower slopes of the mountain, keeping above the bog of the moor. From a distance, the ruined lodge looks like a crag itself, jutting out of the hillside, but as you approach, you begin to see the straight lines and right angles of doorways and window recesses. The lodge was built early in the 1800s but fell out of use by the end of that century. It was once a substantial building, with an enclosed courtyard and stables for ponies, and at over 1,700 feet, it laid claim to being the most elevated shooting lodge in Scotland. It must have been quite the sanctuary in a storm, with the fires stoked and lanterns glowing in the windows. It's desolate now, the chimneys collapsed and the fireplaces reduced to a few buckled scraps of iron, and isolated, lying halfway between Rannoch Station and Corrour.

Early in the twentieth century, a new Corrour Lodge was built on the far side of Carn Dearg, at the east end of Loch Ossian. As for the old lodge, a story persists that, after World War I, it became a sanitorium or isolation hospital for the convalescence of troops gassed in the trenches. There are no records or evidence to support this, although it is possible that a camp of prefabricated huts was erected nearby and used for such a purpose. If true, I pitied the patients, being carted along the Road to the Isles and deposited on the slopes of Carn Dearg, with the wastes of Rannoch Moor to contemplate whilst ill. It would certainly have fulfilled the remit of isolation.

Dried stalks of yarrow and rosebay willowherb speared up amongst tumbled stone, and a stream bubbled past the ruined lodge cheerfully. I drank from it, filled my water bottle, and then carried on along the road to where a small cairn marks the start of the path to Lubnaclach.

The path would once have taken a horse and cart, but now it's rarely used and has, in places, sunk back into the moor, the line of it erased from the land and no longer marked on OS Landranger maps. I followed as best I could, dodging bogs and picking up the trail on firmer ground where ruts could still be traced. It was late in the afternoon by the time I approached the house at Lubnaclach, following the course of the Allt a' Choire Odhair Bhig, 'Small Stream of the Dun-coloured Corrie'.

The gable ends of Lubnaclach still stand, and the walls are mostly intact, though the roof is gone. In a small back room, a cast-iron bath lies on its side, and in the main room, the fireplace is stuffed with the detritus of recent visitors: an abandoned training shoe, tin cans, plastic wrappers. The house is named after a bend in the stream overlooked by an elephant-sized boulder – Lùb na Clach, 'Bend of the Stone'. It was built in the nineteenth century and was still habitable in the 1970s, when the family who owned it allowed staff and students of Glasgow University to use it as a bothy. It sits 500 yards from the railway line, and students remember the guard stopping the train there so that they could climb down and save themselves the two-mile walk back from Corrour Station.

I left Lubnaclach and followed the Allt a' Choire Odhair Bhig to where it merges with the Allt na Caim, the 'Crooked Stream'. More of a river than a stream, the Allt Caim passes beneath the West Highland Line, under an iron bridge, and then snakes its way across the moor until it reaches the Blackwater Reservoir.

The river was lost amongst the ridges and furrows of peat hag and bog, the light was thinning, and I was walking into a remote part of the moor, hoping to reach a place that I knew of only as a name in a story. Half a moon had risen, like a cowled face, reminding me of a different story, one concerning

An Duine Eagalach, 'The Fearsome Man', who is occasionally seen on the moor: tall, grey, his head enlarged and distorted, moon-like.

A traveller is crossing the moor from the King's House Inn at the head of Glencoe. Halfway across, mist thickens around him, and he loses sight of the path. Surrounded by bog, he stops to gather his wits, and in the silence, he hears footsteps behind him.

A hooded figure appears out of the mist and strides past without a word. As the figure passes, the traveller catches sight of a face beneath the hood: hideous, deformed, scowling.

Lost, fearful of being mired in the bog, the traveller has no choice but to follow the hooded figure, who seems able to pick a path despite the mist. After many miles, his guide leads him over the brow of a hill. The traveller, struggling to keep up, crests the hill to find that the hooded figure has disappeared.

On this occasion, An Duine Eagalach has shown kindness: ahead of the traveller, the lanterns of the inn at Rannoch Station are glowing.

I was picking my own way amongst the pools and bogs and peat hags. Pine roots, thousands of years old, protruded from banks, like antlers, pallid against the black of the peat. It would be easy to be lost, and whenever I stopped walking, I heard nothing but the gurgle of the Allt Caim, somewhere out of sight. I thought again about how disturbed I'd been, crossing the moor on the train in winter, in my twenties; and I was grateful there was no recurrence, no dislocation of self, despite being here on my own in the last of the light.

The cottage at Caim is roofless, and its walls are tumbling. It sits amongst a sward of grass on the bank of a bend in the river. The moor rises around the bank, so that you would never know the cottage was there until you stumbled on it. The grass was green and fey amongst the dun colours of the moor.

When I first heard Caim mentioned in a story relating to the Cailleach of Beinn a' Bhric, I searched for it on my OS map and eventually spotted a tiny rectangle set amidst the twists of the river and the swirling contour lines of the moor. The rectangle was like a statement: here we are, or were, even in this remote place.

Caim was a permanent dwelling only after the introduction of sheep farming, and latterly it was used as a keeper's cottage. Estate records show that the last inhabitant was John MacDonald, Corrour gamekeeper, who moved to Lubnaclach when the house was built there in 1893. But the gabled cottage at Caim sits on an old shieling site, and there are other shielings to the south, by the Black Water, evidence that, for centuries, people herded their cattle here for the summer grazing.

I pitched my tent in front of the cottage and unpacked my gear, along with a bundle of kindling and branches that I'd carried from my previous camp. I had also strapped a few lengths of wood onto my rucksack, scavenged from a pile at Lubnaclach, enough for a small fire.

It's difficult now to grasp the life of those who made their home at Caim. A slower-paced life, I imagine, with time metered in seasons, not days. Some who lived here might have hated it; others, perhaps those who accommodated themselves to the pace and to the spaciousness, might have experienced a rare sensitivity to the moor's moods and presences.

The shepherd at Caim is careful of his milk-cow, living in the shadow of Beinn a' Bhric, the witch's mountain. He and his wife must go to Rannoch for supplies, a two-day journey, and their son is left in charge.

In the evening, the boy sits by the fire with his dog, the cow safe in the byre, the wind howling outside, rain lashing at the glass of the cottage window. He hears scratching at the door and dismisses it as a stalk of heather or bracken, blown by the wind, but the scratching persists. The shepherd's son has a measure of courage in him. He rises and lifts the latch, and is surprised to find a bedraggled, black hen outside. The hen hops across the threshold and fusses its way to the warmth of the fire. Snarling, hackles raised, the dog lunges, and it's all the shepherd's son can do to hold it back from savaging the hen. She dries and preens herself in the warmth of the fire, keeping a beady eye on the dog, and as she ruffles out her feathers, it seems to the shepherd's son that she begins to swell.

Sure enough, the hen grows bigger, taller, shifting form to become a bony, crony, black-clad woman who plucks from her head a wiry hair and shrieks above the barking of the dog, 'Use this cord to bind that hound, or I will take the life out of it.'

The shepherd's son pretends to tie one end of the hair around the dog's neck, binding it around the leg of the bed instead, and hands back the other end to the witch.

Immediately, she attacks the boy, clawing at his throat. The dog leaps to the boy's defence, and the witch pulls hard on the wiry hair, thinking to break the dog's neck, but succeeds only in snapping the leg of the bed. Foiled, infuriated, she grapples with boy and dog but cannot match their combined youth and strength. In a flash, she takes back the form of the black hen and escapes up the chimney, shrieking down at the shepherd's son, 'Were it not for your fierce dog this night, I would have taken the life out of you.'

Another encounter with the Cailleach in which she is, once again, reduced to the status of witch; another variant of a tale found throughout the Highlands. But this one is attached to Caim, and that matters: the story rescues meaning from a small rectangle on an Ordnance Survey map.

I lit my fire in the cottage's hearth, beneath its ruined chimney, paying all due attention to the sacrament of the act, aware that it was probably the first fire lit there in decades and that it would be the last fire of my journey. The wood sparked, and flames rose, warming the lintel stone in remembrance of the people who lived here. Despite the isolation, despite the tales of risen witches and evil black hens, I was calm by the fire, as though some etiquette of place, some lingering hospitality, soothed the day's unease. Later, from the cocoon of my tent, the sound of a train on the West Highland Line was like the churn of a boat's engine, ploughing the night sea.

Grouse woke me at dawn, chuckling on the moor, their voices sinister, witchy, and I tried not to think about black hens fussing around outside the tent. After breakfast, I washed my dishes in the pool that swirled at the bend in the river then packed my gear into my rucksack. Before leaving Caim, I knelt before the cottage chimney and spread the ashes of the previous night's fire, as though I was smooring the ruin's hearth.

Chapter 21

Taking Quartz to the Cailleach

What's the use of stories that aren't even true. I asked that question and it broke my father's heart.

So says Haroun near the beginning of Salman Rushdie's allegorical novel, *Haroun and the Sea of Stories*. Haroun's father is a renowned storyteller who has been silenced by his son's dismissal of his craft, and thus begins Haroun's quest to right his wrong and restore to his father the gift of stories.

I don't think it's true that a shepherd's son at Caim encountered a witch in the form of a black hen, scratching at his door to be let in, or that Diarmaid fought with a boar on the summit of Ben Loyal and was killed by one of its poisonous bristles. Nor do I think that Mac Mhic Ailein, Laird of Arisaig, met and married a stag that took the form of a woman in the oak woods of Moidart. But sometimes it's possible – perhaps whilst out walking on a remote and rugged moor that brims with culture – to blur the distinction between literal and mythic truth. You never know, as Barry Lopez said, when he stopped to honour road-kill on the freeways of North America. In tracking these tales, in honouring them, I've expanded my understanding of how story and place are intertwined and been encouraged to read the landscape in a new – or rather, very old – way.

It was the last full day of my journey, and I was looping back to Beinn a' Bhric, following my own ellipse, like the swallow

I'd met contouring the crags on the first morning of May. I felt fit for it, physically and psychically, approaching the mountain after a month's rapport between my body, my mind and the land. Tomorrow would be the eve of Samhain, the festival that marks the turning point of the Celtic year.

I found and followed a stalkers' path that curved its way beneath a craggy ridge below Leum Uilleim, Beinn a' Bhric's eastern peak The bones of trees protruded from every peat hag, some of them so smoothed and polished by wind and rain that they gleamed like mother of pearl. The slope beneath the ridge is called Sealg Gharbh, the 'Rough Hunting Ground', and a stream tumbled down from it, crossing the path and weaving a course amongst the folds and pleats of the moor. The water was clear and clean, bubbling amongst stones, catching and refracting sunlight as the clouds shifted. It was a typical Highland stream, a simple confluence of precipitation and topography, indistinct from so many that I had stepped across or stopped to drink from during my month's walk, but it was a stream that I'd come a long way to find.

The Allt Nighean Mhic Dhomhnuill, the 'Stream of Donald's Granddaughter', is said to flow past the grave of the hunter who honoured and found favour with the Cailleach and who stalked deer as though it was a dance on the ridge of Beinn a' Bhric – the hunter who is identified, historically, as Dòmhnall mac Fhionnlaigh nan Dàn, the sixteenth-century bard of Fersit, but who is, more truthfully, Dòmhnall Donn-shùileach, 'Brown-eyed Donald', a hunter outside of time.

There was no grave, and I didn't expect to find one, but it was only when I stood by the stream and looked up at Beinn a' Bhric that I understood fully: the mountain itself is the grave. Dòmhnall Donn-shùileach, wrapped in the skin of the dun-coloured stag, sleeps inside the dun-coloured mountain; the Allt Nighean Mhic Dhomhnuill doesn't wash away the tears of his grieving granddaughter, it *is* her tears. This is how myth dwells in the land – this is the dreaming of the ancestors.

*

Perhaps it is irrelevant whether or not a few stories cling on to a denuded moor below a denuded mountain, both stripped of much of their flora and fauna. Or perhaps we might tend to those stories in the same way that the young ghillies of Glen Lyon tend to Tigh nam Bodach: respectfully, diligently, stewarding a tradition even if they don't hold to its cosmology. Perhaps that way, the stories won't be lost from the land, and an ability to think beyond modernity will be maintained, like a muscle kept supple for the day when it's needed once more; or like those spindly rowan and birch trees that grow on steep crags or on top of boulders, beyond the reach of sheep and deer, faithfully casting seed, trusting that a time will come when trees can spread again.

Biodiversity and cultural diversity go hand in hand. It's no surprise that the flourishing of one encourages the flourishing of the other, or that the opposite is also true. Across the world, and here in Scotland, when indigenous cultures and traditional land practices are supressed, a loss of biodiversity soon follows and the monoculture of consumerism echoes through agro-industry, strip-mining and deforestation. Meanwhile, stories, clinging on, ringing down through the years, remind us how to live in right relationship with place and with the other beings that we share place with – and they warn us when that relationship is out of kilter. A story collected in the nineteenth century is prophetic:

A hunter is returning from Beinn a' Bhric. At the foot of the mountain, he hears a sound like the cracking of two stones, or the rattling of a stag's horns against a rock. He sees, crouched by a large stone beside the path, the semblance of a woman with a green shawl

about her shoulder, and in her hands two shank-bones of a deer,
which she's striking, one against the other, without ceasing. The
hunter asks, 'What are you doing there, poor woman?' But the
only reply she gives is: 'O'n loisgeadh a' choille, o'n loisgeadh a'
choille' – 'Since the woods were burnt, since the woods were
burnt.' And she keeps striking the bones, one against the other,
again and again, until he walks out of hearing.

So much woodland has been lost, so many habitats and species
gone, while the remaining red deer are stunted, living on poor
land, their numbers kept high so that wealthy men can shoot
them, doing so with none of the intimacy and respect of
Dòmhnall Donn-shùileach. Culture and nature have been
segregated, a deep connection forfeited, so that, for many of
us, our relationship to the natural world is one of consumption
rather than reciprocity.

But change is afoot. In Scotland, and particularly in the
Highlands, renewed attention is being given towards the
restoration of the physical landscape. 'Rewilding' is all the
rage, though there's suspicion that many of the new 'green
lairds' are more interested in bringing back wolf and lynx
than they are in supporting local, human communities. Or
else, increasingly, it's the profits to be made from carbon-
offset markets and government grants that have persuaded
wealthy businesses and individuals to invest their capital in
Highland estates. Change, but not really change: the land
still commodified, its worth still measured in income streams
and investment yields.

My own best hope is that land reform in Scotland will
continue apace, building on the success of community buy-
outs like at Assynt and Eigg and Knoydart, so that biodiversity
and cultural diversity might, once more, begin to correspond,
the land restored *and* re-storied, the weight of loss lifted. But
that will only happen if we are guided forward by those

perennial questions: Who owns the land? How might it best be stewarded? Has owning anything to do with love?

Upstream from where it crosses the stalkers' path, the Allt Nighean Mhic Dhomhnuill curves beneath a gravel bank overhung by heather. Opposite the bank, on the other side of the stream, a flat boulder lies half-submerged in turf, its surface cushioned with moss. Sheltered from the wind by the bank, warmed by the autumn sun, I curled up on the moss of the boulder and listened to the clatter of the stream against stones. It sounded like the hooves of a column of deer, passing me and passing me until I fell asleep to their beat.

I woke up cold. Cloud blocked the sun, and the stream no longer sparkled. When I stood up, I saw that the shape of my body was imprinted on the boulder's moss, as though I was leaving behind the weight of me. I knelt and scooped water from the Allt Nighean Mhic Dhomhnuill, drinking down the sorrow and the joy of the tale, then I shouldered my rucksack and followed the stalkers' path as it skirted below Coir' a' Bhric Beag, where in summer the deer graze the sweet grasses and mountain herbs.

*

Corrour train station is a pretty sight from a distance, perched on the moor at a height of over a thousand feet, with its station house clad in painted weatherboarding and with a steep-pitched, alpine-style roof, designed to stop snow accumulating. Walking past on the other side of the railway track, I saw that the platform was empty and that the station café was closed for the season. It looked deserted, a place where trains never stopped, though I hoped not – tomorrow I would be waiting there for one to take me south and home.

By the time I reached the ridge that rose to the main summit of Beinn a' Bhric, it was mid-afternoon. Mindful of my sleepless night on the mountain in spring, and aware that the hoped-for train from Fort William arrived at Corrour early in the morning, I pitched my tent at the foot of the ridge, on level ground by the side of the path, stowed my rucksack and gear, and then began to climb up onto the mountain.

Gaining height, the moor expanded around me. There were no deer on the ridge, or none that I could see, but three grouse took off, stealth-bombing down into the corrie, and a couple of grey stones, mottled with white lichen, began to wobble and then shuffle off the track ahead of me. I laughed aloud, relieved, when I saw that they were ptarmigan, perfectly camouflaged amidst the scree, their feathers the colours of the stone. Away to the west, the sun was wedged between the mountains either side of Loch Leven.

In 1880, at the foot of one of those mountains, at North Ballachulish, close to the shore of the loch, a carved wooden figure was discovered in deep peat. The figure has been radio-carbon-dated and found to be around 2,600 years old. It's known as the Ballachulish Goddess and is currently kept at the National Museum of Scotland on Chambers Street in Edinburgh. I try to visit whenever I'm in the city, making my way down to the Early People gallery in the museum's base-ment, where some of the oldest evidence for the presence of human culture on these islands is on display. There's funerary pottery, an Iron Age carnyx, carved Pictish stones, with their secret symbol language, and a wealth of material culture hint-ing at beliefs and practices now lost.

The basement gallery is dimly lit, like a cave – a bone cave of artefacts and memory – and the entrance is guarded by the Ballachulish Goddess, encased in glass and cradled in a nest of branches. The figure is a little bit smaller than adult life-sized, with a narrow torso that has been created out of a single piece of alder. There's something compelling about its form, the ancient wood twisted and distorted – human, but not human – like a terrifying, skeletal marionette: the body of a crone, an

ancestor, a *khoziain*, an 'animal-master'. I think it's a represen-
tation of the Cailleach, carved by people who paid homage to
her, and it has quite the presence, even incarcerated behind
glass in a museum. The eyes are two quartz pebbles set into the
alder, pale white, unsettling, animate.

From Beinn a' Bhric's summit I dropped down onto the
western slope of the ridge. The low sun cast shadows across its
folds and gullies, and Fuaran Cailleach Beinn a' Bhric was as
elusive as it had been in the spring. Eventually, I recognised the
profile of a protruding rock, the contours of the slope began to
fit with my memory of them, and I was able to find the way.

Tucked in the hollow, the pool was a shield, polished by the
light so that I couldn't see beneath its surface. I didn't stay long,
with the sun dropping and the wind blowing cold, but kneeling by the pool I was fiercely present. *What can be shaken /
Shall be shaken and disappear / And only the unshakable be left.*
I took from my pocket a piece of quartz that I'd gathered at the
foot of the mountain and dropped it into the Cailleach's well
– a last, small gift, a stone to see by. It cast a perfect circle of
ripples as it dropped beneath the surface. The water I scooped
to drink was bronze in my hands.

Walking back along the ridge, the evening thickened around
me. Ahead, away to the north and east, beyond Loch Ossian, a
cleft between the dark masses of Ben Alder and Aonach Beag
marked the pass through towards Loch Ericht and Dalwhinnie,
where I'd stepped off the train at the beginning of October. For
a dizzy moment, I sensed that if I spun myself around, I might
lose my footing and find myself back there, that after a month
of loose attachment to calendars and clocks, it would be easy
enough to slip a few days or weeks, to flicker my eyelids and
find myself setting out again.

Time equals distance divided by speed, we are told, but
sometimes there's no distance; sometimes the past quickens
into the present, especially at the cusp of the year, approaching

Samhain, that thin time when the living and the dead might congregate.

I didn't meet the Cailleach on the ridge, or her deer-women, but I carried their stories with me, returning them, and I did have a sense of other lives pressing up against my own, somehow there through me: my dad with his red gaiters guiding me on; my old friend Mo who asked me to say hello to the hills for her; other friends who have shared my love for these remote, intractable mountains. Ahead of me on the ridge, indistinct in the gloom, I glimpsed a boy with an orange nylon rucksack that was too big for him, a boy who lost his father and didn't find him again for twelve years. I took his hand, told him he would be fine, and we climbed down off the mountain together.

A Note on the Stories

Folktales aren't fixed – they are part of the carrying stream, they flow – and every time a tale is told, even by the same teller, there are subtle differences that can depend on the audience, the venue or the inclination of the storyteller. The stories in this book have the character of my own telling, but at the same time, they are told 'true' – which is to say that I've been faithful to their sources, following the same narrative arc and including the same key details. By doing so, I hope I've honoured the storytellers that have come before and helped to revivify their tales – many of them were languishing in long-out-of-print books. The following is a list of all the stories and their primary sources.

Chapter 1: Cleaning the Cailleach's Well

p. 1 'Brown-eyed Donald and the Cailleach': As well as hearing this tale from Jamie MacDonald Reid, I've gathered versions from the archive of the Calum Maclean Project, available online, and from *Tales of Rannoch* by A.D. Cunningham.

Chapter 2: The Stag and the Blade

p. 12 'Muireach Mac Iain and the Maid of An Dùn': My main source for this tale is *The Deer Forests of Scotland* by A. Grimble.

p. 15 'Big Young Donald and the Peat Cutters': *Tobar an Dualchais* is the archive of the School of Studies. It contains thousands upon thousands of recordings from fieldwork in Gaelic, Scots and English, from the 1950s onwards. It is a great service to Scottish culture that the archive is freely available online. This tale comes from John MacDonald of Highbridge, Lochaber, who was interviewed by Calum Maclean in the 1950s. MacDonald's repertoire includes many fine tales and songs rooted in Lochaber.

Chapter 3: The Loch beneath the Loch

p. 23 'Saint Columba and the Loch Ness Monster': Adomnán was abbot of Iona in the late seventh century. His *Vita Columbae*, or *Life of Columba*, is a hagiography of the saint, and contains the first mention of a monster in Loch Ness.

p. 24 'The Two Fishermen and the Monster': I heard this in an interview with Douglas Mackay on Rhyddian Knight's podcast *Glenan Radio*.

pp. 27 29, 33 'Brown-eyed Donald and the Cailleach': See Note for chapter 1.

Chapter 4: West Coast Male

p. 42 'The Heavenly Currach': I first came across this tale in Kenneth Jackson's *A Celtic Miscellany*, a wonderful anthology of early Celtic literature. The tale was recorded in an Irish manuscript, author unknown, in the fourteenth or fifteenth century, though the earliest reference to it is in the eighth century.

p. 47 'The Cailleach and the French Sailing Ship': This local legend was gathered by Eleanor Hull in the 1920s and paraphrased in *Visions of the Cailleach* by Sorita d'Este and David Rankine.

Chapter 5: The Bell in the Bone Cave

p. 58 'Muireach Mac Iain and the Fairy Women': William Scrope's *Days of Deer-stalking* provides the main source for this tale.

Chapter 6: Conival

p. 65 'Big Young Donald and the Wounded Hind': There are many recorded versions of this tale in Gaelic. The best printed translation I've found is in Volume 5 of Alexander Carmichael's *Carmina Gadelica*. Carmichael heard it from John Fraser of Lochaber in 1883.

p. 69 'Polson and the Last Wolf': William Scrope gives a full account of this tale in *Days of Deer-stalking*.

Chapter 8: Cranstackie

p. 92 'Na Fir-chlis': Ronald Black talks about the Nimble Men in 'Signs in the Sky', in *The Quern-Dust Calendar*, his series of articles from 1986–2008 for the *West Highland Free Press*, available online.

p. 96 'The Cailleach and the Old Sergeant': I found this tale in *Short Sketches of the Wild Sports and Natural History of the Highlands* by Charles St. John.

Chapter 9: A' Mhòine

p. 103 'The River Conon Kelpie': I've based my telling on Graeme Johncock's account of the tale, on his website Scotland's Stories.

p. 106 'The Fair-haired Drover and the Deer of Sutherland': From *Lays of the Deer Forest* by John Sobieski and Charles Edward Stuart.

p. 109 'The Rope of Sand': Alan Temperley was the teacher at Farr Secondary School who encouraged his pupils to gather local stories. They have been collected in his book *Tales of the North Coast*.

Chapter 10: Diarmaid's Grave

pp. 113, 117, 120 'Diarmaid and Gráinne': I've heard this story told by the Edinburgh-based storyteller David Campbell, and I've read countless versions of it, including in J.F. Campbell's *Popular Tales of the West Highlands*.

Chapter 11: Welcoming the Stranger

p. 129 'The Hospitality of Grant of Invermoriston': A version of this can be found in Otto Swire's *The Highlands and Their Legends*.

Chapter 12: Rubh' Arisaig

pp. 130, 132 'Mac Mhic Ailein and the Deer-woman': This story is the first part of a longer tale, 'MacPhie's Black Dog'. The best version I've found is in *The Gaelic Otherworld*, Ronald Black's masterly, annotated edition of J.G. Campbell's *Superstitions of the Highlands and Islands of Scotland*. The tale was collected by Campbell in 1863, from Donald Cameron of Ruaig on Tiree.

Chapter 13: Carlotta's Eyrie

p. 145 'MacPhie's Fairy Lover': This is from *Tobar an Dualchais* and a recording of Nan MacKinnon of Vatersay, in 1964. I also found a version of the tale in *Carmina Gadelica*.

Chapter 15: The Post Road

p. 166 'Macleans v. MacDonalds': The tale is cited in various histories of Clan Maclean. A condensed version can be found in Charles Maclean's *The Isle of Mull: Placenames, Meanings and Stories*.

p. 170 'The Cailleach at Loch Bà': A full account of this tale is given in Gearóid Ó Crualaoich's excellent study *The Book of the Cailleach*.

Chapter 16: Poison in the Poet's House

p. 179 'The Cailleach and the Ben Cruachan Well': This tale is so well known, I'm not sure where I first heard it. A version can be found in Ronald Black's *Quern-Dust Calendar*, in the article 'The Earth Mother and the Cailleach'.

p. 181 'Duan na Ceàrdaich', 'The Lay of the Smithy', is from the Fenian Cycle. In Scotland, the smith is often associated with Beinn Dòrain. I based my telling on an article by the composer John Purser, first published in the *West Highland Free Press* and available online on *Tobar an Dualchais*. A full version of the lay is also to be found in Campbell's *Popular Tales of the West Highlands*.

Chapter 17: Tigh nam Bodach

p. 186 'The Bodach and the Cailleach': From *Folklore of the Scottish Highlands* by Anne Ross.

Chapter 18: Campbell Generosity

p. 193 'Red Duncan the Hospitable': I found this tale in *The Lairds of Glenlyon* by Duncan Campbell.

Chapter 19: In the Black Wood

p. 199 'The Robertsons of Struan and the Wolves at St Michael's Graveyard': An excellent account of this tale and its context is given in Andrew Wiseman's essay, '"A Noxious Pack"', published in the journal *Scottish Gaelic Studies*.

p. 201 'The Hunter of Tigh na Coille': A.D. Cunningham was a teacher at Rannoch School, an independent boarding school on the shore of Loch Rannoch, which closed in 2002. His *Tales of Rannoch* is a treasure-trove of place specific lore and provides the source for this tale.

p. 207 'The Lone Highlander': From *A History of Rannoch*, also by A.D. Cunningham.

Chapter 20: On the Road to the Isles

p. 211 'The Cailleach and the Crofter of Cruaiche'; p. 217 'The Fearsome Man'; p. 218 'The Cailleach and the Shepherd's Son': Versions of these three stories can all be found in *Tales of Rannoch*.

Chapter 21: Taking Quartz to the Cailleach

p. 223 'The Cailleach and the Deer-shanks': From Rev. James MacDougall's *Folk Tales and Fairy Lore in Gaelic and English*.

Select Bibliography

Adomnán, *Life of St Columba* (London: Penguin Classics, 1995)

Basso, K.H., *Wisdom Sits in Places: Landscape and Language Among the Western Apache* (New Mexico: University of New Mexico Press, 1996)

Black, R., *The Quern-Dust Calendar, West Highland Free Press* (1986–2008); https://querndust.co.uk (accessed May 2023)

Black, R., ed., *The Gaelic Otherworld* (Edinburgh: Birlinn, 2008)

Campbell, D., *The Lairds of Glenlyon: Historical Sketches Relating to the Districts of Appin, Glenlyon and Breadalbane* (Perth: S. Cowan and Co., 1886)

Campbell, J.F., *Popular Tales of the West Highlands, Volumes 1–4* (Edinburgh: Birlinn, 1994)

Carmichael, A., *Carmina Gadelica* (Edinburgh: Floris Books, 1997)

Crumley, J., *The Last Wolf* (Edinburgh: Birlinn, 2010)

Cunningham, A.D., *A History of Rannoch* (Perth: private publication, 1984)

Cunningham, A.D., *Tales of Rannoch* (Perth: Perth and Kinross District Libraries, 1989)

d'Este, S. and Rankine, D., *Visions of the Cailleach: Exploring the Myths, Folklore and Legends of the pre-eminent Celtic Hag Goddess* (London: BM Avalonia, 2008)

Forbes, J.D., *Columbus and Other Cannibals* (New York: Seven Stories Press, 2008)

Grimble, A., *The Deer Forests of Scotland* (London: Kegan Paul, Trench, Trübner & Co., 1896)

Jackson, K.H., *A Celtic Miscellany* (London: Penguin Classics, revised edition, 1988)

Jacob, V., *Bonnie Joann, and Other Poems*, (London: John Murray, 1921)

Johncock, G., https://scotlands-stories.com (accessed May 2023)

Kane, S., *Wisdom of the Mythtellers* (Peterborough, Canada: Broadview Press, 1998)

Knight, R., 'Douglas MacKay & the Makers of Dreams', *Glenan Radio* (podcast), https://soundcloud.com/rhyddian-knight/glenan-radio-douglas-mackay-the-makers-of-dreams (accessed May 2023)

Laing, R.D., *The Politics of Experience and The Bird of Paradise* (London: Penguin Books, 1990)

Lopez, B., *Apolagia* (Athens, Georgia: University of Georgia Press, 1997)

MacCaig, N., *Collected Poems* (London: Chatto & Windus, 1990)

MacDiarmid, H., *The Complete Poems*, Vol. 1, eds Grieve, M. and Aitken, W.R. (London: Penguin Books, 1985)

MacDougall, Rev. J., *Folk Tales and Fairy Lore in Gaelic and English* (Edinburgh: John Grant, 1910)

McKay, J.G., 'The Deer-Cult and the Deer-Goddess Cult of the Ancient Caledonians', *Folklore*, Vol. 43, Issue 2 (London: 1932)

Maclean, C., *The Isle of Mull: Placenames, Meanings and Stories* (Dumfries: Maclean Publications, 1997)

Maclean, C.I., http://calumimaclean.blogspot.com (accessed May 2023)

Neat, T., *The Summer Walkers: Travelling People and Pearl-fishers in the Highlands of Scotland* (Edinburgh: Birlinn, 2002)

Ó Crualaoich, G., *The Book of the Cailleach: Stories of the Wise-Woman Healer* (Cork: Cork University Press, 2006)

Ross, A., *Folklore of the Scottish Highlands* (Cheltenham: The History Press, 2000)

St John, C., *Short Sketches of the Wild Sports and Natural History of the Highlands* (London: John Murray, 1846)

Scrope, W., *Days of Deer-stalking in the Forests of Atholl, with Some Account of the Nature and Habits of the Red Deer* (London: John Murray, 1847)

Sobieski, J. and Stuart, C.E., *Lays of the Deer Forest. With sketches of olden and modern deer-hunting; traits of natural history in the forest; traditions of the clans; miscellaneous notes* (Edinburgh: William Blackwood & Sons, 1848)

Swire, O.F., *The Highlands and Their Legends* (Edinburgh & London: Oliver & Boyd, 1963)

Temperley, A. and the pupils of Farr Secondary School, *Tales of the North Coast* (London: The Research Publishing Co., 1978)

Tobar an Dualchais, https://www.tobarandualchais.co.uk (accessed May 2023)

Willerslev, R., *Soul Hunters: Hunting, Animism, and Personhood among the Siberian Yukaghirs* (California: University of California Press, 2007)

Wiseman, A., ' "A Noxious Pack": Historical, Literary and Folklore Traditions of the Wolf (*Canis lupus*) in the Scottish Highlands', *Scottish Gaelic Studies,* Vol. 25 (Aberdeen: Aberdeen University Press, 2009)

Acknowledgements

I'd like to thank all the team at Birlinn, and especially Jamie Crawford and Andrew Simmons. Thanks too to Jenny Brown for nudging me in their direction.

The Bone Cave began life as a handful of essays, with early versions of Chapters 1 and 5 published by *Dark Mountain*, and Chapter 8 published by *Bella Caledonia*. I'm grateful to Charlotte Du Cann, Nick Hunt and all the *Dark Mountain* crew, past and present, for their support, editorial wisdom, and enduring friendship. Likewise, Mike Small at *Bella* has been a fine editor, encourager and friend.

I wrote about my visit to Diarmaid's grave in Chapter 10 from a different perspective in the anthology *Antlers of Water*, edited by Kathleen Jamie and published by Canongate in 2020. Again, I was grateful for this opportunity to explore in advance some of the themes in this book.

For early reading and thoughtful feedback on the manuscript, thank you to Nick Hunt, Jonny Randall and Gemma Smith (whose expertise on Gaelic place-names was much appreciated). Thanks too to Kate Rawles for sharing the journey of both our books, and to the many other friends who have given encouragement and support along the way, especially all those involved in Life's Too Short and the Kairos Collective, and to Moon Men Jack, Ben and Jonny; and to Rachel and Roger. Honourable mentions too to Neil Harvey, for all our journeying together; Rona MacDonald, for sharing her deep knowledge of Gaelic language and culture; Ann Shukman, former employer and friend; Kayne Coy, for his Fenian lore and ballad enthusiasm; and Alastair McIntosh, for inspiration and occasional hosting of the 'Late Night Whisky Club'.

I'm grateful to the Scottish Book Trust for my year as a New Writer Awardee, and in particular to my mentor, Sarah Ream, who has been a significant help in the final shaping of this book.

Finally, my biggest thanks are to my family – my two wonderful daughters, Fern and Mara, and my wife Em: first reader, best friend, great love.